Intermediality, Life Writing, and American Studies

Buchreihe der ANGLIA/
ANGLIA Book Series

Edited by
Lucia Kornexl, Ursula Lenker, Martin Middeke,
Gabriele Rippl, Hubert Zapf

Advisory Board
Laurel Brinton, Philip Durkin, Olga Fischer, Susan Irvine,
Andrew James Johnston, Christopher A. Jones, Terttu Nevalainen,
Derek Attridge, Elisabeth Bronfen, Ursula K. Heise, Verena Lobsien,
Laura Marcus, J. Hillis Miller, Martin Puchner

Volume 61

Intermediality, Life Writing, and American Studies

—

Interdisciplinary Perspectives

Edited by
Nassim Winnie Balestrini and Ina Bergmann

DE GRUYTER

For an overview of all books published in this series, please see
http://www.degruyter.com/view/serial/36292

ISBN 978-3-11-070962-9
e-ISBN (PDF) 978-3-11-057925-3
e-ISBN (EPUB) 978-3-11-057681-8
ISSN 0340-5435

Library of Congress Control Number: 2018947208

Bibliographic information published by the Deutsche Nationalbibliothek
The Deutsche Nationalbibliothek lists this publication in the Deutsche Nationalbibliografie;
detailed bibliographic data are available on the Internet at http://dnb.dnb.de.

© 2020 Walter de Gruyter GmbH, Berlin/Boston
This volume is text- and page-identical with the hardback published in 2018.
Printing: CPI books GmbH, Leck

www.degruyter.com

Table of Contents

Acknowledgments —— VII

Nassim Winnie Balestrini and Ina Bergmann
Intermediality, Life Writing, and American Studies: A Brief Introduction —— 1

Christopher J. Lukasik
Making an Entrance, Illustrating a Life: Remediating Benjamin Franklin's *Autobiography* in Nineteenth-Century America —— 9

Hélène Quanquin
Illustrations "More Numerous Than We Could Have Expected": Biography as "Mixed Media" in *William Lloyd Garrison, 1805–1879: The Story of His Life Told by His Children* (1885–1889) —— 35

Margit Peterfy
Performing Lives in Nineteenth-Century US-American Culture: From Paratheatricals to Early Cinema —— 51

Dennis Bingham
Lenny: (Auto-)biography, Black-and-White, and Juxtapositional Montage in Bob Fosse's Hollywood Renaissance Biopic —— 75

Ina Bergmann
The Remediation of Little Edie: From It-Girl to Loony Cat Lady to Cultural Icon —— 99

Daniel Stein
Graphic Musical Biography: An Intermedial Case of Musico-Comical Life Writing —— 119

Gabriele Rippl
Ekphrastic Encounters and Word–Photography Configurations in Contemporary Transcultural American Life Writing —— 147

Danuta Fjellestad
"A Figment of Someone Else's Imagination": Intermedial Games in Paul Auster's *Report from the Interior* —— 167

Silvia Schultermandl
Auto-Assembling the Self on Social Networking Sites: Intermediality and Transnational Kinship in Online Academic Life Writing —— 191

Nassim Winnie Balestrini
Intermedial On/Offstage Auto/Biography: Lin-Manuel Miranda's *Hamilton*, Hip Hop, and Historiography —— 211

Ina Bergmann
Emily Dickinson, Intermediality, and Life Writing: An Interview with Susan Snively —— 233

Nassim Winnie Balestrini
The Respectful Biographer's Empathetic Imagination: An Interview about Intermediality and Life Writing with Brenda Wineapple —— 245

Note on the Contributors —— 253

Index —— 255

Acknowledgments

We would like to thank all the authors and interviewees for their thought-provoking contributions to this volume, their unflagging enthusiasm for the project, and their excellent cooperation. We also wish to express our gratitude to the efficient staff at de Gruyter, especially Dr. Ulrike Krauß, Katja Lehming, and Nancy Christ. Furthermore, thanks are due to the Anglia Book Series editors, particularly Prof. Dr. Martin Middeke, Prof. Dr. Gabriele Rippl, and Prof. Dr. Hubert Zapf, for their interest in and their support of this publication project. Last but not least, a very special thank you to Juliann Knaus, B.A., for her eagle-eyed expertise and patient assistance in preparing the manuscript for publication and to Sonja Bonneß, M.A., for compiling the index.

Nassim Winnie Balestrini and Ina Bergmann   Graz and Würzburg, May 2018

Nassim Winnie Balestrini and Ina Bergmann
Intermediality, Life Writing, and American Studies: A Brief Introduction

Since the mid-2000s, intermediality studies has spawned numerous publications in which scholars from various disciplines discuss theories and new vistas aimed at (re-)defining their burgeoning and contentious field.[1] Current intermediality scholarship has been incorporating a growing number of perspectives informed by cultural studies, media studies, and narratology – perspectives that foreground processes rather than products as well as contextual extrinsic phenomena in conjunction with intrinsic analysis. Such perspectives on intermediality highlight the necessity of understanding medium-specific sign systems as well as the impact of combining them in one work, of adapting contents across medial boundaries, of thematizing one art form in another art form, and of imitating the meaning-making techniques of one medium through the semiotic system of another medium. In all of these instantiations of intermediality, it is crucial to consider the implications of the production, inherent characteristics, and reception of specific types of artifacts.

Far surpassing the traditional Enlightenment autobiography, penned by white men whose social standing was used to justify written and published depictions of exemplary lives that readers were meant to emulate, countless types of (self-)life narratives have been integrated into the purview of the vast field of life writing studies. Simultaneous with recent developments in interdisciplinary intermediality research, the study of life writing has opened up towards myriad medial forms and their interaction in autobiographical and biographical discourse. Such (self-)life narratives comprise a wide range of written and printed media that focus on verbal signification only. Moreover, they include combinations of two or more media, for instance, in comic books, graphic narratives, television programs, documentary films, video clips, radio programs, songs, musi-

---

[1] See, for example, Balestrini 2011, 2017; Bergmann 2010, 2018a; Bolter and Grusin 2000; Bruhn, Gjelsvik, and Hanssen 2013; Eilittä 2012; Emden and Rippl 2010; Hallet 2014; Hutcheon 2006; Lukasik 2010; Murray 2012; Nicklas and Lindner 2012; Petermann 2014; Rajewsky 2002, 2006; Rippl 2005, 2015; Ryan and Thon 2014; Sanders 2006; Starre 2015; and Wolf 2003, 2005a, 2005b, 2011.

https://doi.org/10.1515/9783110579253-002

cals, photo books, video games, blogs, vlogs, and currently evolving forms of self-representation in online social media.[2]

Particularly the concepts of "performativity, positionality, and relationality" (Smith and Watson 2010: 214) have contributed to theorizing and contextualizing this immense variety of (auto-)biographical forms of self-expression. Intermediality offers an analytical vantage point for working with these concepts, as the relational approach of interweaving an individual autobiographical voice with biographical depictions of important persons in the autobiographer's experience frequently goes along with indicating different voices and lives through contrasting semiotic features. This can be done within a written and printed verbal text by, for instance, varying font types and sizes or by developing a page design that indicates multiple voices and relationships. In other words, research in relational life writing benefits from dissecting discursive features that are rooted in medium-specific characteristics. Such subtlety of multiple voices has contributed to expanding the generic range of life narratives, particularly through media combinations and intermedial imitation of medium-specific sign systems. This fine-tuned usage of intermedial intersections of meaning-making possibilities also facilitates performative life writing in the sense that the autobiographical trajectory is directed towards the artistry of the depiction as much as or possibly more than the ostensible completeness of narrating a life. Positionality – as a specific form of relationality – foregrounds the situatedness of an individual within a society's ideological matrix. By critiquing widely accepted histories such as national master narratives (Hall 1998; Costantino and Egan 2003), these autobiographies also transcend the focus on the individual. The power of undermining, for instance, local, regional, or national myths can, again, rely on verbal, visual, and possibly auditory representations which must be scrutinized regarding intermedial strategies of meaning-making.

Questions and topics addressed in this essay collection include: how can we reevaluate traditional forms of life writing, produced *avant la lettre*, through the lens of contemporary intermediality studies? In which ways has printed life writing changed in terms of the relationship between verbal texts and visual images and possibly also added audio or audiovisual material? How do social media and the specific forms of self-expression they elicit expand our understanding of intermedial life writing in the digital age? What is the current state of affairs regarding the evolution of documentary biopics? What are the socioeconomic

---

[2] See, for example, Balestrini 2013, 2015a, 2015b; Bergmann 2018b; Bingham 2010; Birkle 2006; Friedman and Schultermandl 2018; Hornung 2010, 2013; Lebow 2012; McNeil 2003; McNeil and Zuern 2015; Poletti 2012; Smith and Watson 2002, 2010; Stein 2012; Stein and Butler 2015; and Whitlock 2006, 2015.

implications of the parallel worlds of open access versus commercial verbal texts, visual images, videos, and films? How is life writing impacted by the evolution of specific media and by being transferred from one medium to another? Which cultural connotations and repercussions do such changes entail? What do these shifts imply about target audiences? Are these changes instrumental in the process of creating a cultural icon? How can the theoretical perspectives and the terminologies of intermediality and life-writing scholarship be made compatible? Which understanding(s) of media and life writing are fruitful in this context? Which new options does this area of interdisciplinary research offer to the field of American studies, particularly in its transnational orientation?

This collection of essays gathers the multi- and interdisciplinary trajectories and insights of an international group of scholars who engage in innovative and compelling research on intermedial forms of life writing. Most of the authors are internationally and/or nationally renowned experts in studies of adaptation, intermediality, and/or life writing. Others are practitioners in the field, such as film makers, biographers, and novelists. This group of contributors approaches the issue of intermediality and life writing in American culture from various disciplines, among them cultural studies, literary studies, media studies, and history. Among their subjects of scrutiny are biographies, memoirs, graphic novels, performances, paratheatricals, musicals, silent films, movies, documentary films, and social media. The collection covers a time frame ranging from works produced in the nineteenth century to artifacts from the immediate present. In addition to a shared focus on theories of intermediality and life writing, the authors apply to their subjects both firmly established and cutting-edge theoretical approaches such as cultural narratology, cultural history, biographical studies, social media studies, performance studies, and visual culture studies.

Several essays provide new perspectives on biographical genres and their use of intermedial features. Christopher J. Lukasik focuses on the 'image ecology' in American print culture during the 1840s and 50s. In his essay "Making an Entrance, Illustrating a Life: Remediating Benjamin Franklin's *Autobiography* in Nineteenth-Century America" he analyzes the intermedial operations of image/text as they appear in illustrations found within various nineteenth-century editions of Benjamin Franklin's *Autobiography*. He applies the theories of the image articulated by W. J. T. Mitchell and Jacques Rancière, which insist that the image is neither the visible nor its textual equivalent, but is instead a nuanced relationship between text and image. In her essay "Illustrations 'More Numerous Than We Could Have Expected': Biography as 'Mixed Media' in *William Lloyd Garrison, 1805–1879: The Story of His Life Told by His Children* (1885–1889)," Hélène Quanquin concentrates on the functions of media combination, of block quotations and engravings made from original photographs, paintings, and sculptures, in the four-volume biography of the American abolitionist leader written by two of his sons. The aims of Quanquin's essay are to enrich the diachronic perspective on intermediality by focusing on nineteenth-century life writing and thereby to reevaluate the novelty of the 1990s 'new biography.' Margit Peterfy explores a very popular and prevalent manifestation of intermediality in the nineteenth century in her contribution "Performing Lives in Nineteenth-Century US-American Culture: From Paratheatricals to Early Cinema." Here Peterfy offers a new perspective on the reception and effect of biographical drama and early silent films. Dennis Bingham focuses on a largely neglected film by Hollywood director Bob Fosse. In his essay "*Lenny:* (Auto-)biography, Black-and-White, and Juxtapositional Montage in Bob Fosse's Hollywood Renaissance Biopic", Bingham uses the concept of intermediality to reveal the significance of this film about stand-up comedian Lenny Bruce as an innovative biopic. Ina Bergmann's contribution "The Remediation of Little Edie: From It-Girl to Loony Cat Lady to Cultural Icon" unravels how media changes are vital factors in the creation of public images or in practices of 'iconizing.' A documentary film, a Broadway musical, and an HBO biopic serve as the main indicators of the shifting public image of Edith Bouvier Beale, infamous first cousin of Jackie Kennedy.

Narratives that combine words and still images are at the center of further essays which are, however, not concerned with film. Daniel Stein connects autobiography studies, intermedia theory, and comics studies in his "Graphic Musical Biography: An Intermedial Case of Musico-Comical Life Writing," exploring the ways in which a combination of these areas of analysis can advance the understanding of contemporary forms of life writing. Stein does so by offering a case study of Philip Paquet's graphic narrative, which illustrates the life of the famous jazz singer and trumpeter Louis Armstrong. Gabriele Rippl investigates "Ekphrastic Encounters and Word–Photography Configurations in Contemporary Transcultural American Life Writing" with a particular focus on the function of photographs for the intermedial aesthetics of 'hyphenated' life writing. Rippl focuses on autobiographical and -fictional texts by authors with a transnational and -cultural identity, covering a time frame from the 1990s to today. In her essay "'A Figment of Someone Else's Imagination': Intermedial Games in Paul Auster's *Report from the Interior*," Danuta Fjellestad unravels the function of photographs in the context of the visual-textual games meant to engage the reader. Fjellestad points out how Auster creates a complex web of intermedial relations in this memoir and how he breaks with the 'autophotographic pact' associated with earlier traditions of self-life writing.

Two essays contemplate relational features of self-definition through kinship and nation as found in widely diverging contemporary forms of (auto-)biographical expression. Silvia Schultermandl discusses personal self-expressions in digital form in her contribution "Auto-Assembling the Self on Social Networking Sites: Intermediality and Transnational Kinship in Online Academic Life Writing." Schultermandl particularly scrutinizes online academic life writing on social network sites (SNSs) and the intermedial nature of these 'everyday autobiographies.' Nassim Balestrini argues in "Intermedial On/Offstage Auto/Biography: Lin-Manuel Miranda's *Hamilton*, Hip Hop, and Historiography" that the innovative intermedial characteristics of this biographical musical reinterpret the life and times of a Founding Father in ways that reflect on the contemporary social climate and its fear of immigrants. Balestrini discusses how the musical per se and Miranda's co-authored book about its genesis and production connect an iconoclastic view of a possibly not-so-usable past with encouraging audiences and readers to revitalize democracy through diversity.

In the forum section, we bring together scholars and practitioners of intermedial life writing. John Carlos Rowe encourages scholars to foster awareness of "the interpretation of cultural narratives that enable such fictions as the State, the market, the nation, and citizenship to be accepted as real" (2012: 21). The interviews presented here connect this outlook to discourses of authenticity and historicity in intermedial life writing, and address the concerns which plague artists, artist-scholars, and scholars working in and on (auto-)biographical material that is in the process of expanding its medial phenotypes as well as its transnational appeal. In the first interview Susan Snively, co-screenwriter of *Angles of a Landscape* (2008–2012), a series of biographical films on Emily Dickinson and author of a biographical novel about the poet, shares her insights about intermediality and life writing from a practitioner's perspective. A poet herself, she highlights the connections between Dickinson's poetry, her life, and intermediality. Snively also discusses the enhancement of practices of life writing through intermedial references. The second interview features renowned literary scholar, essayist, and nonfiction writer Brenda Wineapple, who authored prize-winning biographical monographs – for instance – about Nathaniel Hawthorne and about Emily Dickinson's friendship with Thomas Wentworth Higginson. Wineapple reflects on how she distinguishes between choosing a biographical narrative mode and the much more expansive trajectory of political and literary issues covered in her books. She thus raises points that again confirm the significance of the triad of relational, positional, and performative life writing.

The essays and interviews in this volume constitute an unprecedented collection of research which productively combines intermediality and life writing studies with diverse American studies concerns. The broad historical range and the multiplicity of intermedial forms and life narratives covered by the contributions in this collection clearly indicate the usefulness of medium-specific semiotic analyses which take into account traditions and evolving formats of auto/biographical (self-)expression within their respective artistic and social contexts. These essays will hopefully initiate further debate and dialogue as to the ways in which interdisciplinary approaches to cultural products offer epistemological possibilities that transcend the compartmentalized subdivisions practiced in contemporary academic environments. The fields of intermediality, life writing, and American studies reject limitations posed by boundaries of genre, mode of expression, and nation. As a result, they provide welcome opportunities for interdisciplinary exchange and for honing theories and methodologies that strive to reveal hitherto undiscovered layers of and intersections among ever-evolving representational and communicative formats.

Works Cited

Balestrini, Nassim Winnie. 2017. "Intermediality". In: Timo Müller (ed.). *The American Novel of the Twentieth and Twenty-First Centuries*. Berlin: De Gruyter. 68–83.
Balestrini, Nassim Winnie. 2015a. "Life Writing in the Internet Age: Miranda July and the Limits of Art as Social Practice". *Arbeiten aus Anglistik und Amerikanistik* 40 (1–2): 127–150.
Balestrini, Nassim Winnie. 2015b. "Strategic Visuals in Hip-Hop Life Writing". *Popular Music and Society* 38 (2): 224–242.
Balestrini, Nassim Winnie. 2013. "Photography as Online Life Writing: Miranda July's and Harrell Fletcher's *Learning to Love You More* (2002–2009)". In: Alfred Hornung (ed.). *American Lives*. Heidelberg: Winter. 341–353.
Balestrini, Nassim Winnie (ed.). 2011. *Adaptation and American Studies: Perspectives on Research and Teaching*. Heidelberg: Winter.
Bergmann, Ina. 2018a (forthcoming). "Eine *Divine Comedy* für das 21. Jahrhundert: Matthew Pearls *The Dante Club*". In: Irmgard Scharold (ed.). *Dante Intermedial: Die Divina Commedia in Literatur und Medien*. Würzburg: Königshausen & Neumann.
Bergmann, Ina. 2018b (forthcoming). "Historical Biofiction: Writing Lives in Diane Glancy's *Stone Heart* (2003) and John May's *Poe & Fanny* (2004)". In: Michael Basseler and Ansgar Nünning (eds.). *The American Novel in the 21st Century: Cultural Contexts – Literary Developments – Critical Analyses*. Trier: Wissenschaftlicher Verlag Trier.
Bergmann, Ina. 2010. "Reanimated Classics: Canon Appropriation and Serialization in Contemporary Fiction". In: Jörg Helbig and René Schallegger (eds.). *Proceedings: Anglistentag 2009 Klagenfurt*. Trier: Wissenschaftlicher Verlag Trier. 135–151.
Bingham, Dennis. 2010. *Whose Lives Are They Anyway? The Biopic as Contemporary Film Genre*. New Brunswick: Rutgers University Press.
Birkle, Carmen. 2006. "Conference Report: Auto/biography and Mediation". *International Auto/Biography Association (IABA)*. <https://sites.google.com/a/ualberta.ca/iaba/archives/2006-mainz-germany> [accessed 17 March 2018].
Bolter, Jay David and Richard Grusin. 2000. *Remediation: Understanding New Media*. Cambridge: MIT Press.

Bruhn, Jørgen, Anne Gjelsvik, and Eirik Frisvold Hanssen (eds.). 2013. *Adaptation Studies: New Challenges, New Directions*. London: Bloomsbury.
Costantino, Manuela and Susanna Egan. 2003. "Reverse Migrations and Imagined Communities". *Prose Studies* 26 (1–2): 96–111.
Eilittä, Leena. 2012. "Introduction: From Interdisciplinarity to Intermediality". In: Leena Eilittä (ed.). *Intermedial Arts: Disrupting, Remembering and Transforming Media*. Newcastle: Cambridge Scholars. vii–xiii.
Emden, Christian and Gabriele Rippl (eds.). 2010. *Imagescapes: Studies in Intermediality*. Oxford: Lang.
Friedman, May and Silvia Schultermandl (eds.). 2018 (forthcoming). *Autobiography 2.0*. Special issue of *Interactions: Studies in Culture and Communications* 9 (2).
Hall, Jacquelyn Dowd. 1998. "'You Must Remember This': Autobiography as Social Critique". *The Journal of American History* 85 (2): 439–465.
Hallet, Wolfgang. 2014. "The Rise of the Multimodal Novel: Generic Change and Its Narratological Implications". In: Marie-Laure Ryan and Jan-Noël Thon (eds.). *Storyworlds Across Media: Toward a Media-Conscious Narratology*. Lincoln: University of Nebraska P. 151–172.
Hornung, Alfred (ed.). 2013. *American Lives*. Heidelberg: Winter.
Hornung, Alfred (ed.). 2010. *Auto/biography and Mediation*. Heidelberg: Winter.
Hutcheon, Linda. 2006. *A Theory of Adaptation*. London: Routledge.
Lebow, Alisa. 2012. *The Cinema of Me: The Self and Subjectivity in First Person Documentary*. London: Wallflower Press.
Lukasik, Christopher J. 2010. *Discerning Characters: The Culture of Appearance in Early America*. Philadelphia: University of Pennsylvania Press.
McNeill, Laurie. 2003. "Teaching an Old Genre New Tricks: The Diary on the Internet". *Biography* 26 (1): 24–47.
McNeill, Laurie and John David Zuern (eds.). 2015. *Online Lives 2.0*. Special issue of *Biography* 38 (2).
Murray, Simone. 2012. *The Adaptation Industry: The Cultural Economy of Contemporary Literary Adaptation*. New York: Routledge.
Nicklas, Pascal and Oliver Lindner (eds.). 2012. *Adaptation and Cultural Appropriation: Literature, Film, and the Arts*. Berlin: De Gruyter.
Petermann, Emily. 2014. *The Musical Novel: Imitation of Musical Structure, Performance, and Reception in Contemporary Fiction*. Rochester: Camden House.
Poletti, Anna. 2012. "Reading for Excess: Relational Autobiography, Affect and Popular Culture in *Tarnation*". *Life Writing* 9 (2): 157–172.
Rajewsky, Irina O. 2006. "Intermediality, Intertextuality and Remediation: A Literary Perspective on Intermediality". *Intermédialités* 6: 43–64.
Rajewsky, Irina O. 2002. *Intermedialität*. Tübingen: Francke.
Rippl, Gabriele (ed.). 2015. *Handbook of Intermediality: Literature – Image – Sound – Music*. Berlin: De Gruyter.
Rippl, Gabriele. 2005. *Beschreibungs-Kunst: Zur intermedialen Poetik angloamerikanischer Ikon-Texte (1880–2000)*. München: Fink.
Rowe, John Carlos. 2012. *The Cultural Politics of the New American Studies*. Open Humanities Press. <http://openhumanitiespress.org/books/download/Rowe_2012_Cultural-Politics-of-the-New-American-Studies.pdf> [accessed 21 November 2014].

Ryan, Marie-Laure and Jan-Noël Thon (eds.). 2014. "Storyworlds Across Media: Introduction". In: Marie-Laure Ryan and Jan-Noël Thon (eds.). *Storyworlds Across Media: Toward a Media-Conscious Narratology*. Lincoln: University of Nebraska Press. 1–21.

Sanders, Julie. 2006. *Adaptation and Appropriation*. London: Routledge.

Smith, Sidonie and Julia Watson. 2010. *Reading Autobiography: A Guide for Interpreting Life Narratives*. Minneapolis: University of Minnesota Press.

Smith, Sidonie and Julia Watson (eds.). 2002. *Interfaces: Women, Autobiography, Images, Performance*. Ann Arbor: University of Michigan Press.

Starre, Alexander. 2015. *Metamedia: American Book Fictions and Literary Print Culture after Digitization*. Iowa City: University of Iowa Press.

Stein, Daniel. 2012. *Music Is My Life: Louis Armstrong, Autobiography, and American Jazz*. Ann Arbor: University of Michigan Press.

Stein, Daniel and Martin Butler. 2015. "Musical Autobiographies: An Introduction". *Popular Music and Society* 38 (2): 115–121.

Whitlock, Gillian. 2015. *Postcolonial Life Narratives: Testimonial Transactions*. Oxford Studies in Postcolonial Literatures. Oxford: Oxford University Press.

Whitlock, Gillian. 2006. "Autographics: The Seeing 'I' of the Comics". *Modern Fiction Studies* 52 (4): 965–979.

Wolf, Werner. 2011. "(Inter)mediality and the Study of Literature". *CLCWeb: Comparative Literature and Culture* 13 (3): 1–9.

Wolf, Werner. 2005a. "Music and Narrative". *Routledge Encyclopedia of Narrative Theory*. London: Routledge. 324–329.

Wolf, Werner. 2005b. "Pictorial Narrativity". *Routledge Encyclopedia of Narrative Theory*. London: Routledge. 431–435.

Wolf, Werner. 2003. "Intermedial Iconicity in Fiction: Tema con variazioni". In: Wolfgang G. Müller and Olga Fischer (eds.). *From Sign to Signing*. Amsterdam: John Benjamins. 339–360.

Christopher J. Lukasik
Making an Entrance, Illustrating a Life: Remediating Benjamin Franklin's *Autobiography* in Nineteenth-Century America

Abstract

As one of the most frequently reprinted and often lavishly illustrated life stories of the nineteenth century, Benjamin Franklin's *Autobiography* provides an exemplary case study for considering intermediality and life writing within the American context. Although it is one of the most extensively discussed texts in the American canon, little has been said about the hundreds of illustrations that accompanied Franklin's *Autobiography* throughout the nineteenth century. Critical discussion of Franklin's relationship to visual culture invariably returns to either the pictorial representations that Franklin made or the painted portraits in which he appeared. This essay will be the first diachronic analysis of the intermedial operations of illustrations depicting Franklin within the context of mass visual culture in the United States. Drawing upon the theories of the image articulated by W. J. T. Mitchell and Jacques Rancière, this essay analyzes the image/text operations in three nineteenth-century children's editions of Franklin's *Autobiography*. The arc of these three case studies reflects a historical transformation in how the visibility of Franklin's text was imagined to operate, from the active imagination of individual readerly visualization to the passive mass consumption of optical media.

1 The Remediation of Franklin's *Autobiography*

The nineteenth-century transatlantic world saw an array of innovations in printing and imaging technology, a revolution in transportation, and an expansion of the literary and pictorial market that transformed the publishing industry as well as the nascent consumer culture of which it was a part. These changes resulted in images being produced and reproduced more rapidly, with more sophistication, and in unprecedented numbers; and it turned illustration, over the course of the century, from an expensive ornament to a crucial component of print culture. As literary and art historians have documented recently, it was illustration

– specifically the optical technology of engraving – and not photography which fueled the rise of a mass visual culture across the nineteenth century (Patterson 2010; Kooistra 2011; Leja 2011). In America, illustrations were central to the development of what art historian Michael Leja calls a new "image ecology" (2011: 83) in print culture as publishers began to target mass audiences during the 1840s and 1850s. As the predominant optical medium for nineteenth-century publishers, engraved illustrations propelled the enormous popular success of gift books and literary annuals during the 1830s and 1840s, and the media combinations found within them established the formula that popular pictorial histories and biographies, illustrated magazines, and pictorial weeklies would later adapt in the following decades as the print culture market expanded. "Text and image, text alongside image, text as image," Laurel Brake and Marysa Demoor observe, "– these are the combinations one is confronted with when one studies nineteenth-century print culture" (2009: 12). In short, mid-nineteenth-century print culture on either side of the ocean was a highly complex and evolving intermedial environment.

While scholars of illustration have long known that images and words are intimately related, the methods that have been historically brought to bear upon them have tended either to discuss them separately (as comparative studies of the arts do when they reduce the image to the optical) or subordinate one to the other (as cultural semiotics does when it reduces the image to a text). Yet, the notion of a purely visual or optical medium implicit in each method is radically incoherent. Visual media are always mixtures of sensory and semiotic elements and are thus hybrid formations. "All media," W. J. T. Mitchell asserts, "are mixed media" and this is certainly true for nineteenth-century illustration in which the image–text relationship is explicit (2005: 215). Similarly, when the images found within these illustrations are understood as visual language – as they are in cultural semiotics – their potentialities dwindle to what Jacques Rancière refers to as a reversible equivalence between the silence of images and what they say. In either case, the image is conceived, as Rancière puts it, as "speech which holds its tongue" (2007: 7). Vision, however, "is not reducible to language," Mitchell asserts, "pictures want equal rights with language, not to be turned into language" (2005: 47). What I believe Rancière and Mitchell want us to keep in mind – and what I would like to emphasize in the following pages – is that the image is neither merely the visible nor simply its textual equivalent; it is instead a nuanced relationship between them, a media combination, an intermedial environment in which the seeable and the sayable coalesce and operate.

It is within these two historical and theoretical contexts – the explicit intermediality of nineteenth-century illustrated print culture, on the one hand, and the limitations of comparative and cultural semiotic approaches to that print culture, on the other – that I wish to situate this essay's discussion of intermediality in Benjamin Franklin's *Autobiography*. Drawing upon the theories of the image articulated by Mitchell and Rancière, this essay analyzes the image/text operations of illustrations as they appear within three nineteenth-century children's editions of Franklin's *Autobiography*. The arc of these three case studies, I argue, reflects a historical transformation in how the visibility of Franklin's text was imagined to operate, from the active imagination of individual readerly visualization to the more passive consumption of identical optical remediations. Despite the fact that Franklin's *Autobiography* is one of the most extensively discussed and widely reprinted texts in the American canon, virtually nothing has been said about the hundreds of illustrations that accompanied his text during the period when it became one of the most popular life stories of the nineteenth century. When the subject of Franklin's relationship to visual culture has been addressed by scholars, the critical conversation invariably returns either to the pictorial representations that Franklin made himself or the painted portraits, engravings, and sculptures in which he appeared. In either case, the emphasis is on Franklin the biographical person as opposed to the remediation of his image across the nineteenth century.

In contrast, this essay will be the first to analyze the intermedial operations of the illustrations of Franklin diachronically within the context of a developing mass visual culture in the United States. In addition to using an intermedial methodology, this essay also departs from traditional studies of book illustration by not organizing its analysis around familiar art and book historical frames (such as the illustrator, the author of the illustrated text, the biographical person depicted in the illustration, the publisher, or even a coherent reading of the illustrated text as a whole). Instead, I will discuss how a single verbal image from the *Autobiography* was remediated through illustrations over time. The intermediality and visibility of Franklin's *Autobiography* will thus be understood and addressed through the three kinds of images it produces: first, through an analysis of the verbal image generated by Franklin's description of his first entrance into Philadelphia; second, through an analysis of the subsequent media combinations that accompanied and remediated that specific verbal image in illustrated editions published during the nineteenth century; and third, through a comparative analysis of those media combinations with each other as they appeared across the nineteenth century. This last form of analysis, I believe, will allow us to see how these illustrations not only remediated the verbal image created by Franklin's text, but also responded to later optical remediations of that same verbal image. While the decision to address the visibility of the *Autobiography* through the optical remediation of just one of its verbal images may seem arbitrary and unrepresentative, I am less interested in providing a comprehensive reading of the *Autobiography* or any of its individual illustrations than I am in trying to trace a historical relationship among them through those remediations. The point of looking at historically discrete visualizations of the same narrative moment, I want to suggest, is to ask whether it is possible to analyze image/text operations diachronically and, if so, to determine what can be said about them.

2 The Visibility of Franklin's *Autobiography*

Franklin's *Autobiography* was and, in many respects, remains the quintessential biography of the American self-made man. His plain-spoken narrative of hard work and upward social mobility was reproduced through countless editions and adaptations. By the middle of the nineteenth century, "the unfinished memoir, sometimes then called his *Autobiography*, was reprinted piecemeal nearly one hundred and twenty times" (Huang and Mulford 2008: 150). Throughout said century, it was widely "available to Americans in a multitude of sources: full-length editions, magazine profiles, collective biographies, as well as sketches in schoolbooks and almanacs" (Casper 1989: 89). In fact, when "early readers talk about reading Franklin's 'life,' we often do not know whether they mean a version of the *Autobiography* or one of those biographies," Stephen Carl Arch notes, but "in one form or another [...] Franklin's life circulated widely in the United States and Europe during the nineteenth century" (Arch 2008: 164). The ubiquity of Franklin's life story during the second half of the nineteenth century has led one scholar to conclude that he was "the most important figure in the writing of American biography between 1860 and 1890" (Miles 1957: 139). Undoubtedly, its remarkable popularity had much to do with how the voluntary and instrumental nature of Franklin's social performances in the *Autobiography* resonated with the liberal notion of a free and autonomous subject at the center of America's new democracy and its emergent market economy. Generations of aspiring nineteenth-century Americans read Franklin's life story and were inspired to emulate its rendering of the self-made man.

Yet, Franklin's image in print was at first more documentary than representative. In the ten years following his death, the story of Franklin's life served more as a historical monument to America's origins than as a role model for America's youth. Thus, the particular Franklin, the specific historical person, more than the representative Franklin appeared in the *Autobiography*'s first illustrations. Whether due to the high costs of illustration, the dearth of engravers, or the democratic-republican principles of an impersonal public sphere free from particular interest, illustrations of Franklin rarely occurred alongside his life story; and when they did, they were frequently based on physiognomically-detailed profile portraits such as those by Louis Carmontelle (artist) and François Denis Née (engraver) (1780), John Norman (1781), and Daniel Berger (1783). "When his *Autobiography* initially appeared in France and England between 1791 and 1793, none of the publishers thought it necessary to include his portrait," Nian-Sheng Huang notes; it was only in "the first American editions printed in New York and Philadelphia in 1794 that a picture of Franklin was used as a frontispiece. Thereafter his writings were rarely published without a portrait" (Huang 1994: 63). At the beginning of the nineteenth century, what few optical images there were inside Franklin's *Autobiography* were portraits of the particular man as opposed to exemplary scenes from his life.

During the first quarter of the nineteenth century, however, as Franklin's life story began to circulate more widely and cheaply throughout print culture, a wider range of illustrations began to accompany the *Autobiography*. The physiognomically-detailed portrait frontispieces were now joined by more generic images of Franklin depicting various episodes from his life. The resulting conjunction of the portrait frontispiece – which established a likeness to the particular person of Franklin the biographical author and founding father – with the subsequent narrative illustrations – which more often than not bore no discernible resemblance to the particular Franklin – reflects the way in which the two bodies of Franklin functioned within the text itself. These images of Franklin's two bodies (his particular corporeal self, on the one hand, and his more generic performative one, on the other) not only dovetail with the different ways in which Franklin represents himself in the *Autobiography* (was his success a product of the social capital of his particular, corporeal person or the cultural capital of his de-corporealized, performative self?), they confirm what Joseph Fichtelberg describes as the transformation of Franklin into an exemplary image. Fichtelberg contends that the shift in the memoirs from the intimate 'you' of Franklin's son to the universal 'you' of posterity – one that is typically identified as occurring between Parts 1 and 2 – transforms Franklin into "a national cynosure" (1988: 205).

This image of Franklin as an emulative national icon was nowhere more forcefully illustrated and widely distributed than in the many bowdlerized versions of his memoirs which began to appear in America during the second quarter of the nineteenth century. Books such as Mason Weems's *The Life of Doctor Franklin* (1815), Mahlon Day's *Brief Memoir of the Life of Dr. Benjamin Franklin* (1824), and Samuel G. Goodrich's *The Life of Benjamin Franklin* (1832) (also known as Parley's Franklin) sought to market Franklin's story to an emergent and upwardly mobile middle class, particularly to its youth. While these frequently fictionalized biographies placed varying degrees of emphasis on Franklin's piety, frugality, and filial obedience, they also had the effect of establishing which narrative moments from Franklin's life would be remediated through illustrations. Starting in the 1830s, some of the more iconic episodes from his life story – such as his work as a printer, his first entrance to Philadelphia, his walking through the streets with a wheelbarrow, and his electrical experiments with a kite – began to be illustrated consistently from edition to edition, and these optical images would become, over the course of the century, the ones most often visually associated with his life story.

The highly visible nature of Franklin's memoirs undoubtedly made the choice of these episodes somewhat easier for publishers and illustrators. Even when printed without any illustrations, the *Autobiography* provided readers with a series of memorable verbal images demonstrating the importance of appearance in the signification of gentility and the social perception of character. For this reason, it is important to remember that the *Autobiography*'s visibility was initially a product of its words; and it confirms what Rancière has asserted elsewhere, that "the image is not exclusive to the visible" (2007: 7). The intense visibility of the *Autobiography* created "iconic pictures that eventually entered American folklore," and it undoubtedly facilitated its subsequent illustration (Arch 2008: 159). As Lemay remarks, Franklin was "among the most visually conscious writers of eighteenth-century America [...] and he deliberately attempted to create visual effects through his writing" (1987: 495). "Franklin's knack for painting a portrait in words," for example, is perhaps nowhere more on display, Arch maintains, than when the young Franklin first comes to Philadelphia (2008: 159). Franklin's dramatic entrance into the city of brotherly love would become one of the most frequently illustrated moments from his memoirs, even in those very earliest editions which contained only a few cuts. Eventually, Franklin's arrival into Philadelphia would, at least according to Lemay, become "the most famous single scene in all American literature" (Lemay 1987: 495).

Indeed, it is difficult to imagine a more enduring and influential coming-to-America picture than Franklin's written description of his first entrance into Philadelphia in 1723. Yet, what makes its visibility so extraordinary is that the vivid verbal image Franklin creates for his readers is one that self-reflexively describes a moment of intense looking itself. It is similar to what Mitchell calls a meta-picture, in that it self-reflexively reflects on seeing even as it generates a verbal image for its readers (1994: 61). It does so, however, through language rather than an optical medium. In the episode, Franklin draws our attention not only to his personal appearance, but to how it was seen by others, especially his future spouse, Deborah Read. Early in Part 1 of the *Autobiography*, Franklin relates how, after a long night of rowing, he walks down Market Street seemingly oblivious to the image he presents before the eyes of strangers. "Tired" and "dirty" from the journey, Franklin staggers into Philadelphia with his pockets bursting with dirty laundry (Franklin 1986: 27). Famished, he spends what little money he has left on "three great Puffy Rolls" (27) and then proceeds to walk down Market Street with one under each arm and a third rapidly disappearing into his mouth. The three large puffy rolls not only intensify the image of Franklin's ignorance, obscurity, and poverty at this moment, but they also help draw the scrutiny and judgment of his future wife. "Thus I went up Market Street," Franklin recalls, "passing by the door of Mr. Read, my future wife's father; when she, standing at the door, saw me, and thought I made, as I certainly did, a most awkward, ridiculous appearance" (27). For Franklin, the point of this episode is to enable the reader to contrast the verbal image of this ravenous runaway apprentice with the exemplary public gentleman and founding father that he would later become. As he explains to his son, "I have been the more particular in the description of my journey and shall be so of my first entry into that city, that you may in your mind compare such unlikely beginnings with the Figure I have since made there" (Franklin 1986: 27). Franklin invites readers to visualize those two bodies of Franklin discussed above – the generic youthful figure of his obscure past and the particular older man of his extraordinary present – so that readers might attribute the magnitude of his accomplishments to what he did rather than who he was, what he had, or where he came from.

Yet, part of what makes the verbal image of Franklin's first entrance so compelling is that he projects the differences between these two selves – between the general, universal figure of Franklin the national role model and the specific, historical actor of Franklin the particular person – onto a temporal difference between an unformed common boy and the distinguished man he would become. Moreover, there is nothing particular to Franklin's awkward and ridiculous appearance that cannot be changed over time. As I have argued elsewhere, part of the great attraction of Franklin's *Autobiography* for his readers is that he presents the relationship between the visibility of his person and the legibility of his public character in terms of performance (Lukasik 2010: 2–6). By de-corporealizing his person and explaining his success in the generalized terms of pure genteel performance, Franklin allows the acquisition of his social mobility to seem as available as the acquisition of his conduct.

What makes the visibility of Franklin's verbal image of his first entrance to Philadelphia so memorable and effective for delivering his message of upward mobility, however, is how he is able to depict both Franklins, the particular and the general, at the same time. In the narrative present of the memoir, Franklin appears as an obscure and ignorant boy, awkward and ridiculous. Yet, the particular Franklin of the future, "the Figure I have since made" and which would inspire the emulation of America's youth, is also present. Franklin, however, condenses the mental comparison, which we as readers are invited to do retrospectively, through the eyes of Deborah Read, who performs the same task as we do, but proleptically. *The Autobiography*, in other words, amplifies the significance of appearances in the social perception of character by invoking two different temporalities simultaneously, and it does so by focalizing readers on the exchange of glances between Franklin and Read. As we are about to find out, Franklin's decision to register this mental comparison, the before and after images of his appearance, would become an important element in subsequent remediations of the famous scene through the optical medium of illustration.

3 Mahlon Day's *A Brief Memoir of the Life of Dr. Benjamin Franklin*

One of the earliest remediations of Franklin's iconic first entrance into Philadelphia appeared as an illustration in Day's *A Brief Memoir of the Life of Dr. Benjamin Franklin*. First published in 1824, Day's text would be reprinted several times throughout the next decade, including the 1830 edition reproduced here (figure 1). As one of the first children's book publishers in America, Day operated a children's book store in New York where he sold works emphasizing piety and virtue (Weiss 1941: 5). In general, Day's little books, or 'toys,' as he called them, were profusely illustrated (Weiss 1941: 5). Although J. A. Adams and Alexander Anderson were both known to have engraved for Day, Anderson most likely designed the illustration of Franklin's first entrance to Philadelphia since his name appears on the signed frontispiece for the 1824 edition of the book and since the illustration stylistically resembles small inset engravings Anderson is known to have made from the turn of the century.

As one of the first, if not the first, to illustrate the famous episode, Anderson's engraving hews more closely to the verbal image in Franklin's text than later remediations would. In fact, Day's biography intensifies this effect by switching from the third to the first person as the image/text operation sutures Franklin's own verbal image to the optical equivalent in the engraving. The engraving follows the text's focalization of the scene on the exchange of glances between Franklin and Read. In Anderson's image, no other people are depicted on the street, as would be the case in subsequent illustrations. As a result, the spectacle of Franklin's appearance is somewhat reduced, or, more precisely, the social dimension of Franklin's appearance still depends upon its visibility within the verbal image itself. Indeed, Anderson's engraving closely conforms to the text in its picture of Franklin as an impoverished runaway. It duplicates the visibility of Franklin's text through its depiction of his dirty laundry, puffy rolls, and, in Day's words, "a very singular and grotesque appearance" (1830: 15).

Yet, by minimizing the social nature of that appearance, Anderson's engraving also mutes the force of the public in producing the revisable nature of that image. Anderson's engraving restricts the legibility of Franklin's malleability to the two figures staring at him: Read and the implied reader. Indeed, the optical remediation presents the episode as if nobody else is around. The buildings of Market Street are missing and thus also the social observation that Franklin otherwise implies within the text (and that later illustrations will accentuate; see figure 4, for instance). While there are looming windows – a detail not specifically mentioned in Franklin's text – no faces are peering out from them. The sole figure, framed by the front door from which she emerges, is Read. In Anderson's remediation, Franklin's appearance matters not so much for what it says to the public, but for what it says to her. Staring from her father's doorway, surrounded by a wall of windows, her stiff figure channels the social effects of appearance into the realm of a subsequent marital choice and domestic life.

Anderson's condensation of the scene to Franklin and Read is magnified by the distance from which we, as readers and viewers, behold the scene before us. Unlike later remediations in which Franklin appears much closer to the picture plane (see figures 3, 5, and 6), Anderson's engraving places him further from the picture plane in the middle of the street. Despite our distance, the absence of other figures in the engraving has the effect of placing us in the position of those early Philadelphians who first saw Franklin enter the city. Indeed, Franklin looks nervously over his left shoulder as if reluctantly acknowledging the force of our stares. With no other people looking at Franklin besides Read, the spectacle Franklin makes, in the sense of registering its public as opposed to its private effects, falls to our eyes. The implied spectators who are represented through the staring and pointing figures in later remediations (see figure 4) are missing here. The distance also allows for the particularity of Benjamin Franklin, the eminent founding father, to recede more easily into a universal boyish figure (universal, that is, to those who share his race and gender). Although engraved portraits – typically based on well-known oil portraits of Franklin – had been standard frontispieces for his memoirs since at least the 1790s and, in fact, one serves as the frontispiece for Day's biography, Anderson's engraving inaugurates a tradition in which the optical image functions to illustrate a moment from an exemplary life story more than an incident in the life of an exemplary man.

The intermedial operation of word and image in Anderson's engraving for Day's *A Brief Memoir of the Life of Dr. Benjamin Franklin* is one of conjunction in the production of the visibility of the revisable and voluntary nature of Franklin's physical appearance. Yet, the optical remediation of that verbal image minimizes the social effects of the spectacle by restricting the force of that gaze to Deborah Read and us as readers/spectators. These two entities are the only ones who can simultaneously compare both Franklins mentally, the former prospectively, the latter retrospectively. Anderson's illustration amplifies the visibility of the verbal image produced by the text itself by following its invocation of multiple temporalities. The most significant and enduring effect of Anderson's remediation of Franklin's verbal image, however, might well be the reduction of the episode to the narrative moment when Read sees Franklin from the doorway. More often than not, subsequent nineteenth-century illustrators would remediate this precise narrative moment when illustrating Franklin's first entrance to Philadelphia.

4 Samuel G. Goodrich's *The Life of Benjamin Franklin*

Goodrich's *The Life of Benjamin Franklin* also remediates Franklin's first entrance into Philadelphia with an illustration of Deborah Read staring at Franklin walking down the street. The illustration, simply titled, "Franklin Walking in the Streets of Philadelphia" (figure 2) first appeared in the 1832 edition. This illustration, like all the others in the book, is unsigned and remains unattributed (Pfitzer 2002: 14). Goodrich, a pioneer in pictorial histories, published a series of illustrated children's books in America during the 1830s and 1840s under the pen name of Peter Parley. *The Life of Benjamin Franklin* or Parley's Franklin, as it was better known at the time, was the third number in his American School Biography series and, like Day's book, it was intended for a juvenile audience. Parley's Franklin, like other biographies in Goodrich's series, contains numerous engravings. At a time when "nearly two thirds of all illustrated works proved heavy financial failures or barely covered the costs of production," Goodrich's conviction in the pedagogical value of images came with considerable risk (Pfitzer 2002: 14).

Goodrich's insistence on illustrating children's school books challenged longstanding educational theories that iconoclastically accused picture books of catering to the senses rather than the understanding. Goodrich, however, believed that children should learn through the "senses, and especially by the eye" (1856: III, 309). Years later, in his memoirs, he would describe how his illustrated children's books were at first criticized for being "too materialistic," "too utilitarian," and "too easy" (Goodrich 1856: III, 311). Nonetheless, Goodrich maintained that illustrations were indispensable for childhood learning and literacy acquisition. Optical images did not indulge the senses, he argued; they rather enabled the mind to engage in distinct ideas. "Let children look upon pictures, not as pictures *merely*; but as lessons to be *studied*," his *Parley's Magazine* declared in 1834, "What can be more rich in valuable instruction than a good engraving" (1834: n.pag.)? In Goodrich's books, the image precedes the word and serves to delimit the range of subsequent ideas associated with it. "These views," he points out, "led me in a direction exactly opposite to the old theories in respect to nursery books" (Goodrich 1856: III, 311). The problem with nursery books and fairy tales, Goodrich reasons, was that their verbal images could make too strong of an impression on the child's imagination and thus they could be mistaken for reality. Instead of imagining shocking, violent scenes from the verbal images they read – and then mistaking them for "a picture of life" (1856: I, 166) –, the young mind could avoid such mental pictures by looking at distinct images generated by the illustrations they saw. Thus, for Goodrich, the optical image was a means to limit, if not replace, the child's capacity to imagine and picture images evoked by words. The implicit image/text operation was a delimitation of the imagination in reading practice in exchange for the production of a homogenous and distinct series of images that all readers would experience similarly. As a publisher of children's literature, Goodrich's illustration practice was thus grounded in ideas that sought to de-individuate readerly visualization through the mass consumption of optical imagery.

The media combination of caption and illustration in Goodrich's *The Life of Benjamin Franklin* reflects his views in that it works to limit the imagination in the production of the visibility of Franklin's verbal image. Where young minds might have imagined themselves in the otherwise generalized illustration of an impoverished runaway walking down Market Street – as they might have done while looking at the caption-less Anderson illustration in Day's biography – the caption, "Franklin Walking in the Streets of Philadelphia," reminds the young reader that the foreground figure is Franklin and the background scene is Philadelphia – as if the reader has somehow been inattentive and forgotten what he is reading or who has written it. As a result, the media combination works against the simultaneous multiple temporalities that Franklin's verbal image otherwise invokes through the gaze of Deborah Read. Although Goodrich's illustration remediates the exact same narrative moment as Day and Anderson, its caption anchors the image's meaning to the particular Franklin. The caption's reminder that this is the particular Franklin serves to produce a visibility in which his image serves as a behavioral model more than an aspirational goal.

The media combination of caption and illustration is therefore disjunctive in so far as the caption anchors the illustration's otherwise generalized representation of Franklin's youth so that the optical image functions more to inculcate moral lessons than to inspire social mobility.

The illustration also departs in several ways from the text that is consistent with Goodrich's broader intention of having the optical technology of engraving (rather than the reader's imagination) generate distinct images for children. Even though the illustration remediates the same narrative moment as Day and Anderson did, it introduces several elements into the scene not specifically mentioned in the text. Perhaps the most striking and enduring addition is the introduction of four figures into the picture. In the far left middle-ground, a strolling couple emerges from the shadows to catch Franklin crossing their path. Next to them and to the left of Franklin, a small boy stands – no longer interested in the hoop to be trundled – eyes fixed, gaping at Franklin. To the right of Franklin, a stunned Read leans out of her front door tilting her head forward just enough to peek, as if unsure she even wants to be seen herself. Finally, to her left and to our far right, a man with a cane walks in the opposite direction of Franklin. He turns his head slightly backwards as if doubling back in amazement at the appearance Franklin is making.

Nearly all of their eye lines direct our attention to Franklin himself who is spotlighted in the center of the image directly in front of us. His cast shadow enhances this effect by creating yet another implied line directing our visual attention to him. That all of these figures share more or less the same middle-ground depth as Read does within the picture intensifies the public nature of the spectacle that Franklin makes. While there is background space behind them (indeed, the couple walks towards us from it), not a single person dares to look that way. All of the figures have their eyes fixed on Franklin. They form a wall of spectators separating the middle from the background while we, as readers/spectators and parallel to the picture plane, complete the circle of eyes that surround him. We, too, participate in the spectacle, adding our gaze to those of the middle-ground figures.

Yet, we no longer look alone as was the case in Day and Anderson's remediation. Although we are much closer to the picture plane than we were in Day and Anderson's illustration, our role has been lessened because it is now shared. Where Day and Anderson's illustration depicted a solitary Franklin – almost lost on the street – before the eyes of Read, Goodrich's illustration emphasizes and distributes the sociality of the gaze through the additional figures. And, consequently, it mitigates our participation in it even as it invites us to look all the same. Even though we are encouraged to stare, our look is nonetheless guided by Goodrich's media combinations. In addition to the caption, the inclusion of a monitorial footnote at the bottom of the page contributes to the illustration's function in limiting the visibility of Franklin's verbal image. At the beginning of the paragraph describing the scene, Goodrich prints a number 7 which leads presumably young readers to the bottom of page 29 where they are instructed to "describe [Franklin's] appearance on his first arrival there." Thus, the readerly imagination is restrained three times in Goodrich's biography; once, by the illustration whose distinct image operates disjunctively with Franklin's verbal image; twice, by the caption which emphasizes one temporality (the past) over another (the future) in Franklin's text; and third, by the paratextual number and endnote command which literally directs readers where to look.

Just as Goodrich's media combinations work to limit the reader's imagination, so, too, does the engraving, whose odd depiction of Franklin's appearance disrupts how the multiple temporalities implicit in Franklin's verbal image operate. The illustration, however, does not entirely dispense with them. Instead, it separates the past and the future, the general and the particular Franklins, and relocates them through the optical image of the engraving. The illustration switches the location of the future Franklin from the prospective gaze of Read (and the implicit retrospective looking of ourselves) onto the represented figure of Franklin himself. We as readers no longer have to mentally compare and imagine the figure Franklin has since become, because Goodrich's illustration does this for us.

Indeed, the illustration is oddly disjunctive, even somewhat incoherent, in its rendering of Franklin's ridiculous appearance in that the visibility of his awkwardness is communicated more strongly through the staring and pointing figures of those who surround Franklin, than through what they stare and point at: Franklin himself. The introduction of these four additional figures helps Goodrich to relocate the future, distinguished Franklin onto the depicted boyish figure in the illustration. The iconographic details of Franklin's supposedly awkward appearance are more legible, but they also depart from the unkempt appearance that Franklin's verbal image otherwise emphasizes. While certain aspects of the verbal image are reproduced – Franklin's puffy rolls for instance – others are muted, such as the dirty laundry emphasized both in the text and in Day and Anderson's engraving. Where Day and Anderson drew attention to the revisable nature of the self by faithfully reproducing all the details of Franklin's physical appearance, Goodrich makes Franklin appear less ridiculous than the verbal image suggests. In it, Franklin is hardly stuffing his mouth. Instead, he is shown holding one puffy roll rather carefully in his left arm with a second firmly in his right hand as if returning from the market, rather than arriving hungry, penniless, and friendless. The third roll has presumably already been eaten and consequently the illustration avoids having to display Franklin's simultaneous surplus of hunger and lack of *politesse* (a point memorably illustrated through Franklin's stuffed cheeks in the 1850s *The Child's Life of Franklin*; see figure 5). This less ridiculous impression of Franklin is supported by Goodrich's biographical text which, besides being told in the third person, softens Read's judgment. Whereas, in Franklin's memoirs, Deborah "standing at the door, saw me, and thought I made, as I certainly did, a most awkward, ridiculous appearance," in Goodrich's biography she "*probably* thought he made an awkward appearance" (Goodrich 1836: 31; emphasis added).

To be clear, this less ridiculous depiction of Franklin's first entrance in Goodrich's illustration is not a matter of the engraver or the designer 'interpreting' the verbal image (a claim that assumes that the effect of the reception of the image/text is identical to its production); it is a matter of the visibility produced by the operation of the image/text. We do not read one, then see the other, but rather read and see them simultaneously. By picturing a less awkward figure than the verbal image of Franklin's text otherwise suggests, the optical image of Goodrich's illustration also allows the arc of Franklin's social mobility to become more immediately visible, but it does so in ways that reduce the reader's role in imagining that trajectory. Here, it is as if the optical image is already anticipating the distinguished figure Franklin will become even as he is in the process of becoming it (which is, to be sure, consistent with the narrative trajectory that Franklin himself encourages when he asks us to compare the figure he has since made with the one he describes as a youth). Yet, the difference is that Goodrich's illustration seeks to minimize the perceived gap between these two Franklins optically, in part, to minimize the role of the imagination in visualizing that image, but, perhaps also, to avoid alienating an audience who may identify with Franklin's obscurity, poverty, and ordinariness, but may not wish to be reminded of it before the public.

5 John Frost's *Pictorial Life of Benjamin Franklin*

By the time Frost's *Pictorial Life of Benjamin Franklin* appeared in the late 1840s, Goodrich's use of the optical medium of engraving to limit the role of the imagination in readerly visualization was more prevalent as illustration became more and more widespread in American print culture. Frost's book includes yet another optical remediation of Franklin's first entrance into Philadelphia. The engraving, now entitled "Franklin's Arrival in Philadelphia" (figure 3), was likely designed by William Croome and engraved by the Philadelphia engravers R. S. Gilbert and William Gihon. Croome's illustration follows Goodrich's engraving in presenting a far more refined image of Franklin than his memoirs suggest.

Yet, even more than Goodrich's illustration did, Frost and Croome's engraving works against the mental comparison that Franklin's verbal image otherwise solicits from readers by blurring the line between the two Franklins (obscure boy and distinguished man) in its optical remediation.

First published in 1846, Frost's *Pictorial Life of Benjamin Franklin* was part of a series of pictorial biographies and histories that he authored throughout the 1840s. Frost was in many ways an even greater advocate for the power of illustration in children's books than his predecessor Goodrich. Frost shared Goodrich's view that the value of optical images lay in the distinct impressions they made upon the young minds of their readers. In his lavishly illustrated *Pictorial History of the United States of America* (1844), for example, Frost promotes the idea that "well-conceived and ably executed" pictures can impress "historical events upon the mind" (1844: vii). "The portrait," he continues,

> of a distinguished man gives additional force and distinctness to our recollection of his character: the picture of a battle, although it is necessarily incomplete and imperfect, *takes a stronger hold of the imagination than any effort of descriptive power*; and even the sketch of a remarkable place will give it a local habitation in the mind, which will remain longer and produce a livelier satisfaction than any mere record of language. (Frost 1844: vii; emphasis added)

Pictures were the ideal teachers of history for Frost because they delivered distinct and lasting impressions to the young mind. For this reason, he illustrated his books copiously. For Frost, illustrations were indispensable for the study of history since they facilitated the reader's memory by providing it with permanent images.

The "force and distinctness" of images, however, were unquestionably the result of optical, not textual, media. By the time Frost's *Pictorial Life of Benjamin Franklin* was published in 1846, illustration was no longer an expensive embellishment; instead it was an integral component to the production, circulation, and consumption of antebellum print culture. For Frost, this transformation in how images appeared within print culture was something to be embraced, not feared. Where a cautious Goodrich could still point to the verbal image's capacity to act "strongly upon [the] imagination" and excite "the most painful impressions" as a justification for illustrating children's books during the 1830s, by the mid 1840s the force of such visibility was less and less likely to be granted to the descriptive power of words alone. As Frost put it, the optical technology of engraving now possessed "a stronger hold of the imagination than any effort of descriptive power" and their images produced longer lasting and livelier impressions "than any mere record of language" (1846: vii).

Frost maintained that no genre was better suited to impress "distinct ideas and vivid impressions" (1846: iii) on young minds than biography. Indeed, his *Pictorial Life of Benjamin Franklin* was published so that the adolescent reader would receive "the benefit of his good example" (iv). As we saw above, no single episode epitomized the force of Franklin's example more for mid-nineteenth-century American publishers than his first entrance into Philadelphia. Like Day and Goodrich before him, Frost pictured this moment for his readers with an engraved illustration of the episode. Yet, unlike Goodrich, who changed the narrative voice to the third person, Frost chose to have Franklin "describe his first appearance in Philadelphia in his own words" (45).

The resulting image/text operation of Croome's engraving and Franklin's verbal image in Frost's *Pictorial Life of Benjamin Franklin* is one of profound disjunction. Similar to Goodrich's work, Croome's "Franklin's Arrival in Philadelphia" works to suppress the visibility of Franklin's verbal image as it presents an even more genteel image of the young Franklin. Like earlier remediations, Franklin remains the compositional focus of Croome's engraving. He stands near its center, walking to our left, his head turned slightly to the picture plane, as he looks directly at us. The severe receding orthogonals of the buildings and city streets place the vanishing point directly behind Franklin and thus further draw our attention to him. Where Franklin's verbal image emphasizes the visible cues betraying his lack of civility and genteel distinction, Croome's optical image presents the same information, but mutes their social significance. Franklin still holds puffy rolls, but he does so elegantly – even more so than in Goodrich's remediation – as if returning from the market. Moreover, he is not caught eating in the street and thus does not appear hungry at all. His pockets are full, but his "shirts and stockings" (Frost 1846: 45) are discretely hidden from our view. He does not appear dirty or tired as he does in Franklin's verbal image. The self-assured strut of Croome's young Franklin is a far cry from the meek hobble featured in Day and Anderson's engraving. The young Franklin looks confident, not lost. His face lacks any trace of embarrassment. Hardly "a most awkward, ridiculous appearance," Franklin parades around as if he is already a gentleman. Indeed, the caption, "Franklin's Arrival in Philadelphia" eliminates the word "first" that would be found in later remediations (see figures 4, 5, and 6).

The background elements in Croome's engraving further diminish the spectacle of Franklin's verbal image by rendering him utterly pedestrian; nobody even notices that he is there. In the far-right immediate background, two gentlemen chat without even bothering to turn their heads. Likewise, in the left background, the couple first seen in Goodrich's engraving continues their stroll, this time walking their dog. Unlike later engravings (such as the 1868 Bigelow edition of Franklin's *Autobiography*; see figure 6), in which a stray dog, undoubtedly attracted by Franklin's fallen breadcrumbs, wanders into the episode, Croome's dog completely ignores him. To the left of the couple, two more people in the far distance walk away from Franklin toward the background seemingly unaware of his presence. In addition, the engraving's odd execution of the perspective – in which the size of the background figures is incorrect – creates the impression that these figures do not share the same pictorial space and suggests that Franklin is literally in his own world. The absence of eye contact between the background figures and the foregrounded Franklin further minimizes his ridiculous appearance and instead focuses the exchange of glances exclusively between Franklin and us.

In general, Croome's engraving departs significantly from both previous optical remediations of Franklin's verbal image and from those that will follow. Perhaps the most striking departure is what is not shown, but nonetheless present. In nearly every other nineteenth-century engraving of this episode (see figures 1, 2, 4, 5, and 6, for instance), we find Deborah Read prominently depicted, typically standing in or near her father's doorway, staring at Franklin. In Croome's engraving, however, she is conspicuously absent. Or, rather, her absence within the picture allows us to see it through her eyes. Croome cleverly collapses the vantage point of Read with that of the picture itself. We stand in the doorway, but rather than see Franklin strictly as he was – that is, as he describes himself in the past – we also see him as he will be. What Deborah sees at this moment is 'hidden potential.' As a result, the type of mental comparison that Franklin's verbal image seeks to obtain from its readers is relocated from the reader's imagination and condensed into the single optical image of the young Franklin entering Philadelphia. Past and present, obscure boy and distinguished man, the general and the particular Franklin are all combined into Croome's illustration. We see him in the future perfect, as it were. No longer a mental comparison generated by Franklin's verbal image, Frost and Croome's engraving relocates the visibility of Franklin's social mobility from the active imaginations of his individual readers to their passive consumption of de-individuated optical media.

6 Intermediality, Remediation, and Media History

In the years following Frost's *Pictorial Life of Benjamin Franklin*, numerous illustrated editions of Franklin's *Autobiography* would be published as the market for illustrated biographies continued to expand in the United States. O. L. Holley's

The Life of Benjamin Franklin (1848), Horatio Hastings Weld's *Benjamin Franklin: His Autobiography* (1849), and John Bigelow's massively illustrated *The Autobiography of Benjamin Franklin* (1868), to name but a few – all would remediate Franklin's famous first entrance into Philadelphia through engraved illustrations (see figures 4, 5, and 6). Yet, it was in the period between 1830 and 1846 – when the first optical remediations of the episode were published alongside Franklin's verbal image – that the visibility of the text would undergo the most significant transformations of its image/text operations.

I began this essay by asking what we can learn through a diachronic analysis of optical remediations of the same verbal image. I offer the following four points by way of conclusion. First, the historical arc of these three case studies documents a transformation in how the visibility of Franklin's text was understood to operate in terms of media history (and, in particular, in terms of literature's relationship to that media history). Where, in the first quarter of the nineteenth century, the visibility of Franklin's *Autobiography* is generated by the active imagination of an individual reader visualizing the verbal images of his text, by the end of the second quarter of the nineteenth century that visibility shifts significantly to the passive, mass consumption of identical optical media. Second, this transformation is consistent with broader trends within the publication of nineteenth-century print culture, which saw not only a substantial increase in illustration, but an acknowledged decrease in the pictorial power of words. Third, as the case studies of Goodrich and Frost suggest, the production of a distinct series of optical images that all readers would experience similarly owed more to the educational theories of the proponents of illustrated children's literature than the emergence of cheaper forms of engravings. Despite its inherent financial risk for publishers during the 1830s, the illustration practice of Goodrich (and later Frost) nonetheless sought to de-individuate readerly visualization through the mass consumption of homogenous optical imagery. Fourth, and as a result of this last point, the rise of the optical image within nineteenth-century print culture may have been the effect of, rather than a cause in, the rise of a mass visual culture in print media. Even as optical media began to displace the dual operations of literary pictorialism and readerly visualization – as I hope the history of the remediation of Franklin's first entrance to Philadelphia has shown –, its rise was intricately tied to the visibility that was generated by and expected from its predecessor media form: the verbal images of literature. In short, might we consider the rise of the optical image in media history as a technologization of that prior mode of literary pictorialism and its graphic descriptive power?

As I hope the preceding pages have suggested, an intermedial approach to nineteenth-century literature has the potential to establish the foundation for articulating a new history of the dominance of modern optical media during the twentieth century and beyond. By using a dialectical account of media in studying the rise of illustration, for instance, we may be able to reverse our familiar understanding of the relationship between technology and culture – one in which technological innovations always drive cultural transformations – by showing how prior cultural forms, when conceived in terms of media environments, might generate practices which facilitate (or, alternatively, restrict) the introduction and acceptance of new cultural technologies. As the example of illustrated editions of Franklin's *Autobiography* suggests, the representational and reading practices of nineteenth-century literary culture, with its emphasis on the production and reception of images, is precisely such a media environment. Clearly, the extraordinary growth of literary illustration during the nineteenth century and across a range of print media affords us an opportunity to consider how literature might have participated in a more general historical transformation of the image – from the imaginary to the optical – one undoubtedly expedited by the technologizing of culture, but not necessarily inaugurated by it.

Works Cited

Arch, Stephen Carl. 2008. "Benjamin Franklin's *Autobiography:* Then and Now". In: Carla Mulford (ed.). *The Cambridge Companion to Benjamin Franklin*. Cambridge: Cambridge University Press. 159–171.
Brake, Laurel and Marysa Demoor (eds.). 2009. *The Lure of Illustration in the Nineteenth Century: Picture and Press*. London: Palgrave.
Casper, Scott. 1989. *Constructing American Lives: Biography and Culture in Nineteenth-Century America*. Chapel Hill: University of North Carolina Press.
[Day, Mahlon]. 1830. *Brief Memoir of the Life of Dr. Benjamin Franklin. Completed for the Use of Young Persons*. New York: Mahlon Day.
Fichtelberg, Joseph. 1988. "The Complex Image: Text and Reader in the *Autobiography* of Benjamin Franklin". *Early American Literature* 23(2): 202–216.
Franklin, Benjamin. 1986. *The Autobiography of Benjamin Franklin*. Kenneth Silverman (ed.). New York: Norton.
Frost, John. 1844. *Pictorial History of the United States of America, from the Discovery by the Northmen in the Tenth Century to the Present Time*. 4 vols. Philadelphia: B. Walker.
Frost, John. 1846. *The Pictorial Life of Benjamin Franklin: Embracing Anecdotes Illustrative of His Character. Embellished with Engravings*. Philadelphia: Lindsay and Blakiston.
Frost, John. 1852. *Historical Collections of All Nations*. Hartford: Case, Tiffany, & Co.
[Goodrich, Samuel G.]. 1834. "Circular". *Parley's Magazine*. 2:1 (part 1, no. 1): n.pag.
Goodrich, Samuel G. 1836. *The Life of Benjamin Franklin*. Philadelphia: Desilver, Thomas & Co.
Goodrich, Samuel G. 1856. *Recollections of a Lifetime*. 3 vols. New York: Miller.

Huang, Nian-Sheng. 1994. *Benjamin Franklin in American Thought and Culture, 1790–1990*. Memoirs of the America Philosophical Society Volume 211. Philadelphia: American Philosophical Society.

Huang, Nian-Sheng and Carla Mulford. 2008. "Benjamin Franklin and the American Dream". In: Carla Mulford (ed.). *The Cambridge Companion to Benjamin Franklin*. Cambridge: Cambridge University Press. 145–158.

Kooistra, Lorraine. 2011. *Poetry, Pictures, and Popular Publishing: The Illustrated Gift Book and Victorian Visual Culture, 1855–1875*. Athens: Ohio University Press.

Leja, Michael. 2011. "Fortified Images for the Masses". *Art Journal* Winter: 61–83.

Lemay, J. A. Leo. 1987. "The American Aesthetic of Franklin's Visual Creations". *Pennsylvania Magazine of History and Biography* 111(4): 465–499.

Lukasik, Christopher J. 2010. *Discerning Characters: The Culture of Appearance in Early America*. Philadelphia: University of Pennsylvania Press.

Miles, Richard D. 1957. "The American Image of Benjamin Franklin". *American Quarterly* 9(2): 117–143.

Mitchell, W. J. T. 1994. *Picture Theory*. Chicago: University of Chicago Press.

Mitchell, W.J.T. 2005. *What Do Pictures Want? The Lives and Loves of Images*. Chicago: University of Chicago Press.

Patterson, Cynthia. 2010. *Art for the Middle Classes: America's Illustrated Magazines of the 1840s*. Jackson: University Press of Mississippi.

Pfitzer, Gregory M. 2002. *Picturing the Past: Illustrated Histories and the American Imagination, 1840–1900*. Washington, DC: Smithsonian IP.

Rancière, Jacques. 2007. *The Future of the Image*. Translated by Gregory Elliott. London: Verso.

Weiss, Harry B. 1941. *Mahlon Day: Early New York Printer, Bookseller and Publisher of Children's Books*. New York: New York Public Library.

Figure 1: This is one of the earliest remediations of Franklin's iconic first entrance into Philadelphia. Source: *Brief Memoir of The Life of Dr. Benjamin Franklin. Compiled for the use of young persons*. 1830. NY: Mahlon Day. Courtesy, American Antiquarian Society.

Franklin walking in the streets of Philadelphia.

Figure 2: "Franklin Walking in the Streets of Philadelphia." Source: Samuel G. Goodrich [Peter Parley]. 1832. *The Life of Benjamin Franklin.* New York: Collins and Hannay. Courtesy, American Antiquarian Society.

Making an Entrance, Illustrating a Life — 31

FRANKLIN'S ARRIVAL IN PHILADELPHIA.

Figure 3: "Franklin's Arrival in Philadelphia." Page opposite page 46. Designed by William Croome and engraved by R. S. Gilbert and William Gihon. Source: John Frost. 1847. *The Pictorial Life of Benjamin Franklin: Embracing Anecdotes Illustrative of His Character. Embellished With Engravings.* Philadelphia: Lindsay and Blakiston. Courtesy, New York Public Library.

Figure 4: "Franklin's First Visit to Philadelphia." Designed and Engraved by Alexander Anderson. Source: O. L. Holley. 1848. *The Life of Benjamin Franklin*. New York: George F. Cooledge & Brother. Stereotyped by C. C. Savage. Courtesy, American Antiquarian Society.

Figure 5: "Franklin's First Entry Into Philadelphia." Source: *The Child's Life of Franklin*. With Eight Illustrations. c.1850. Philadelphia: Fisher & Brother. Courtesy, American Antiquarian Society.

Figure 6: "Franklin's First Entrance Into Philadelphia." Source: *Autobiography of Benjamin Franklin*. Edited from his manuscript, with notes and an introduction, by John Bigelow. 1868. Philadelphia: J. B. Lippincott. Courtesy, Historical Society of Pennsylvania.

Hélène Quanquin
Illustrations "More Numerous Than We Could Have Expected": Biography as "Mixed Media" in *William Lloyd Garrison, 1805–1879: The Story of His Life Told by His Children* (1885–1889)

Abstract

The four volumes of *William Lloyd Garrison, 1805–1879: The Story of His Life Told by His Children*, the biography of the American abolitionist leader written by his two sons and published in 1885 and 1889 include numerous illustrations, mostly portraits made by wood-engraver Gustav Kruell. The use of "mixed media" (Higgins 2001 [1965]: 52) in this biography is not meant only to complement, but also to interact with the text in order to draw a more accurate picture of Garrison's life and work as well as of the authors' own roles as guardians of their father's legacy. The analysis of the portraits published in the biography and of the intentions of the two authors, however, shows that the intermediality of the project revealed as much as it obscured. The story of intermediality in *William Lloyd Garrison, 1805–1879* is a story of omissions as much as it is a story of revelations.

1 Media in William Lloyd Garrison's Biography

The four volumes of abolitionist William Lloyd Garrison's biography, written by his sons, were published in 1885 and 1889, each dealing chronologically with a period in the American abolitionist leader's life: from 1805 to 1835 (volume I), from 1835 to 1840 (volume II), from 1841 to 1860 (volume III), and from 1861 to 1879 (volume IV).[1] For approximately ten years, the two authors, Francis Jackson Garrison and Wendell Phillips Garrison, collected a considerable amount of papers and documents related to their father's life and work (Alonso 2002: 274–275). The biography, entitled *William Lloyd Garrison, 1805–1879: The Story of His Life Told by His Children*, was published at a time when the memory of the Civil War was still dominating the political debate (Tetrault 2014: 7). It was also part of

---

[1] Volumes I and II of the biography were published in 1885; volumes III and IV in 1889.

https://doi.org/10.1515/9783110579253-004

a "Garrison revival," encouraged by his children and fellow abolitionists between 1865 and 1910, which promoted "an ideal narrative of anti-slavery protest, sacrifice, and righteous suffering" regarding the abolitionist leader's life (Santana 2016: 57). Generally well-received by friends of the family and critics (Alonso 2002: 277), it was also a commercial success, which led to the appointment of the two authors to city commissions "that were charged with the very task of deciding how to best commemorate their father" in Boston (Santana 2016: 89).

In telling their father's story, Francis Jackson and Wendell Phillips Garrison's avowed goal was to draw "a faithful portrait of his life" (1885a: xi). In order to achieve that goal, they interspersed their narrative with letters, articles, and other primary documents reproduced partially or in full in the body of the text. They also inserted the references to their sources in the margins in an effort to emphasize the reliability of their narrative, confirming that theirs was a serious endeavor, not to be confused with abolitionists' memoirs published after the Civil War, some of which were "eulogies" (Sinha 2014).[2] Garrison's biography by his sons, Manisha Sinha writes, was thus representative of "the transition from the proliferation of abolitionist memoirs to full-fledged efforts to write the history of slavery, abolition, and the war by the participants themselves."[3]

In the preface to the first volume, Francis Jackson and Wendell Phillips Garrison advised the reader to peruse the four volumes of the biography "consecutively," as this was the only proper way to "arrive at a just conception of the man, the cause, or the times" (1885a: xii). The result, they argued in the third volume, was closer to "an Autobiography – but one guarded from the defects of reminiscence by constant employment of and reference to the contemporary records in print and in manuscript, and by a thousand disinterested illustrations, corrections, and criticisms, from which the truth can hardly fail to emerge" (1889a: iii).[4] "The force of this narrative is cumulative," they claimed (1885a: xii), and it was out of the aggregation of different sources that "the truth" was to come to light.

The two authors believed that it was through the combination of abundant written archives and what they called "disinterested illustrations" (Garrison

---

[2] In the third volume, they noted that "not a material error of fact ha[d] been pointed out" in the first two volumes (Garrison 1889a: iii).

[3] For a chronology of the abolitionist autobiographies that were published after the Civil War, see Jeffrey 2008: xi–xii.

[4] In 1866, William Lloyd Garrison had agreed to write a history of abolitionism but returned the advance he had been given by a Boston publisher (Jeffrey 2008). Wendell Phillips Garrison had also wanted his father to write an autobiography after the Civil War and the abolition of slavery (Wendell Phillips Garrison January 19, 1868).

1889a: iii), most of which were portraits, that the essence of their father's life and work could be made accessible to the public. They were particularly proud of having enlisted the services of Gustav Kruell (1843–1907), a wood engraver well known for his mastery of portraiture (Smith 1929).[5] Noting that the pictures were "more numerous than [they] could have expected" (Garrison 1885: x), they profusely thanked the publishers for "their unstinted liberality in the manufacture of these admirable specimens of the printer's art, which only the highest literary excellence could parallel" (1885: v). According to them, the wood engravings were integral to their intermedial project and could not be considered apart from the biographical text itself for at least two reasons. First of all, they were thought to impart information that was essential to an accurate depiction of Garrison. Secondly, their quality testified to the high standard that the two authors aimed at when writing the biography of their father and pointed to the kind of readership they wanted to reach. In 1889, Wendell Phillips Garrison thus thanked one of his colleagues, poet and academic George E. Woodberry, for writing a review that was "all the praise [he] could desire" (1908: 79), which shows that it was important for him to appeal to an educated and literate audience.

Biographies and wood engravings were popular forms of expression in the United States in the second half of the nineteenth century, both resonating with national concerns and sharing similar goals that pertained to the edification and education of the public in a still young country. Biography was celebrated for its "power to shape individuals' lives and character and to help define America's national character" (Casper 1999: 2), while wood engraving, Woodberry claimed, was "a democratic art," with "unlimited capacities for usefulness in the future in both the intellectual and artistic education of the people" (1883: 179, 209). These two forms, whose aims were to shape and educate, coincided in *William Lloyd Garrison, 1805–1879: The Story of His Life Told by His Children*. Far from the long-established "separation of words from pictures" (Heffernan 2002: 37), the latter were harnessed by Wendell Phillips and Francis Jackson Garrison in order to serve their life-writing enterprise. They probably were first and foremost considered by the authors as complements to and illustrations of the written narrative, but they ended up being elements whose interaction with the text created and revealed tensions, gaps, and weaknesses in the representation of Garrison as a public figure.

This paper will investigate the use of "mixed media" – defined as "works executed in more than one medium" (Higgins 2001 [1965]: 52) – as a way to achieve biographical "truth," Garrison's sons' avowed goal in their father's biography, and

---

5 Gustav Kruell also co-founded the American Wood Engravers' Society in 1881.

the tensions it revealed. The use of "mixed media" is visible not only in the role played by pictures in the biographical enterprise but also in the circulation of media those very illustrations evince. It is present in the variety of media and techniques used for the original prototypes, from oil and crayon paintings, mezzotint and steel engravings, and photography to daguerreotypes and sculptures. The frontispiece of the first volume of the biography (figure 1) is a prime example of such circulation. A portrait of Garrison at the age of thirty, it was based on a cabinet oil painting, the replica of which was "painted for [British abolitionist] George Thompson." In addition, it was "engraved in mezzotint," as well as "engraved on wood, with the added accuracy of having been photographed upon the block" (Garrison 1905: 114).

Meant as a contribution to a "diachronic perspective" on intermediality (Rajewsky 2005: 47), this essay will analyze the use of pictures in *William Lloyd Garrison, 1805–1879* and the paradox of a biography whose avowed goal was to show the definitive "truth" of the man Garrison. The absence of ekphrastic elements in the text does not mean that there was no correlation between the text and the pictures or that the authors believed that the latter would speak for themselves. Wendell Phillips and Francis Jackson Garrison were fully aware of the two, sometimes contradictory, purposes of portraits, which composed the majority of the pictures we find in the biography: "a *revelatory* aim, requiring accuracy and faithfulness to the subject, and a *creative* aim, presupposing artistic expression and freedom" (Freeland 2007: 95–96). Kruell's wood engraving of Garrison that serves as the frontispiece of the fourth volume of the biography was thus reviewed by the authors as follows: "As a work of art, of the highest order; as a likeness, variously esteemed" (Garrison 1905: 116). Although the pictures used in the biography were carefully selected, the imperfect likenesses they sometimes provided point to the limits and elusiveness of a biographical project carried out from both a "disinterested" – objective – and a personal perspective.

2 Portraits: Copies and Originals

Garrison's biography by his sons incorporates more than forty illustrations, most of which are "head-and-shoulder" portraits[6] of Garrison and of his associates in the fight against slavery; furthermore, the biography features pictures of Garrison's birthplace and grammar school (Garrison 1885a: 28), facsimiles of his abo-

---

[6] Portraits are classically categorized as follows: "full-length," "three-quarter-length," and "head-and-shoulder" (Schneider 2002: 6).

Figure 1: William Lloyd Garrison, at the age of 30. Source: Frontispiece, Wendell Phillips Garrison and Francis Jackson Garrison. 1885. *William Lloyd Garrison, 1805–1879: The Story of His Life Told by His Children*, volume I: 1805–1835. New York: The Century Company.

litionist periodical *The Liberator* (Garrison 1885a: 232) and of his handwriting (Garrison 1889b: 310) as well as maps of Boston, where he lived for most of his life (Garrison 1885b: 19, 25). In the preface to the first volume, the two authors explained that priority had been given "to portraits, and among these to such as ha[d] never been engraved before" (Garrison 1885a: x), in keeping with their belief that the biography of their father was to be unprecedented in terms of the amount of sources compiled and the ambition of the project. "In the field to which we now invite the general reader we have had almost no predecessors," they boasted (Garrison 1885a: xii).

From the very first lines of the first volume, they acknowledge the duality of their readership and show they believed in "the distinction between the 'professional' and the 'amateur,'" which was essential to the standard of "historical 'objectivity'" that was becoming dominant among historians in the last third of the nineteenth century (Casper 1999: 8). Explaining their use of references in the margin, they allude to their desire "to effect a division between the specialist and the general reader." The latter, who was "not intent on enlarging his information or proving the veracity of the narrative," could very well overlook the list of sources, they argued (Garrison 1885a: ix). On the contrary, "those who study history not for amusement, but for its practical bearing on conduct in the formation of principle," they reiterated in the third volume, "may well linger over these pages" (Garrison 1889a: iv). They added that they had wanted "to secure portraits most nearly contemporaneous with the beginnings of the anti-slavery cause" (Garrison 1885a: xi). The likenesses they included could thus appeal to the general reader through their ability to create empathy with the subject as well as the historian through their historical precision.[7]

Wendell Phillips and Francis Jackson Garrison had the same high standards of accuracy for the portraits they included in the biography as they had for the written text, and they were very thorough in their presentation of the works enumerated at the beginning of each volume. The "lists of illustrations" thus detail the location, ownership, and original medium of each prototype used and, when known, the age of the subject at the time it was represented. They also sometimes include judgments on the original or the reproduction itself. One comment on the portrait of Boston abolitionist Maria Weston Chapman in the second volume mentions that it "f[ell] short of the rare beauty of the original" (1885b: vii). A similar remark is made about Garrison's likeness in the third volume: it "falls short of the spirited original, and is not quite true in expression" (1889a: vii). In both cases, however, the term "original" is ambiguous as it might refer to the prototype or the subject, an indication of the difficulty of representing someone in writing as well as in pictures. The paradox of Garrison's portraits inserted in the biography and the desire for accuracy expressed by the authors is that his children were of the opinion that his face and expression

---

[7] Despite their intentions, they however did not always manage to include portraits produced at the time of the early abolitionist movement.

eluded accurate representation. In a short biographical essay about him, his daughter Fanny Villard deplored that "[t]he photographs and portraits of [her] father g[a]ve no idea of his mobile countenance," which she described as "the despair of photographer, painter and sculptor" (Villard 1924: 12, 4) – incidentally, photography, painting, and sculpture were three media forms used as models for Garrison's portraits included in *William Lloyd Garrison, 1805–1879*. Some of the remarks added in the lists of illustrations show the high, and perhaps impossible, standard according to which Garrison's likenesses were judged. One published in the first volume was thus described as "a 'crude' practice portrait, chiefly valuable for its general testimony as to the hair and dress of the subject" but, it was mentioned, had "no resemblance in it" (Garrison 1885 a: xv).[8]

This attention to resemblance is important as it resonated with Wendell Phillips and Francis Jackson Garrison's desire to write a depiction of the life of their father that would be as comprehensive and reliable as possible. This aspiration was later exhibited again in a compilation entitled *The Words of Garrison*, which was published on the occasion of their father's centennial, in 1905. The book included a list of "[s]elect portraits and statuary of Garrison," some of which were inserted in the biography, along with a few comments that often pertained to the resemblance between the picture and the subject. Similarities were established by various means – "striking resemblance in a son and grandson" (113), being "recognized as such, in the print, by Garrison's infants" (114),[9] or "the favorable opinion [...] of Mrs. Maria Weston Chapman" (114). About an oil painting dated from 1846, the Garrison brothers claim that "[i]t ha[d] never been esteemed as a likeness by Garrison's family" (114). In another instance, that of an oil painting by Nathaniel Jocelyn in 1833, it was Garrison himself who was invoked as a judge and quoted as "regard[ing]" the portrait "a very tolerable likeness" (113). The reference to the instant reaction of "Garrison's infants" when presented with a portrait of their father, though odd it may have been, was meant to prove that it was Garrison's family members who were deemed to be the best judges of his like-

---

[8] Garrison's hair seems to have been oddly important for his sons, as they later wrote that a portrait of their father at the age of twenty published in the first volume of the biography was "the only one showing a full head of hair" (Garrison 1905: 113). "As my hands were exceptionally cold in winter," his daughter also recalled, "I often warmed them on my father's bald head. For a long time I could not understand why he said: 'You come to my incendiary head, my darling, to warm your cold hands?' One day he said to me: 'I met a man this morning who thought that I had horns.' I was greatly puzzled and did my best to find them" (Villard 1924: 6).

[9] The list of illustrations of the first volume of Garrison's biography also mentions that an engraving made around the same time as the original painting "was readily recognized as a likeness by all the Garrison infants in arms" (Garrison 1885a: xv).

nesses and were, as a consequence, the people who could provide the public with the most accurate narrative of his life and work, which was confirmed by the allusion to the already mentioned "striking resemblance in a son and grandson" (113). While these remarks contradicted to some extent Wendell Phillips and Francis Jackson Garrison's claim for objectivity and rationality when narrating their father's life, the reference to "infants in arms," i. e., children too young to walk and certainly to talk, as the best tests of the accuracy of Garrison's portraits shows that pictures were meant to arouse emotions beyond and apart from the text.

Physical resemblance was not the only quality marker perceived in portraits. In the 1905 compilation, Francis Jackson and Wendell Phillips Garrison remarked about a statuette of their father made in 1884 – five years after his death – that "this likeness st[ood] at the head of all the prints of Garrison as truly bodying forth the spirit of the resolute reformer, and it was universally approved by his co-workers and by his family" (Garrison 1905: 116), thus confirming that conveying the character of the subject depicted was equally important when judging a portrait. As the literary editor of the *Nation*, Wendell Phillips Garrison was probably in charge of the choice of illustrations, and especially portraits, and he often expressed his admiration for Kruell's likenesses, which, he believed, were true, not only to the physical appearances of his subjects, but also, and perhaps more importantly, to their personalities.[10] "Take Kruell's whole series," he wrote a friend about the engraver's work *The Portfolio of National Portraits; Eight Portraits of Historic Americans* published in 1899, "and you will find a fresh treatment of each in point of technique. This was not because [Ulysses S.] Grant and [Abraham] Lincoln and [Daniel] Webster and [James Russell] Lowell had different complexions, but because the character of each called for a different handling of the graver. Hence the wonderful absence of mannerism in his works" (Garrison 1908: 39).[11] Therefore, he praised Kruell for his ability to adapt his technique to his subjects' unique personalities – a quality the engraver's contemporaries often noted (Smith 1929: 15).

Wendell Phillips Garrison's opinions of Kruell were in tune with the development and reception of both portraiture and wood engraving in the nineteenth century. Portraits had been for some time expected to "convey [the sitter's] 'per-

---

[10] In letters written to his brother in 1889, Wendell Phillips Garrison mentioned several conversations with Kruell about the engravings that were to be included in the biography. See, for instance, Garrison February 10, 1889; March 15, 1889; March 17, 1889. A book he published in 1889 was illustrated by 21 woodcuts made by Kruell (Garrison 1898).

[11] *The Portfolio of National Portraits; Eight Portraits of Historic Americans* included his best-known work, a portrait of Lincoln.

son-ness'" (Freeland 2007: 98) or "identity" (Schneider 2002: 15). This was evident when a daguerreotype of Lincoln in his thirties was published for the first time in *McLure's* magazine in 1895, just a few years after the publication of Garrison's biography by his sons. Analyzing the viewers' reactions to it, Cara A. Finnegan notes that they "saw in the image not only a Lincoln they recognized physically, but one whose psychology and morality they recognized too" (2005: 33). In addition, the invention of the white line by Englishman Thomas Bewick at the end of the eighteenth century and its adoption in the United States in later decades gave the engraver, who was "no longer restricted to a servile following of the designer's work, line for line" (Woodberry 1883: 151), more freedom in his work within the constraints of the art, thus making it the best form for portraits.[12] Such tension between freedom and limitations is evident in Woodberry's judgment, according to which "[o]f all the work of recent years [...] the best, it is generally admitted, is in the portraits, possibly because the artists are restrained by the definiteness of the form and expression to be conveyed" (1883: 200).

3 "Public Character[s]" and Portraits

For Francis Jackson and Wendell Phillips Garrison, the biography was driven as much by their desire to pay tribute to their father as by their wish to illuminate "one of the greatest movements in the annals of mankind," i. e., the fight for the abolition of slavery (Garrison 1885a: xi). With that in mind, the choice of the figures who were represented was carefully made according to their dual goal. The placement of images throughout the volumes follows the chronology of the narrative. In the preface of the first volume, it is mentioned that "[s]ome [of the portraits] that might, from the close personal relations of the subjects of them to Mr. Garrison, have appeared here, w[ould] find an appropriate place in subsequent volumes" (Garrison 1885a: x–xi). Except for the frontispieces at the beginning

---

12 Here, George E. Woodberry compares the old and new methods of wood engraving: "[...] by the old method, [...] the block [of wood] was treated as a white surface, on which the designer drew with pen and ink, and obtained grays and blacks by increasing the number of cross-strokes, as if he were drawing on paper; by the new method the block was treated as a black surface, and the color was lessened by increasing the number of white lines" (1883: 152). He adds: "Formerly the effects were given by the designers' lines, now they were given by the engravers' lines; in other words, the old workman followed the designer's drawing, the modern workman draws himself with his graver. With the old method the design was reproduced by keeping the same line arrangement that the artist employed; by the new method the design is not thus reproduced, but is interpreted by a line arrangement first conceived by the engraver" (153). Also see Carrington 1927: 415.

of each volume and the maps of Boston in the first volume, all the pictures are placed on the right page and illustrate figures or moments mentioned in the narrative. Apart from Helen Benson Garrison, the people whose portraits were included in the biography were all well-known male and female abolitionists, among whom we find Garrison's early associates Benjamin Lundy (1885a: 88),[13] Arthur Tappan (1885a: 190), Isaac Knapp (1885a: 272) as well as fellow travelers Samuel J. May (1885a: 466), Maria Weston Chapman (1885b: 34), Sarah M. and Angelina E. Grimké (1889b: 134, 214), Abby Kelley Foster (1889b: 348) and her husband Stephen S. Foster (1889b: 30), and Parker Pillsbury (1889b: 110), among others. Francis Jackson and Wendell Phillips Garrison, however, decided to do without famous figures like Lincoln and Brown, whom they seem to have originally intended to include. Their role in the fight against slavery had been important, but they had not been close associates of their father. The insertion of their portraits would also have taken the focus away from the abolitionist movement and Garrison's leadership as well as from the centrality of his and his associates' actions in the abolition of slavery.

Originally, the authors had intended to "couple" the portraits included in the biography (Garrison March 15, 1889). Wendell Phillips Garrison recommended to pair his father with his long-time associate Wendell Phillips (Garrison March 15, 1889), which was a surprising suggestion as, by the time of Phillips's death in 1884, Wendell Phillips Garrison's originally close relationship with his namesake had turned into one of strong resentment (Quanquin 2014: 190–191). He wrote to his brother and co-author, Francis Jackson, about some of the "couples" he had in mind: "I renewed my intimation that he had better forego engraving Mother, but rather couple Phillips with W[illiam]L[loyd]G[arrison] & John Brown with Lincoln" (Garrison March 17, 1889). "Coupled" portraits were to create links between figures that would have been unmistakable to the readers, such as the martyrdom suffered by John Brown and Abraham Lincoln in the fight against slavery.[14]

When Kruell made the unsurprising suggestion that Garrison should be represented with his wife, Helen Benson Garrison, Wendell Phillips Garrison resisted the idea, claiming that his mother "was not a public character & there could be no commercial gain from portraying her" (Garrison February 10, 1889). Although such a remark – the value of his mother's portrait being judged according to the

---

[13] Garrison and Lundy met in 1828 and Garrison called their encounter "the primary link" that accounted for his conversion to immediatist abolitionism (*Helen Eliza Garrison. A Memorial* 1876: 7).

[14] I want to thank Nassim Winnie Balestrini for pointing this out.

expected sales of the book – might appear unusually cynical, it also referred to Helen Benson Garrison's place in the abolitionist movement and to the Garrisons' rather traditional marriage. She was the daughter of George Benson, a prominent Providence abolitionist, and Garrison had very early found in her family great support for his activities (Merrill 1956: 185).[15] When, in 1834, he had asked her to organize a women's abolitionist society in Providence, she however had answered that her "influence" was "extremely limited" and that her "efforts" would be "inefficient" (Benson February 18, 1834).[16] Such diffidence on her part meant that, right from the start of their relationship and in the years to come, she adhered to the idea that her role as a wife would be to help Garrison fulfill his mission, an arrangement her husband accepted and even encouraged. On their first wedding anniversary, he thus wrote his brother-in-law that he had not "marr[ied] her, expecting that she would assume a prominent station in the anti-slavery cause, but for domestic quietude and happiness." In the same letter, he conceded that he was "completely absorbed" in the antislavery fight, and "that it was undoubtedly wise in [him] to select as a partner one who, while her benevolent feelings were in unison with [his], was less immediately and entirely connected with it" (qtd. in Merrill 1956: 200).

Wendell Phillips Garrison's reluctance to include his mother both in the text and in the pictures might thus be explained by his belief that her abolitionist activism outside of the limelight would not be an efficient component of the overall argumentative trajectory of the biography of his father, but it could just as well mean that, for him, her contribution to the cause was not central to the movement. He also believed that only people who knew her would have found value in her likeness, which would have limited the appeal to potential readers.

The other motive he invoked to account for his unwillingness to publish a portrait of his mother had to do with the emotive function of pictures in relation to norms of female beauty. He wrote his brother that "the case would have been different if Mother had been a person of such beauty that her portrait would have been admirable even to a stranger," adding that Kruell "defended her beauty, though admitting it was not of the conventional kind" (Garrison March 17, 1889). He thus might have believed that only his mother's good looks could have made up for her activism outside of the public eye.

Wendell Phillips Garrison's misgivings are evidence of his desire to write the biography of his father as an activist, thus excluding all relationships, including

---

[15] On the Benson family, see Garrison 1872.
[16] The society was later formed in April 1835 on the occasion of British abolitionist George Thompson's visit to Providence.

his marriage, that were deemed private and did not provide an unmistakable focus on abolitionism. His goal had thus been to write a biography of his father as a public figure, more than as a man in all his dimensions, including the more private one. His strong opinion about his mother's portrait (figure 2), which was eventually published as the frontispiece of the second volume, is to be linked to the place he made for her in his father's biography. While the great bulk of the narrative was devoted to Garrison the "historical personage" (Garrison 1889b: 308) and showed his private life "only incidentally" (Garrison 1885a: xiv), the last chapter of the fourth and last volume entitled "Inner Traits" was devoted to "his private and domestic life" (Garrison 1889b: 308), its very position suggesting that it was more like an afterthought. It was written by Wendell Phillips Garrison, who claimed that he was aware of "a sense of insufficiency," as he felt that he could not "giv[e] a free rein to filial feeling" and had on the contrary to show "restraint" in his depiction of his father (Garrison 1889b: 308) – a possible allusion to his aim to write a book that would conform to standards of objectivity. This chapter was the subject of numerous letters exchanged by Garrison's children and was criticized by Fanny Villard, who believed that her mother had been short-changed by her brother (Alonso 2002: 277–278; Quanquin 2014: 285).

Overall, the portraits published in the biography are misleading because they give the impression that Garrison's world was populated solely by white men, when it was not. Out of the thirty-two people other than Garrison whose likenesses are included, we find no person of color, and only seven white women – Helen Benson Garrison (1885a: frontispiece), Prudence Crandall (1885a: 316), Maria Weston Chapman (1885b: 34), Sarah M. and Angelina E. Grimké (1885b: 134, 214), Abby Kelley Foster (1885b: 348), and Elizabeth Pease (1889a: 322). Such a selection does not provide an accurate description of Garrison's relationships and actions as a militant. As noted by his sons, he urged women to join the temperance movement before he became an active abolitionist (Garrison 1885a: 85–86). When he joined the fight against slavery, he also encouraged women's participation. His role was that of a "catalyst who changed the nature of the antislavery movement and helped to transform women's role in it" (Hersh 1978: 10). One year after the creation of the *Liberator*, in January 1832, he started a section devoted to women called the "Ladies Department," which he placed under the editorial responsibility of poetess Elizabeth Chandler. During his trip to England in April 1833, he was further impressed by the agitation of British female abolitionists (McDaniel 2013: 50).

Garrison's relations with black abolitionists were also central to his activism. His promotion of female participation in the abolitionist movement included both black and white women. He thus published and advertised the writings of African American abolitionist and lecturer Maria Stewart in the *Liberator*

Figure 2: Helen Benson Garrison, at about the age of 42. Source: Frontispiece, Wendell Phillips Garrison and Francis Jackson Garrison. 1885. *William Lloyd Garrison, 1805–1879: The Story of His Life Told by His Children*, volume II: 1835–1840. New York: The Century Company.

(Jones 2007: 24). He also encouraged literary contributions from members of the Female Literary Association, a black women's literary society founded in Philadelphia in 1831 (Winch 2007: 143). Black readership was certainly essential to the success of the *Liberator* (Jacobs 1971). "Black abolitionists were integral to the broader, interracial milieu of the [abolitionist] movement," Manisha Sinha argues, adding that "[t]o read them out of the abolitionist movement is to profoundly miss the part they played in defining traditions of American democratic radicalism" (2016: 2). The whitewashing present in the selection of the portraits included in Garrison's biography speaks not so much to Garrison's prejudices as to his sons' views. Wendell Phillips Garrison thus defended a very conservative view of Reconstruction, supporting the end of the occupation of the South by Northern troops and refusing to see the question of black suffrage as an urgent matter (Alonso 2002: 272).

4 Omissions and Widening Horizons

The use of "mixed media" in *William Lloyd Garrison, 1805–1879: The Story of His Life Told by His Children* thus tells a story Francis Jackson and Wendell Phillips Garrison could only have alluded to if they had solely relied on the written text, i. e., a historical account of a movement centered around the figure of their father and of his circle. It also pointed to their legitimacy as the authors of Garrison's biography and, ultimately, as the guardians of his legacy. This is especially clear in the case of Wendell Phillips Garrison, whose predominant contribution to the biography cannot be denied. "I have a sentimental reason for wishing to make the 70th [index of the *Nation*], for the *Nation* will be as old as the *Liberator*, and the two journals will stand for seventy years of editorial labor in one family without a break," he wrote a friend in 1899, as his tenure as literary editor of the *Nation* was drawing to a close (1908: 40).

The story of intermediality in *William Lloyd Garrison, 1805–1879* is a story of omissions and absences as much as it is a story of improvements and widening horizons. Garrison's sons believed that the addition of pictures would expand the scope of their project and give a more accurate description of their father's life. They however obscured some important aspects of his activism and of his personal life, revealing their own limitations as authors with both personal and political interests.

Works Cited

Alonso, Harriet Hyman. 2002. *Growing up an Abolitionist: The Story of the Garrison Children*. Amherst: University of Massachusetts Press.

Benson, Helen Eliza. February 18, 1834. Letter to William Lloyd Garrison. Garrison Family Papers, Houghton Library.

Carrington, James B. 1927. "American Wood-Engravers". *The American Magazine of Art* 18 (8): 414–423.

Casper, Scott E. 1999. *Constructing American Lives: Biography and Culture in Nineteenth-Century America*. Chapel Hill: University of North Carolina Press.

Finnegan, Cara A. 2005. "Image Vernaculars in Nineteenth-Century Visual Culture". *Rhetoric and Public Affairs* 8 (1): 31–57.

Freeland, Cynthia. 2007. "Portraits in Painting and Photography". *Philosophical Studies: An International Journal for Philosophy in the Analytic Tradition* 135(1): 95–109.

Garrison, Wendell Phillips and Francis Jackson Garrison. 1885a. *William Lloyd Garrison, 1805–1879: The Story of His Life Told by His Children*, volume I: 1805–1835. New York: The Century Company.

Garrison, Wendell Phillips and Francis Jackson Garrison. 1885b. *William Lloyd Garrison, 1805–1879: The Story of His Life Told by His Children*, volume II: 1835–1840. New York: The Century Company.

Garrison, Wendell Phillips and Francis Jackson Garrison. 1889a. *William Lloyd Garrison, 1805–1879: The Story of His Life Told by His Children*, volume III: 1841–1860. New York: The Century Company.

Garrison, Wendell Phillips and Francis Jackson Garrison. 1889b. *William Lloyd Garrison, 1805–1879: The Story of His Life Told by His Children*, volume IV: 1861–1879. New York: The Century Company.

Garrison, Wendell Phillips and Francis Jackson. 1905. *The Words of Garrison: A Centennial Selection (1805–1905) of Characteristic Sentiments from the Writings of William Lloyd Garrison with a Biographical Sketch, List of Portraits, Bibliography and Chronology*. Boston: Houghton, Mifflin and Company.

Garrison, Wendell Phillips. 1872. *The Benson Family of Newport, Rhode Island. Together with an Appendix Concerning the Benson Families in America of English Descent*. New York: The Nation Press.

Garrison, Wendell Phillips. 1898. *Parables for School and Home*. New York: Longmans, Green, & Co.

Garrison, Wendell Phillips. 1908. *Letters and Memorials of Wendell Phillips Garrison, Literary Editor of "The Nation," 1865–1906*. Cambridge: Riverside Press.

Garrison, Wendell Phillips. February 10, 1889. Letter to Francis Jackson Garrison. Wendell Phillips Garrison Papers, Houghton Library.

Garrison, Wendell Phillips. January 19, 1868. Letter to Francis Jackson Garrison, Wendell Phillips Garrison Papers, Houghton Library.

Garrison, Wendell Phillips. March 15, 1889. Letter to Francis Jackson Garrison. Wendell Phillips Garrison Papers, Houghton Library.

Garrison, Wendell Phillips. March 17, 1889. Letter to Francis Jackson Garrison. Wendell Phillips Garrison Papers, Houghton Library.

Garrison, William Lloyd. 1876. *Helen Eliza Garrison: A Memorial*. Cambridge: Riverside Press.

Heffernan, James. 2002. "Literacy and Picturacy: How Do We Learn to Read Pictures?". In: Erik Hedling and Ulla-Britta Lagerroth (eds.). *Cultural Functions of Intermedial Exploration*. Amsterdam: Rodopi. 35–66.

Hersh, Blanche Glassman. 1978. *The Slavery of Sex: Feminist-Abolitionists in America*. Urbana: University of Illinois Press.

Higgins, Dick. 2001 [1965]. "Intermedia". *Leonardo* 34 (1): 49–54.

Jacobs, Donald M. 1971. "William Lloyd Garrison's *Liberator* and Boston's Blacks, 1830–1865". *The New England Quarterly* 44 (2): 259–277.

Jeffrey, Julie Roy. 2008. *Abolitionists Remember: Antislavery Autobiographies and the Unfinished Work of Emancipation*. Chapel Hill: University of North Carolina Press.

Jones, Martha. 2007. *All Bound Up Together: The Woman Question in African American Public Culture, 1830–1900*. Chapel Hill: University of North Carolina Press.

Kruell, Gustav. 1899. *The Portfolio of National Portraits; Eight Portraits of Historic Americans*. New York: R. H. Russell.

McDaniel, W. Caleb. 2013. *The Problem of Democracy in the Age of Slavery: Garrisonian Abolitionists and Transatlantic Reform*. Baton Rouge: Louisiana State University Press.

Merrill, Walter McIntosh. 1956. "A Passionate Attachment: William Lloyd Garrison's Courtship of Helen Eliza Benson". *The New England Quarterly* 29 (2): 182–203.
Obituary. 1907. *American Art News* 5 (12): 4.
Quanquin, Hélène. 2014. "William Lloyd Garrison par ses Enfants : Une Correspondance Familiale Politique". *Epistolaire* 40: 185–194.
Rajewsky, Irina. 2005. "Intermediality, Intertextuality, and Remediation: A Literary Perspective on Intermediality". *Intermédialités* 6: 43–64.
Santana, Brian Allen. 2016. *William Lloyd Garrison and American Abolitionism in Literature and Memory.* Jefferson, NC: McFarland & Company.
Schneider, Norbert. 2002 [1992]. *The Art of the Portrait: Masterpieces of European Portrait Painting, 1420–1670.* Köln: Taschen.
Sinha, Manisha. 2014. "Memory as History, Memory as Activism: The Forgotten Abolitionist Struggle after the Civil War". *Common-Place* 14 (2): n. pag.
Sinha, Manisha. 2016. *The Slave's Cause: A History of Abolition.* New Haven: Yale University Press.
Smith, Ralph Clifton. 1929. *Gustav Kruell, American Portrait Engraver on Wood.* Champlain: Winfred Porter Truesdell.
Tetrault, Lisa. 2014. *The Myth of Seneca Falls: Memory and the Women's Suffrage Movement, 1848–1898.* Chapel Hill, NC: The University of North Carolina Press.
Villard, Fanny Garrison. 1924. *William Lloyd Garrison on Non-Resistance, Together with a Personal Sketch by his Daughter Fanny Garrison Villard and a Tribute by Leo Tolstoi.* New York: The Nation Press Printing.
Winch, Julie. 2007. "Sarah Forten's Anti-Slavery Networks". In: Kathryn Kish Sklar and James Brewster Stewart (eds.), *Women's Rights and Transatlantic Antislavery in the Era of Emancipation.* New Haven, CT: Yale University Press. 143–157.

Margit Peterfy
Performing Lives in Nineteenth-Century US-American Culture: From Paratheatricals to Early Cinema

Abstract

In this essay, I consider the cultural work of theatrical and cinematic performances with biographical content in nineteenth-century America, as well as a further 'turn' within this fundamental interest in biographies: the way audiences paid attention not just to the enacted historical figure's life on the stage but also to the actors' biographies, sometimes even looking for the same virtues in the performers as in the roles they represented on stage. The necessary condition for this second, derivative interest was the existence of a discursive field from which one could learn about the lives of the 'real persons' behind the roles. This discourse was provided by newspaper reports about famous and popular actors as 'stars.'[1] The interaction between newspapers and the stage resulted in productive intermedial cooperation, from which both could benefit: the papers published stories of interest and hereby raised their circulation, while the publicity was welcome advertising for the theater companies – even though reports sometimes conflicted with the expectations attached to stardom.

1 Legitimizing Drama through Life Writing

Serious misgivings about drama as a merely superficial form of entertainment, or even worse, a truly harmful influence, remained part of US-American discourse as late as the middle of the nineteenth century.[2] At the same time, some equally dedicated proponents of theater tried to legitimize the form by praising it as an educational medium, in particular as a resource which Americans could draw on

---

[1] The *Oxford English Dictionary* dates the first lexical (i. e., not metaphorical) usage of the term "star" as found in print with the year 1808; theater historian Alfred L. Bernheim identifies the 1820s as the beginning of the US-American "star-system" (Bernheim 1932).
[2] See Edmund S. Morgan (1966) for the origins of the rejection of theater in religious contexts. For later, eighteenth- and nineteenth-century anti-theatrical discourses, see Jürgen C. Wolter's documentary collection of dramatic criticism (1993).

https://doi.org/10.1515/9783110579253-005

to construct and advance the private and the public self. For this, they could rely on the already prevailing consensus about the value of biographies (see Casper 1999). Especially historical drama was expected to be able to inspire with exemplary acts and exemplary lives, against which the audience could not only measure, but also improve themselves.[3] Based on this assumption, many theatrical productions were conceived around historical characters, hoping that audiences would readily part with their money to see a play with both human and educational interest.[4] In the long run, the strategy proved to be successful: even if it was not the only cause of a changed perception of the theater, it encouraged both greater social acceptance, and the development of new forms of intermedial reception.

2 Theoretical Reflections on Intermediality

In current discussions of intermediality and performance, two associations may first come to mind. On the one hand, we might think of performance as the result of an intermedial adaptation process, e. g., from a novel or a poem to a theatrical performance (see Balestrini 2005 and 2011); on the other hand, the association is with the performative use of electronic or digital media – such as film, digital image, video installation, or blogs – either on stage or on various other virtual platforms. As Claudia Georgi emphasizes in her article on "Contemporary British Theatre and Intermediality," theater as an inherently "multi-or plurimedial medium combines language, movement or dance, architectural and pictorial stage designs, music and other media in a way that makes them appear not as individual media but as integral components of the composite theatrical medium" (2015: 530). Her concepts are based not just on Freda Chapple and Chiel Kattenbelt's more recent definitions, but go hand in hand with classic discussions of the theory of theater, such as Martin Esslin's *The Field of Drama: How the Signs of Drama Create Meaning on Stage and Screen* (1987) or Erika Fischer-Lichte's introduction to the semiotics of theater (1998). In the next instance,

---

[3] American drama as an influence on the formation of – mostly national – identity has been examined in publications by J. Mason (1993), S.E. Wilmer (2002), and J. Richards (2005).
[4] The scope of this essay does not allow listing all the existing biographical plays, but some examples might give an impression of how broad-ranging the selection of historical personages was: Alfred the Great, Benjamin Franklin, Catherine Brown, Charles the Twelfth, Xerxes, Ethan Allen, Anne Boleyn, Glaucus, Leonor de Guzman, Francesca da Rimini, Bethlen Gabor, Joan D'Arc, General Montgomery, Spartacus. These are examples culled from a "Selected Play List" in Richard Moody's *America Takes the Stage* (1955).

Georgi argues that the "more recent inventions of analogue and digital media have taken theatrical intermediality to an entirely new level" (2015: 531). Based on a similar interest in current developments, Christina Ljungberg focuses on the presence of various media within "performance art" and discusses semiotics, performativity, and self-reference within this relatively new art form (2015: 547). A number of innovative theoretical approaches starting from the same vantage point can be also found in the collection *Mapping Intermediality in Performance*, approaches which point to hybrid and dynamic practices that emphasize the theoretical challenges of the so-called "intermedial turn" in theater, in particular the question of how a "live performance in the here and now may be in the process of being re-qualified contextually as it accommodates an integrated production, recording and storage medium with its digital disposition to interactivity" (Nelson 2010: 13–14).

Although my following case studies are from a pre-digital period and, as a rule, do not even feature any explicit analogue version of a digital "play-within-the play" performance, they can be seen as conceptual precursors to the notions quoted above. The performances are often (though not always) adaptations and, as practices, they are contextually redefined as "plurimedial" even while they accommodate "an integrated production of hybrid performances" (Nelson 2010: 14). Further, they can be seen, just as in Georgi's and Ljungberg's examples, as multi- or plurimedial manifestations of distinct media (re)presentations. Following Werner Wolf's definition of plurimediality as the fusion of at least two distinct media (Wolf 2005: 254), I would like to suggest an extension of this conceptualization also to the reception side, that is, to the role of the audiences in this process.

In the case of an actual stage routine or play during which actors consciously assume scripted roles, aspects of intermediality as plurimediality extend both beyond and more deeply into the role and its performance. Given that the performers appear on stage by using their own bodies as mediators of verbal and non-verbal texts, any kind of interference between their theatrical and their real identities can be conceptualized as a plurimedial presence of different systems of (performative) signification. In the act of looking at the actors, the audience perceives two performative media: the performance of the scripted role and the actor as the (inadvertent) performer of his or her own extra-theatrical life. (Since the audience needs to learn about the actor's life from other sources than the communication situation of the performance, we have here a secondary, theoretically less complex instance of intermediality in the form of a rather straightforward combination of media in the reception process.)

The foundational principle of theatrical communication requires acknowledging the convention that what audiences see on the stage is a representation and not real life as such – in Coleridge's better-known words: "the willing suspension of disbelief" (Coleridge 1817: 216). Actors are expected to perform according to rehearsed rules, suppressing their own personalities and spontaneous *habitus* for the sake of the embodied characters. Still, especially when it comes to 'stars,' audiences see and perceive both manifestations of the person, for example when they admire 'good acting' – which they could not do if they were completely caught up in the realm of illusion. At the same time, as Denis Diderot pointed out already in 1773, this situation is paradoxical: the success and accomplishment of an actor depends on his own detachment from the emotions of his role so that his own personality is perfectly camouflaged; in extreme cases, he has to 'be' the exact opposite of what he 'seems' ("être" v. "paraître," Diderot 1995 [1773]: 72). In the field of theater studies, this paradox has been examined and studied in great detail, leading to ever more complex distinctions and contested definitions, in particular with respect to the question whether an actor is a 'medium' or not. With respect to the focus of this paper, I follow Kati Röttger's interpretation. She points out that actors can be seen as intermedial and dynamic manifestations of their semiotically ambivalent positions (Röttger 2008: 117). To illustrate this with an example: William Dean Howells observed this phenomenon in 1869 when he reviewed the current theater season in Boston. He was quite taken aback by some new, so-called 'burlesque' productions[5] and in particular by their performers:

> Their faces had merely the conventional Yankee sharpness and waneness [sic] of feature, and such difference of air and character as should say for one and another, shop-girl, shoe-binder, seamstress; and it seemed an absurdity and an injustice to refer to them in any way the disclosures of the ruthlessly scant drapery. A grotesque fancy would sport with their identity: "Did not this or that one write poetry for her local newspaper?" so much she looked the average culture and crudeness; and when such a one, coldly yielding to the manager's ideas of the public taste, stretched herself on a green baize bank with her feet towards us, or did a similar grossness, it was hard to keep from crying aloud in protest, that she need not do it. (Howells 1869: 639)

What Howells describes here is a highly visible conflict between the 'medium' of the actor and of the script (which, among other things, demanded a scant costume) while he is trying to reconcile the two sets of signals emanating from these two media.

This essay's focus on plays with a biographical character at their center further accentuates the interest of audiences in other people's lives – mostly in the

---

5 The "burlesques" of the mid-nineteenth century were mostly parodies of classical works, often performed by actresses dressed in short skirts or as men in tight trousers (see Allen 1991).

lives of 'exceptional' people: heroes or stars. Quite a number of theories try to explain the psychological foundations for the cult of the 'star' or fandom, which cannot be discussed within this essay.[6] I rather intend to show how the dramatic presentations of individual lives fitted with the larger US-American intellectual climate of the nineteenth and early twentieth centuries, which had a specific appreciation for biographies of all kinds. Building on this, I will argue that life writing had its own, distinctive place in the entertainment industry of the time. Emphasis on moral education, patriotism, industry, self-improvement, or other 'republican' virtues was a dominant part of an all-pervasive belief system dedicated to individual achievement.

One of the structurally and institutionally simplest forms to facilitate an individual's self-fashioning could be based on imitation of role models. However, the interest in exemplary lives took also some unexpected forms, which brings me to the second focus of my essay. With the development of certain actors into exceptional performers who were marketed as 'stars,' audiences often came to perceive theatrical performances not just as representations of theatrical roles but simultaneously as manifestations of the real personal identity of the star on the stage. From the point of view of logic, this conflation must count as a category error, but it seems that audiences were capable of suspending their disbelief in a way so that they could follow the drama, even as they also managed to be aware of the histrionic achievements and biographical background of the actors.

During the transition from popular theater to popular cinema, there was a short hiatus in this relationship. In the early days of the industry, film companies withheld the names of the actors, as they did not want to share the attention, the profit, and thus the control over production with the performers. But audiences demanded to learn the names of their favorite actors and actresses, and thus the lives of star performers received renewed attention, either with the help of studio publicity material or with the help of newspaper and magazine reporting (deCordova 1991: 19). While these 'stars' of the twentieth century have received a fair amount of critical interest,[7] scholarship has disregarded the fact that the strangely fluid relationship between representation and real life can be traced back to earlier genres of theatricals. The general popular appeal of biography created

---

[6] Most theoretical reflection on 'stardom' can be found with respect to twentieth-century cinema. Seminal works are studies by Richard Dyer in *Heavenly Bodies: Film Stars and Society* (1987) and Richard deCordova in *Picture Personalities: The Emergence of the Star System in America* (1990). For a more recent bibliographic overview see Katrin Keller's *Der Star und seine Nutzer* (2008).

[7] See, for example, Dyer (1987), Faulstich (1997), Gledhill (1991), deCordova (1990).

a backdrop for the interest in the staged (more or less fictional) life of a historical character on the one hand, and in the biography of the actor on the other, as often reported in the newspapers of the time. In the following I will thus discuss three examples dealing with this intermedial phenomenon: first, amateur performances and paratheatricals, then professional theater performance of the legitimate stage, and finally early cinema performance.

3 General Interest in Biography

The prestigious position of dramatic life writing derived from other cultural forms of the nineteenth century. As Scott E. Casper argues in his study *Biography and Culture in Nineteenth-Century America*, the place of biography or life writing went beyond the publication and reception of biographical works, whether written for, or by Americans. Casper sees a "biographical imagination" at work in many readers, or "a proclivity to see individual lives as stories: not merely sequences of events or episodes, but totalities with a certain coherence" (1999: 14). Casper only refers to traditional or textual biographies. As I will argue in the following, the same impulse can be detected in performative and/or intermedial varieties of life writing.[8]

Even without the aspect of multi- or intermediality, the genre definition of what counts as 'life writing' or 'biography' has been long contested. In his *The Development of English Biography* (1927), Harold Nicolson proceeded to lay down the criteria for a biography proper, in particular rejecting spontaneous and hybrid forms. His advocacy of a certain type of biographical expression depended on the structural features of an ideal example of a textual work. The inclusion of the various performative practices that I am going to present as related to biography would have been unthinkable for him. From a functional perspective however, i. e., considering the question what purpose (or purposes) a given text or performance fulfilled for its audiences, there is no logical reason to exclude performative biographical forms. When an anonymous critic wrote in the *New York Mirror* in 1829 "The stage! It is an abridged copy of human life" (qtd. in Wolter 1993: 85), he was only referring to professional performances. But as Karen Halttunen (1982) shows in her study of middle-class culture in the antebellum period, Americans played explicit roles also in their everyday lives. This practice was historically more specific, as new members of the US-American

---

[8] Casper mentions some examples in his study that would be considered parts of "material culture" nowadays: locks of hair, autographed letters, etc. (1999: 13).

middle class used conduct manuals like actors use prompt books in order to learn their 'roles' in unfamiliar social contexts. It was also closer to actual role playing than the general anthropological and sociological theories about the performative aspect of identity, as put forward, for example, by Erving Goffman.[9]

The step from the necessity of everyday posturing to the general role of biography in American society can be bridged by a summary of the most important positions of historians with respect to the role of biography for Americans in the nineteenth century.[10] Further, we also need to take account of a more popular interest in history and biography – an interest which was still related in some ways to the specialized discourse, but which had its own idiosyncratic interpretations of the role of life writing as part of collective and individual notions of personal history. Many writers also emphasized both the "pleasure" and the "improvement" of biography, and championed biographies even as one of the most preferable literary forms, given that they combined "entertainment with instruction" as S. Backus claimed in 1811 (qtd. in Lanzendörfer and Scheiding 2015: 145). And according to Casper, the popular type of biography in the Early Republic was connected to the notion of reputation, which meant that "one's performance or actions on the public stage revealed one's character in others' eyes" (1999: 6).

These notions become similarly relevant when we look at the development of the role of biographical performances on the private and commercial stage and screen during the nineteenth century and up to the beginning of the twentieth. One popular theory of biography as exemplary and/or inspirational life writing could be found in the following lines of the once ubiquitous poem "A Psalm of Life" by Henry Wadsworth Longfellow, from 1837:

> Lives of great men all remind us
> We can make our lives sublime,
> And, departing, leave behind us
> Footprints on the sands of time;

The meaning of these verses hinges decisively on the modal "can," but this possibility was enough to satisfy the romantic, republican, and individual yearnings

---

[9] Goffman described in *The Presentation of Self in Everyday Life* (1959) how individuals control their public appearances by performances.

[10] See Jan Stievermann's essay "Die Wandlung der traditionellen Exemplarik zum Konzept des Repräsentativen im Geschichtsdenken des 19. Jahrhunderts – eine transatlantische Betrachtung" (2007), which contains a comprehensive discussion of a number of influential historians of the nineteenth century, both American and European.

of the poem's readers, with the idea of the US as a society offering equal opportunities for everybody.[11] Another reason given for the importance of writing biographies in a US-American context was a nationalistic agenda: given the disparagement of American cultural productions by Europeans, it was deemed imperative to "portray to the world, with the pen and the pencil, some of the most distinguished and worthy of our countrymen" (Caldwell qtd. in Lanzendörfer and Scheiding 2015: 195). But it should be kept in mind that in spite of this patriotic rhetoric, the reception habits of American theatergoers were less ideologically and patriotically determined. American audiences were, in fact, not just avid consumers of imported plays, but even showed interest in the biographies of actors from Europe.

The two distinct approaches to nineteenth-century biography in the United States thus pursued "didactic" and "romantic" interpretations of the meaning of a life presented in writing, which would lead to emulation and inspiration respectively (Casper 1999: 7). In the following, I will develop a third, more ambivalent interpretation which is related to the glamour associated with some star-actors, whose offstage lives and biographies became the subject of interest for American audiences. It is important to mention here that the word 'glamour,' which is so familiar to us, is of relatively recent origin in Standard English (American or British). It was originally part of Scottish folklore and dialect and referred to "magic, enchantment, spell, esp. in the phrase 'to cast the glamour over one'" (*OED*) and had more negative than positive connotations. The term was first popularized by Sir Walter Scott in the 1830s and received its contemporary denotation as "charm; attractiveness" in the first decades of the twentieth century in the US. Its conceptual usefulness manifests itself, however, in the original meaning: as an ambivalent category that points to the semiotically equally ambivalent role that actors (professionals, or amateurs, as in the examples discussed in the following sections) incorporate on the stage or the screen, oscillating between their 'real' selves and the characters they performed.

---

11 From today's perspective this was of course not the case: economic standing, race, and gender were powerful inhibitors of a self-made career (see Weiss 1969). But in 1810, for example, an anonymous writer praised "biography" as a reflection of social mobility and thought it "indispensable in a free country, particularly of such extent as our own," whereas "in a monarchy, there is not the same inducement" (qtd. in Lanzendörfer and Scheiding 2015: 139).

4 On the Margins of Institutional Performance: Martha Washington in Paratheatricals

Peter Buckley documents in his essay on popular stage entertainment how nineteenth-century US-American performers created a new, vital form of theatrical culture in which "minor forms were elevated into major cultural successes" (1998: 426). Among these minor forms are public fairs and festivities, including amateur performances in the form of parades and *tableaux vivants*.[12] Only positive and inspiring historical or literary figures were represented in these shows. The performances were based on an intertextual and intermedial discourse that was familiar to performers and audiences alike. The embodiment of the historical figure was life writing in the sense that every feature of the represented person was a deliberately chosen sign, part of a semiotic code.

The figure of Martha Washington, George Washington's wife, was a popular historical character in these performances. Her public exposure was inherent in her role as the first president's spouse, but it really began to grow after 1800 with the appearance of Mason Locke ("Parson") Weems's biography of Washington. Some decades later, a biographical sketch written about her by George Washington P. Custis, her nephew, was widely reprinted.[13] By 1839, she was given a marble sarcophagus, almost identical to her husband's, which provides material evidence of her rise in the hierarchy of historical American dignitaries enshrined in collective memory. In the same year, a "splendid new ship, Martha Washington," was leaving Boston, as announced in *The Daily Atlas* of July 12, while types of flowers, horses, designs of shoes, sewing tables, blends of tea, and similar items were named after her. This interest in her marketable person(a) was accompanied by a sentimental craving for news about her and George Washington's relationship. Ironically (or wisely), Martha Washington had burned all her letters between her husband and herself after the former's death. In fact, this lack of concrete historical traces clearly facilitated the development of quasi-mythical imagery around her character. One of the foundational texts in this process

---

12 *Tableaux vivants*, or 'living pictures,' were popular parlor entertainments, but they were also performed as parts of public rituals and festivities. The participants chose either a famous painting or a scene from a literary work and recreated it by posing in costumes on elaborately prepared platforms. Substantial effort went into visual effects such as lighting, props, makeup, and staging. For a contemporary book on *tableaux vivants* techniques, see William Fearing Gill's *Parlor Tableaux and Amateur Theatricals* (1867).
13 The sketch itself seems apocryphal, but several newspapers quoted the history of George and Martha Washington's courtship.

was the above-mentioned biography of Washington, in which Weems created an image that was summarized as follows in the *Birmingham Age Herald* in Alabama: "There are no names in the list of American women that are regarded with more reverence than those of the mother and wife of George Washington. They have been constantly held up as types of pure and noble womanhood" ("Some Characteristics of Martha Washington" 1898). For almost a century she was considered a model of republican motherhood, complete with a hagiography constructed around her wedding slippers and locks of hair, which were on exhibition in Vermont. By 1873, there was even a yearning for a lost code associated with the first president's wife: "What had become of the type of woman that graced the period of the Revolution? The gentle, yet commanding dignity, the lovely, matronly grace that was the admiration of foreign courts as of the home circle?" ("Something of a Masquerade" 1873).

As part of this collective memory narrative, Martha Washington's life was also frequently dramatized in parlor theatricals and amateur performances. The Centennial of 1776 provided occasion for celebrations such as the "Grand Tea Party" of Philadelphia and the "Grand Centennial Carnival." These events were centered on a very specific and surprisingly colonial "Martha Washington" character, as during the "Martha Washington Reception" at the "Grand Centennial Carnival" in Orkney Springs, Virginia: "to continue two days, embracing diversions of the Olden Time, Promenade Concert, Centennial Oration and Fancy Ball, Historical Sketches" with "Mock Court, Tableaux, etc." ("Grand Centennial" 1876). Another example of such a festivity, which featured the central character as the host of a domestic occasion, was "The Martha Washington Reception and Chinese Tea Party" in Baltimore: "[O]n the night of Washington's Birthday, must be classed rather with professional than social events, the theatrical element being the chief attraction" ("Things Theatrical" 1878). Or, in Healdsburg, California, "[...] a large and refined audience [was] treated to a generous program of musical, tableau, and pantomime exercises, by members of the society and volunteers. Our space will not admit of a description of each piece put upon the stage, but those present at the grand reception of Martha Washington, in costume, and others participating, are as follows" ("Martha Washington Festival on the 22d." 1876). And, indeed, the long list of names provides a public and visible record of the 'actors' who performed in the festival. Their impersonation of historical figures of the American Revolution while being perceived as their everyday selves in their local community was both an enactment and a reflection of their patriotism.

Martha Washington–themed celebrations required "the garb of Colonial times," which meant, paradoxically, that the wife of the first American president was also visually codified as a member of a colonial society rather than of a young republic. A nostalgic yearning for conventional modes of genteel politeness was transformed into scenes in which Mrs. Washington received her guests: "Mrs. Washington, and those who were presented to her, simultaneously curtsying very low to each other as the guests passed her in succession" ("Martha Washington. Second and Closing Evening of the Reception" 1875). The aristocratic custom is modified, however, to suit the republican habits: everybody curtsied, including Mrs. Washington. Often, her husband, the General of the victorious Revolutionary War, was also placed in a colonial context. It seems that in popular culture the symbolic value of Washington and his wife was just as much related to their origins as to their achievements. Thus it can be concluded that these paratheatricals did not fulfill the criteria of a model biography in the form of a complete and balanced manifestation, but had a particular entertainment value and ideological use at the time: that of visually depicting certain socially fixed roles, above all, gender roles. Newspaper reports frequently emphasize the "grace" of the "young ladies" participating in the Martha Washington Receptions – a sense of beauty securely circumscribed by the nostalgic framework of "ye olden times" ("Remembered the Day" 1894). The self-promotion of specific individuals becomes even more obvious in notes such as "Miss Nellie Grant will be among the pretty Martha Washington girls at the centennial tea party." It is more than likely that towards the end of the nineteenth century, coincident with the introduction of divorce, suffragettes, and the New Woman, male desire for a more "old-fashioned" (i. e., submissive) wife was catered to at such events, where "a good deal of tea, and a good many bachelor resolutions were destroyed" ("Martha Washington" 1873). While the reporter is trying to be witty, the casual humor suggests the contemporary understanding of the possible real-life consequences of such public posturing. In amateur performances the oscillating aspect of 'performing lives' became especially obvious, as the performers were, first, not professionals and, second, as members of their local communities, always perceived as appearing in double incarnations, in other words, in an intermedial performance.

5 Life Writing in Historical Romances and Melodramas

The supposedly first American play (though never performed) was of a biographical character: Major Robert Rogers's drama about the Indian chief Pontiac. Other so-called Indian plays on historical characters depicted, for instance, Pocahontas (by James Nelson Barker) and Metacom/King Philipp (by Augustus

Stone). Further historical dramatic productions and early films were based on the lives of Leonor de Guzman, Columbus, Francesca da Rimini, Louis XI, George Washington, Davy Crockett, Billy the Kid, Barbara Frietchie, Ben Hur, Marco Polo, and many others (Moody 1955: 265–307).

In his book on American national identities and the theater, S.E. Wilmer takes the reader through some American historical crises by examining how the contemporary stage responded to key historical events. Thus, when he talks about "staging American identities," he refers not just to the biographies of historical (or historio-mythical) personalities, but to a set of ideological or prescriptive values which constitute 'Americanness.' The values connected with this 'Americanness' were both individual and collective, and – at a time when theatrical performances were still attacked as sinful – it seemed important to emphasize that not just the plays, but also the actors were in the service of morality and virtue. This was not merely a requirement of plays with a nationalistic agenda but extended to theater in general. The New York–based *The Correspondent* thus claimed in 1827: "Propriety of character [of the actor] is, therefore, of infinite consequence on the stage. He who would teach men to live well, should learn to live well himself; for there is no other way to recommend virtue forcibly and effectually. We go to the theatre to be diverted, and we return instructed" (qtd. in Wolter 1993: 66).

The plea for a national theater called for national themes, and one of the most obvious thematic choices following from this was the representation of American heroes on stage. Whereas some theater practitioners contemplated the Aristotelian requirement that tragic heroes needed to belong to the ruling class, others argued that this was not necessary in a republican society: "The dignity of life does not need the outward aid of power or station" ("Prospects of the American Stage," *Arcturus* 1841 qtd. in Wolter 1993: 104). The demand for American heroes was first and foremost fulfilled by soldiers of the War of Independence and, above all, by George Washington. William Dunlap's *André* (1798), a play about a British spy and his treatment by Washington, was later turned into an early form of a musical, *Glory of Columbia* (1803). It was popular as part of Fourth of July celebrations, for example in New York, in 1820, and ended with a spectacle: "End of the play will descend a transparency of an Eagle, holding a crown of laurel, bearing the inscription 'Immortality to Washington'" ("Fourth of July" 1820). Another commentator praises Dunlap's influence on his audiences: "Mr. D. seems to have exerted every nerve in order to inspire all true Americans with that patriotism which the savior of our country, the immortal Washington, ever displayed" ("Mr. and Mrs. Barnes's Benefit" 1812).

When it comes to the staging of American themes, the choice of revolutionary heroes is obvious, but the ideals of the Early Republic were also transferred to historical characters from outside the United States. A case in point is Robert Taylor Conrad's play originally titled *Jack Cade* (1835), which was later revised by the author for the star-performer Edwin Forrest in 1841 with the title *Aylmere, or, the Bond Man of Kent, Jack Cade*. The hero – played by Forrest – is a fifteenth-century Englishman, who incites an insurrection to abolish the feudal structures of his village. Its theme of individual freedom was made popular by Edwin Forrest's star-performance. As one newspaper reviewer from Baltimore put it:

> The spirited and effective personation of the English liberalist by Mr. Forrest is not only one of his most brilliant professional achievements, but conjointly with the dramatist, it rescues the reputation and deeds of Cade from the historical degradation by which they have been falsified and restores the character to the position and status which truth awards. It is an honorable illustration of American fidelity to liberal principles, and a fact worthy of our regard, that an American dramatist has recognized and approved the character of a man whose aspirations for political liberty were so far in advance of the age in which he lived. ("Holliday Street Theatre" 1860)

This and similar reviews drew a clear parallel between American republican values and a figure from fifteenth-century England, using the real-life personality of a US-American performer to complete the chain of patriotic argument.

Forrest thus presents here a prime example for the kind of intermedial merging of stage and personal performance where the 'glamour' of one role impacted the other. As Bruce A. McConachie reports, the public "tended to confuse Forrest's personal qualities with the characteristics of the heroes he presented on stage" (1989: 14). Forrest's strategically practiced charity and benevolence radiated into his roles, while he was praised in turn as a man with the qualities of the heroes he impersonated, most importantly as a self-made man with democratic virtues.[14]

Although Forrest is often seen as one of the most successful and influential US-American star performers, he was not (and could not be) representative of all manifestations of intermedial life writing on American stages. Another example of this specifically US-American case of sentimental democracy was Joseph Jefferson III, who was famous for the role of Rip Van Winkle, and who presented a similar example of a star-performer whose private persona infiltrated his role, and vice versa – at least in the eyes of his audiences, who eagerly followed details of his life not only in newspapers, but also in his self-promotions, such as his autobiography (Balestrini 2005: 120–126).

---

14 McConachie sees here additionally a distinct parallel to the representation of Andrew Jackson (1989: 8–9).

In spite of the frequent nationalistic rhetoric associated with stars such as Forrest or Jefferson, audiences were still highly interested in European productions and performers (Peterfy 2015). A prominent example for this phenomenon is the case of Adelaide Ristori, a celebrated Italian actress whose American tour in 1867/1868 was a great success in spite of the fact that all her appearances were in Italian. When Ristori came to the US in 1866, she was already a well-known and respected actress, as Kate Field remarked in *The Atlantic Monthly* of April 1867: "For the New World, to cry, *Brava!* is to make no discovery: we crown a long-acknowledged queen. America may make fortune, but cannot make fame, for an artist" (Field 1867: 495). In this long, admiring article, Ristori's representation of Francesca da Rimini is singled out as one of her most successful roles: "There is not a note in the register of human passion, but is richly rounded, and bursts forth grandly at the will of the artist" (Field 1867: 495).

Some fourteen years before Ristori performed the role of Francesca in the US, the Philadelphian poet and playwright George Henry Boker had based his romantic tragedy *Francesca da Rimini* (1853) on the doomed love affair of a married woman, told by Dante in his *Divina Commedia*. Although the exact details of the story are unclear today, Dante's verses being the earliest existing source, it is known that Francesca was a historical figure. In the nineteenth century, the anecdotal knowledge about her was considered a true occurrence of romantic love, as well as of misguided passion and tragic death. The protagonists of the story are Francesca da Rimini, her husband Lanciotto, and Paolo, Lanciotto's brother. In his commentary on Dante's *Divina Commedia*, Boccaccio added some details to the episode and created the best-known version of the story, which inspired many other writers, artists, and composers – among them Byron, Keats, D'Annunzio, Ingres, Rodin, Tchaikovsky, and Liszt. In this version Francesca was wedded, for political reasons, to an older, infirm man. Later she fell in love with her husband's brother and carried on an affair with him. When their relationship was discovered by the husband, he killed them both. Ristori's impersonation of this role was one of her most admired performances:

> Madame Ristori renewed her former triumphs and gave an admirable impersonation of Lanciotto's hapless wife. Every cadence of the voice, in the beautiful language of her native clime, every movement, every gesture, every glance, every convulsion of passion, seemed that of Francesca, not of Ristori. ("Ristori-Francesca da Rimini" 1867)

Ristori also performed other roles, but this one, personifying a desire for the freedom to choose one's partner for life, even in opposition to the expectations of class, convention, or simply the wishes of the parents' generation, was not just highly popular in the nineteenth century, but it was also imbued with contemporary notions of republicanism. Thus the romantic marriage of Adelaide Ristori, the person embodying the role of Francesca di Rimini, to an Italian nobleman – a marriage that crossed class boundaries – proved to be of great interest to US-American audiences. Comparable to other, almost daily, newspaper articles, the *New York Herold* reports:

> As might have been expected, the young man's family objected to the alliance. [...] The story goes that while they were both travelling accident brought them together at a small village. They improved the opportunity to renew their vows of love, and resolved to plight them perpetually, as fate had favored them so far. The door of the village church stood open [...] and the ceremony was immediately performed. ("Adelaide Ristori" 1866)

Ristori's personal story did not only confirm the popular belief in the proverbial 'village church' as a sanctuary for true love. The success of the Italian Francesca da Rimini probably also reminded theater directors of an ambitious dramatic version of the story by an American dramatist. Revived in 1882 in Philadelphia, Boker's play became part of the popular repertoire in the middle-brow range, contributing to the general US-American "Dante-craze" around the turn of the century (Uricchio and Pearson 1990: 76).

6 Biography and the (Re-)Discovery of the 'Star' for the Cinema as 'Picture Personality'

In their article "Dante's Inferno and Caesar's Ghost: Intertextuality and Conditions of Early Reception in Early American Cinema" (1990), William Uricchio and Roberta A. Pearson establish the connection between Vitagraph's film *Francesca da Rimini* (1908) and Boker's tragedy. Around the turn of the century, popular fare in cinemas and nickelodeons consisted of short comic films, sensational melodramas, and movies about crime and detection. Working against the image of an exclusively low-culture industry, film companies such as the American Vitagraph Company began to develop programs of so-called "quality films" (see Uricchio and Pearson 1989). One of the important pillars of these programs was biographical film. The main motivation of the company was to "enhance their reputations, linking filmic signifying practices to other 'respectable' cultural expressions" (Uricchio and Pearson 1989: 15). In order to incorporate cultural capital into their products, producers chose topics and forms that were already regarded as prestigious by their target interpretative communities: canonized literary themes and biographies of historical figures. At the same time, the two important early US-American film companies Vitagraph and Biograph Company[15] created their biographical "quality films" on the assumption that their audiences were familiar with the featured topics. The presentation of the lives of well-known characters was in this respect a logical choice, made to combat the documented observation that "a significant number of films left their viewers somewhat mystified and confused" (Musser 1994: 3). The audiences did not watch early biographical films, for example about Washington or Napoleon,[16] primarily to learn about the historical facts of a famous life; rather, they joined the cultural discourse about these characters as commentators, who could compare and contrast their own interpretations with those presented in the moving pictures. It is of course difficult or even impossible to recover the exact content of these mostly oral and ephemeral comments, but – as Uricchio and Pearson argue – critics can rely on "an intertextually based approach for extrapolating historically grounded possible readings" (1993: 13). One of the results of these readings is the discovery that the intention of the film companies to withhold the names of the actors and present their recorded films as pure (and thus arbitrary) 'signs' did not take with the public. In the case of Vitagraph's first 'star,' Frances Turner in *Francesca da Rimini*, audiences spontaneously chose to individualize the actress they saw on the screen and called her the "Vitagraph girl" (deCordova 1991: 14). Later, the film studios released the names of their most popular actors and actresses, and the cinematic star-system, as we know it today, emerged (deCordova 1991: 14). In her case study of the "Vitagraph girl," Kathryn Fuller-Seeley (2012) analyzes one example of a local promotion of Turner as a "'picture personality.'" The whole presentation of the actress hinged on a conflation of her professional roles and her private life. This kind of presentation is obvious also in 'occasional reporting,' for example in a 1912 article about Turner in the *Albuquerque Journal*, where her health and her career plans are laid open as if these were questions of public interest ("Vitagraph Girl on Her Way Back to New York" 1912).

---

[15] The full names were "Edison Vitagraph Company" and "American Mutoscope & Biograph Company." The meaning of 'vitagraph' and 'biograph' in this context is originally wholly technical: it referred to the projector, a device that was praised as being able to 'write' (as in -graph) 'life' (see Musser 1990: 118).

[16] See the chapter "Historical Qualities: Washington and Napoleon" (Uricchio and Pearson 1993: 111–159).

7 Continued Interest in the 'Star' Personality

The cultural capital of biography as a superior form of entertainment continued as an unbroken trend from US-American nineteenth-century theater to early cinema and beyond: the biopic, for instance, is still a major genre in commercial cinema today (Taylor 2002). In this contribution, I hope to have shown that audiences' interest in other people's lives did not stop short with the representations of specific characters on the stage or on the screen, but extended further into the private lives of actors and actresses. I have called this an intermedial phenomenon, with a focus on plurimediality, for two reasons. First, the performers are perceived as belonging to two different media, in the sense that they represent both roles from the scripted play and also their own selves or at least the public versions of these selves. Although recent theories of intermediality in performance have not focused on this aspect of intermedial performance, I have suggested to extend concepts developed for contemporary (theatrical) performance and (digital) intermediality (primarily by Georgi and Ljundberg) to a theoretical conceptualization of this phenomenon, in connection with Wolf's conceptualization of plurimediality.

Second, the perception of this dual role required an additional discursive medium beyond the stage or the screen in the form of extensive newspaper or other textual coverage. Since audiences had an avid interest in the lives of 'model Americans,' they turned to other, mostly printed sources for detailed information and related their gleanings to the performances they watched. In fact, the expansion of such a corpus of various forms of life writing was instrumental for the kind of plurimedial performance that existed from Martha Washington paratheatricals to early cinematic biographies. Finally, the argument that this relationship was not accidental, but rather something that seems to have become part of a modern (i. e., post–nineteenth-century) dramatic experience is evidenced by the star systems of the theater and of cinema. Originally, the movie production companies did not want stars. They tried consciously to avoid the development in their audiences of any association of individuality and personality with their actors and actresses, independent of their specific scripted roles. But they failed in this endeavor: audiences demanded to know not just what sort of person, but what particular person and what particular personal narrative stood in front of the cameras and "cast their glamour" over the roles they played.

Works Cited

"Adelaide Ristori". *New York Herald*. America's Historical Newspapers, 12 September 1866. <http://infoweb.newsbank.com.ubproxy.ub.uni-heidelberg.de/iw-search/we/HistArchive/?p_product=EANX&p_theme=ahnp&p_nbid=X6BC64NXMTUxMzY4NDk0Mi4yOTAzODM6MToxNDoxNDcuMTQyLjE4Ni41NA&p_action=doc&d_viewref=search&s_lastnoni ssuequeryname=2&p_queryname=2&p_docnum=13&p_docref=v2:11A050B7B120D3F8@EANX-128B465D765AA470@2402857-128B465DF45DAB90@3-128B46602B22E478@Adelaide%20Ristori%20Her%20Arrival%20in%20New%20York> [accessed 25 August 2017].

Allen, Robert C. 1991. *Horrible Prettiness: Burlesque and American Culture*. Chapel Hill: The University of North Carolina Press.

Balestrini, Nassim Winnie (ed.). 2011. *Adaptation and American Studies: Perspectives on Research and Teaching*. Heidelberg: Winter Universitätsverlag.

Balestrini, Nassim Winnie. 2005. *From Fiction to Libretto: Irving, Hawthorne, and James as Opera*. Frankfurt: Peter Lang.

Bernheim, Alfred L. 1964 [1932]. *The Business of the Theatre: An Economic History of the American Theatre, 1750–1932*. Rpt. New York: Benjamin Blom, Inc.

Buckley, Peter G. 1998. "Paratheatricals and Popular Stage Entertainment". In: Don Wilmeth and Christopher Bigsby (eds.). *The Cambridge History of American Theatre: Beginnings to 1870*. vol 1. New York: Cambridge University Press.

Caldwell, Charles. 1816. "'Preface' to *Delaplaine's Repository of the Lives and Portraits of Distinguished American Characters*". Rpt. in: Oliver Scheiding und Tim Lanzendörfer (eds.). *American Lives: An Anthology of Transatlantic Life Writing from the Colonies to 1850*. Trier: Wissenschaftlicher Verlag, 2015. 194–196.

Casper, E. Scott. 1999. *Biography and Culture in Nineteenth-Century America*. Chapel Hill: University of North Carolina Press.

Chapple, Freda and Chiel Kattenbelt. 2006. "Key Issues in Intermediality in Theatre and Performance". In: Freda Chapple and Chiel Kattenbelt (eds.). *Intermediality in Theatre and Performance*. Amsterdam: Rodopi. 11–25.

Coleridge, Samuel Taylor. *Biographia Literaria*. 1817. <www.fulltextarchive.com/pdfs/Biographia-Literaria.pdf> [accessed 22 June 2018].

Comeret, Lorraine. 1989. "Edwin Booth's Bertuccio: Tom Taylor's Fool Revisited". In: Judith Fisher and Stephen Watt (eds.). *When They Weren't Doing Shakespeare: Essays on Nineteenth-Century British and American Theatre*. Athens: The University of Georgia Press, 1989. 64–87.

Custis, George Washington P, Esq. of Arlington. 1835. "From the Life of Mrs. Martha Washington". *The Floridian*. 19th Century U.S. Newspapers, 4 July 1835. <http://find.galegroup.com/ncnp/newspaperRetrieve.do?sgHitCountType=None&sort=DateAscend&tabID=T003&prodId=NCNP&resultListType=RESULT_LIST&searchId=R2&searchType=BasicSearchForm&currentPosition=2&qrySerId=Locale%28en%2C%2C%29%3AFQE%3D%28tx%2CNone%2C39%29From+the+Life+of+Mrs.+Martha+Washington%24&retrieveFormat=MULTIPAGE_DOCUMENT&userGroupName=heidel&inPS=true&contentSet=LTO&&docId=&docLevel=FASCIMILE&workId=&relevancePageBatch=GT3011485849&contentSet=UDVIN&callistoContentSet=UDVIN&docPage=article&hilite=y> [accessed 30 September 2017].

deCordova, Richard. 1990. *Picture Personalities: The Emergence of the Star System in America*. Urbana: University of Illinois Press.
deCordova, Richard. 1991. "The Emergence of the Star System in America". In: Christine Gledhill (ed.). *Stardom: Industry of Desire*. London: Routledge. 17–29.
Diderot, Denis. 1995 [1773]. In: Jane Marsh Dieckmann (ed.). *Paradoxe sur le comédien*. Paris: Hermann.
Dyer, Richard. 1987. *Heavenly Bodies: Film Stars and Society*. London: Macmillan.
Esslin, Martin. 1987. *The Field of Drama: How the Signs of Drama Create Meaning on Stage and Screen*. London: Methuen.
Faulstich, Werner (ed.). 1997. *Der Star: Geschichte, Rezeption, Bedeutung*. München: Fink.
Field, Kate. 1867. "Adelaide Ristori". *The Atlantic Monthly* 19 (114): 493–501.
Fischer-Lichte, Erika. 1998. *Semiotik des Theaters: Eine Einführung*. Tübingen: Narr.
"Fourth of July". *The American*. America's Historical Newspapers, 3 July 1820. <http://infoweb.newsbank.com.ubproxy.ub.uni-heidelberg.de/iw-search/we/HistArchive/?p_product=EANX&p_theme=ahnp&p_nbid=X6BC64NXMTUxMzY4NDk0Mi4yOTAzODM6MToxNDoxNDcuMTQyLjE4Ni41NA&p_action=doc&d_viewref=search&s_lastnonissuequeryname=7&p_queryname=7&p_docnum=131&p_docref=v2:10D35048E774E038@EANX-10D7EDB2F44EC328@2385985-10D7EDB389BCC858@2-10D7EDB5A1687D80@> [accessed 29 August 2017].
Fuller-Seeley, Kathryn. 2013. "Local Promotion for a 'Picture Personality': A Case Study of the Vitagraph Girl". In: Karina Aveyard and Albert Moran (eds.). *Watching Films: New Perspectives on Movie-Going, Exhibition and Reception*. Bristol: Intellect. 103–120.
Georgi, Claudia. 2015. "Contemporary British Theatre and Intermediality". In: Gabriele Rippl (ed.). *Handbook of Intermediality*. Berlin: De Gruyter. 530–546.
Gill, William Fearing. 1867. *Parlor Tableaux and Amateur Theatricals*. Boston: J. E. Tilton and Company.
"glamour". *Oxford English Dictionary*. <http://www.oed.com.ubproxy.ub.uni-heidelberg.de/view/Entry/78690?rskey=CeczVX&result=1&isAdvanced=false#eid> [accessed 29 May 2017].
Gledhill, Christine (ed.). 1991. *Stardom: Industry of Desire*. London: Routledge.
Goffman, Erving. 1959. *The Presentation of Self in Everyday Life*. New York: Doubleday.
"Grand Centennial Carnival". *The Sun*. America's Historical Newspapers, 22 July 1876. <http://infoweb.newsbank.com.ubproxy.ub.uni-heidelberg.de/iw-search/we/HistArchive/?p_product=EANX&p_theme=ahnp&p_nbid=X6BC64NXMTUxMzY4NDk0Mi4yOTAzODM6MToxNDoxNDcuMTQyLjE4Ni41NA&p_action=doc&d_viewref=search&s_lastnonissuequeryname=10&p_queryname=10&p_docnum=1&p_docref=v2:11343008E4D07040@EANX-1171219AF2772C98@2406458-1171219B04AAAFD8@0-1171219B5E56AD88@> [accessed 15 May 2017].
Halttunen, Karen. 1982. *Confidence Men and Painted Women: A Study of Middle-Class Culture in America, 1830–1870*. New Haven: Yale University Press.
"Holliday Street Theatre: Jack Cade". *The Sun*. America's Historical Newspapers, 5 September 1860. <http://infoweb.newsbank.com.ubproxy.ub.uni-heidelberg.de/iw-search/we/HistArchive/?p_product=EANX&p_theme=ahnp&p_nbid=X6BC64NXMTUxMzY4NDk0Mi4yOTAzODM6MToxNDoxNDcuMTQyLjE4Ni41NA&p_action=doc&d_viewref=search&s_lastnonissuequeryname=15&p_queryname=15&p_docnum=1&p_docref=v2:11343008E4D07040@EANX-1171111FE811D000@2400659-1171111FF71CB420@0-

1171112092B4A2A0@Holliday%20Street%20Theatre.%20Jack%20Cade> [accessed 25 May 2017].

Howells, William Dean. 1869. "The New Taste in Theatricals". *The Atlantic Monthly* 23 (139): 635–644.

Keller, Katrin. 2008. *Der Star und seine Nutzer: Starkult und Identität in der Mediengesellschaft*. Bielefeld: transcript Verlag.

Lanzendörfer, Tim and Oliver Scheiding (eds.). 2015. *American Lives: An Anthology of Transatlantic Life Writing from the Colonies to 1850*. Trier: Wissenschaftlicher Verlag.

Ljungberg, Christina. 2015. "Intermediality and Performance Art". In: Gabriele Rippl (ed.). *Handbook of Intermediality*. Berlin: De Gruyter. 547–561.

Longfellow, Henry Wadsworth. 1904 [1837]. "A Psalm of Life". Rpt. in: *The Complete Writings of Henry Wadsworth Longfellow. In Eleven Volumes. Craigie Edition*. vol. 1. Boston: Houghton, Mifflin & Co. 18–20.

"Martha Washington". *Daily Constitution*. America's Historical Newspapers, 29 December 1873. <http://infoweb.newsbank.com.ubproxy.ub.uni-heidelberg.de/iw-search/we/HistArchive/?p_product=EANX&p_theme=ahnp&p_nbid=X6BC64NXMTUxMzY4NDk0Mi4yOTAzODM6MToxNDoxNDcuMTQyLjE4Ni41NA&p_action=doc&d_viewref=search&s_lastnonissuequeryname=21&p_queryname=21&p_docnum=2&p_docref=v2:110215FE05459C00@EANX-1110FABC789C7E20@2405522-1110FABCA3FCAD50@1-1110FABD39337A78@[Philadelphia%3B%20Academy%3B%20Music%3B%20December%3B%20State%3B%20Territory%3B%20Philadelphians%3B%20Martha%20Washington> [accessed 19 July 2017].

"Martha Washington. Second and Closing Evening of the Reception". *Philadelphia Inquirer*. America's Historical Newspapers, 16 December, 1875. <http://infoweb.newsbank.com.ubproxy.ub.uni-heidelberg.de/iw-search/we/HistArchive/?p_product=EANX&p_theme=ahnp&p_nbid=I63T5CQPMTUxMzY4MjkxNS45MjA1Mzc6MToxNDoxNDcuMTQyLjE4Ni41NA&p_action=doc&d_viewref=search&s_lastnonissuequeryname=3&p_queryname=3&p_docnum=4&p_docref=v2:110C9BFA1F116650@EANX-111FEDD441EFAE88@2406239-111FEDD4758A8EE8@1-111FEDD6792735D8@Martha%20Washington.%20Second%20and%20Closing%20Evening%20of%20the%20Reception> [accessed 18 December 2017].

"Martha Washington Festival on the 22d". *Russian River Flag*. California Digital Newspaper Collection, 24 February 1876. <https://cdnc.ucr.edu/cgi-bin/cdnc?a=d&d=RRF18760224.2.20&srpos=2&e=-------en-20-RRF-1-txt-txIN-martha+Washington-----1> [accessed 20 July 2017].

Mason, Jeffrey D. 1993. *Melodrama and the Myth of America*. Bloomington: University of Indiana Press.

McConachie, Bruce A. 1989. "The Theatre of Edwin Forrest and Jacksonian Hero Worship". In: Judith Fisher and Stephen Watt (eds.). *When They Weren't Doing Shakespeare: Essays on Nineteenth-Century British and American Theatre*. Athens: The University of Georgia Press. 3–18.

Moody, Richard. 1955. *America Takes the Stage: Romanticism in American Drama and Theatre, 1750–1900*. Bloomington: Indiana University Press.

Morgan, Edmund S. 1966. "Puritan Hostility to Theatre". *Proceedings of the American Philosophical Society* 110 (5): 340–347.

"Mr. and Mrs. Barnes's Benefit". *Rhode-Island American*. America's Historical Newspapers, 21 August 1812. <http://infoweb.newsbank.com.ubproxy.ub.uni-heidelberg.de/iw-search/we/

HistArchive/?p_product=EANX&p_theme=ahnp&p_nbid=U67T5FFSMTUxMzc4MTMxO
C45ODczOTg6MToxNDoxNDcuMTQyLjE4Ni41NA&p_action=doc&d_viewref=search&s_last
nonissuequeryname=4&p_queryname=4&p_docnum=1&p_docref=
v2:10E31851B1F0F920@EANX-10E692A79F78A018@2383112-10E692A80028AA28@2-
10E692A8ED82F870@Mr.%20and%20Mrs.%20Barnes%27s%20Benefit> [accessed 29
August 2017].
Musser, Charles. 1990. *The Emergence of Cinema: The American Screen to 1907*. vol. 1. Berkeley: University of California Press.
Nelson, Robin. 2010. "Introduction: Prospective Mapping". In: Sarah Bay-Cheng, Chiel Kattenbelt, Andy Lavender, Robin Nelson (eds.). *Mapping Intermediality in Performance*. Amsterdam: Amsterdam University Press. 13–23.
Nicolson, Harold. 1959 [1927]. *The Development of English Biography*. London: Hogarth Press.
Peterfy, Margit. 2015. "Transkulturelle Dynamiken im US-amerikanischen Showbusiness des Gilded Age, 1870–1900". In: Jutta Ernst and Florian Freitag (eds.). *Transkulturelle Dynamiken: Aktanten–Prozesse–Theorien*. Bielefeld: transcript Verlag. 63–90.
"Remembered the Day – Colonial Teas and Receptions". *The Daily Inter Ocean*. Nineteenth Century U.S. Newspapers, 23 February 1894. <http://find.galegroup.com.ubproxy.ub.uni-heidelberg.de/ncnp/newspaperRetrieve.do?sgHitCountType=None&sort=DateAscend&ta
bID=T003&prodId=NCNP&resultListType=RESULT_LIST&searchId=R2&searchType=Ad
vancedSearchForm&currentPosition=1&qrySerId=Locale%28en%2C%2C%29%3AFQE%3D
%28tx%2CNone%2C20%29%22remembered+the+day%22%3AAnd%3AFQE%3D%28tx%7
2CNone%2C13%29colonial+teas%24&retrieveFormat=MULTIPAGE_DOCUMENT&user
GroupName=heidel&inPS=true&contentSet=LTO&&docId=&docLevel=FASCIMILE&workId=
&relevancePageBatch=GT3001541821&contentSet=UDVIN&callistoContentSet=UDVIN&doc
Page=article&hilite=y> [accessed 20 July 2017].
Richards, Jeffrey H. 2005. *Drama, Theatre, and Identity in the American New Republic*. Cambridge: Cambridge University Press.
"Ristori – Francesca da Rimini". *New York Herald*. America's Historical Newspapers, 21 September 1867. <http://infoweb.newsbank.com.ubproxy.ub.uni-heidelberg.de/iw-search/
we/HistArchive/?p_product=EANX&p_theme=ahnp&p_nbid=N63F5BYOMTUxMzc4MzM5M
S4yNjc3NDU6MToxNDoxNDcuMTQyLjE4Ni41NA&p_action=doc&d_viewref=search&s_last
nonissuequeryname=29&p_queryname=29&p_docnum=1&p_docref=
v2:11A050B7B120D3F8@EANX-127E775189840900@2403231-127E7751F38A65A0@3-
127E77536AA08960@Ristori-Francesca%20Da%20Rimini> [accessed 25 August 2017].
Röttger, Kati. 2008. "Intermedialität als Bedingung von Theater: Methodische Überlegungen". In: Henri Schoenmakers et al. (eds.). *Theater und Medien / Theatre and the Media: Grundlagen–Analysen–Perspektiven*. Bielefeld: transcript Verlag. 117–124.
"Some Characteristics of Martha Washington". *Birmingham Age Herald*. America's Historical Newspapers, 16 September 1898. <http://infoweb.newsbank.com.ubproxy.ub.uni-heidel
berg.de/iw-search/we/HistArchive/?p_product=EANX&p_theme=ahnp&p_nbid=
N63F5BYOMTUxMzc4MzM5MS4yNjc3NDU6MToxNDoxNDcuMTQyLjE4Ni41NA&p_action=
doc&d_viewref=search&s_lastnonissuequeryname=26&p_queryname=26&p_docnum=
1&p_docref=v2:11EC25AD467AEC15@EANX-11F4758F40FAABE0@2414549-
11F4758F6A91BC50@5-11F4759051C2D830@Woman%20and%20Society> [accessed 24 May 2017].

"Something of a Masquerade". 1873. *Daily Alta California*. California Digital Newspaper Collection, 15 August 1873. <https://cdnc.ucr.edu/cgi-bin/cdnc?a=d&d=DAC18730815.2.50&srpos=1&e=------en-20-1-byDA-txt-txIN-%22Something+of+a+masquerade%22-----1> [accessed 15 May 2017].

"star". *Oxford English Dictionary*. <http://www.oed.com.ubproxy.ub.uni-heidelberg.de/view/Entry/189081?rskey=X9U3tf&result=1#eid> [accessed 27 June 2018].

Stievermann, Jan. 2007. "Die Wandlung der traditionellen Exemplarik zum Konzept des Repräsentativen im Geschichtsdenken des 19. Jahrhunderts – eine transatlantische Betrachtung". In: Bernd Engler and Isabell Klaiber (eds.). *Kulturelle Leitfiguren – Figurationen und Refigurationen*. Berlin: Duncker & Humblot. 207–238.

Taylor, Henry McKean. 2002. *Rolle des Lebens: die Filmbiographie als narratives System*. Marburg: Schüren Verlag.

"Things Theatrical". *The Sun*. America's Historical Newspapers, 2 March 1878. <http://infoweb.newsbank.com.ubproxy.ub.uni-heidelberg.de/iw-search/we/HistArchive/?p_product=EANX&p_theme=ahnp&p_nbid=N63F5BYOMTUxMzc4MzM5MS4yNjc3NDU6MToxNDoxNDcuMTQyLjE4Ni41NA&p_action=doc&d_viewref=search&s_lastnonissuequeryname=24&p_queryname=24&p_docnum=1&p_docref=v2:11343008E4D07040@EANX-11710403A3A2D168@2407046-117104046ABB7018@3-117104055C10AD58@Our%20New%20York%20Letter.%20The%20New%20York%20Press%20and%20the%20Eastern%20War%20-%20Second-Hand%20Foreign%20News> [accessed 15 May 2017].

Uricchio, William and Roberta E. Pearson. 1990. "Dante's Inferno and Ceasar's Ghost: Intertextuality and Conditions of Reception in Early American Cinema". *Journal of Communication Inquiry* 14 (2): 71–85.

Uricchio, William and Roberta E. Pearson. 1993. *Reframing Culture: The Case of the Vitagraph Quality Films*. Princeton: Princeton University Press.

Uricchio, William and Roberta E. Pearson. 1989. "'Films of Quality', 'High Art Films', and 'Films de Luxe': Intertextuality and Reading Positions in the Vitagraph Films". *Journal of Film and Video* 41 (4): 15–31.

"Vitagraph Girl on Her Way Back to New York". *Albuquerque Journal*. America's Historical Newspaper, 22 April 1912. <http://infoweb.newsbank.com.ubproxy.ub.uni-heidelberg.de/iw-search/we/HistArchive/?p_product=EANX&p_theme=ahnp&p_nbid=N63F5BYOMTUxMzc4MzM5MS4yNjc3NDU6MToxNDoxNDcuMTQyLjE4Ni41NA&p_action=doc&d_viewref=search&s_lastnonissuequeryname=4&p_queryname=4&p_docnum=12&p_docref=v2:11C7D0596D228BB9@EANX-11D60F36AF6ADEC8@2419515-11D60F3752C0DB88@5-11D60F3A42160EC0@Vitagraph%20Girl%20on%20Her%20Way%20Back%20to%20New%20York.%20Railroad%20Folk%20Wonder%20Where%20They%20Have%20Seen> [accessed 25 August 2017].

Weems, Mason Locke. 1800. *A History of the Life and Death, Virtues and Exploits of General George Washington*. Philadelphia: J. B. Lippincott.

Weiss, Richard. 1969. *The American Myth of Success: From Horatio Alger to Norman Vincent Peale*. New York: Basic.

Wilmer, S.E. 2002. *Theatre, Society, and the Nation: Staging American Identities*. Cambridge: Cambridge University Press.

Wolf, Werner. 2005. "Intermediality". In: David Hermann, Manfred Jahn, and Marie-Laure Ryan (eds.). *Routledge Encyclopedia of Narrative Theory*. London: Routledge. 252–256.

Wolter, Jürgen C. 1993. *The Dawning of American Drama: American Dramatic Criticism, 1746–1915*. Westport, CT: Greenwood Press.

Dennis Bingham
Lenny: (Auto-)biography, Black-and-White, and Juxtapositional Montage in Bob Fosse's Hollywood Renaissance Biopic

Abstract

Bob Fosse directed *Lenny* (1974), about the profane American comedian Lenny Bruce, at a time when he had won complete artistic control over his films. As an intermedial artist, with equal facility for the stage and movies, Fosse approached film editing with the rhythmic intricacy of his dance style. He developed a film style that eschewed conventional chronology, aiming for an atemporal juxtapositional montage closer to poetry and the live performing arts than the narrative causality and temporality of Hollywood cinema. *Lenny* is an intermedial biographical collage that straddles divergent narrative strands, subjectivities, mid-twentieth-century periods. It contrasts modes of black-and-white cinematography, making them forms into themselves. It tells a story (rather than the story, as biopics conventionally insist) of Lenny Bruce, an irreverent, iconoclastic standup comedian who ran afoul of American obscenity laws in the last years before the cultural revolution of the late sixties, even as he helped to change them. Like Fosse's previous film, *Cabaret* (1972), *Lenny* juxtaposes cinematic and photographic realism with the heightened reality of the stage, where Bruce speaks to us, bursting the chronology of his own biography, and commenting on his own life story.

1 A Key Transition in the Evolution of Cinematic Life Writing

In the New Hollywood, or 'Hollywood Renaissance' of the 1970s, film genres, such as the Western and the *film noir*, were revised and deconstructed. Meanwhile the biopic withered. One of the very few innovative American film biographies of the decade was *Lenny* (1974), which turned out to be influential, leading perhaps to the masterpiece of the New Hollywood at its very end, *Raging Bull* (Martin Scorsese 1980). A biopic of the profane, hip comedian Lenny Bruce (1925–1966), *Lenny* shows that one performing artist, in this instance dancer/choreographer/stage director-turned-film director Bob Fosse (1927–1987), can write in cinema the life of another performing artist, from yet another medium, standup comedy, while expressing aspects of his own life experiences and preoccupations. *Lenny*, Fosse's first non-musical work in any medium and his only black-and-white film, cuts between Bruce's monologues and his personal life, rendering the frame story/flashback conventions of the biopic in dialectical juxtapositions. *Lenny* privileges the private realm, spending the first two-thirds of the film on the remembrances of Honey Bruce, whose six-year marriage to Bruce took place before he became well-known. With this unusual approach the film explores Bruce the person before he began to belong to the public. The film twice plays out a pattern of infatuation, courtship, passion, infraction, decline, and disintegration: the first time between Lenny and Honey, and the second time between Lenny and the public. Drugs and deception conclude the cycle the first time. In the second sequence American puritanism in its last hurrah comes between Lenny and his fans. *Lenny* is a biographical collage that straddles divergent narrative strands, subjectivities, mid-twentieth-century periods, and contrasting modes of black-and-white cinematography. In terms of film genre, Fosse's film is a collision of innovation and biopic conventions.

The biopic is possibly the most intermedial of genres, especially biographies of subjects of the past century and a half, from the eras of photography, audio recording, and cinema. Clichés, including newspaper headlines supplying narrative information, newsreels (for example, in *Wilson* [1944] or *Patton* [1970]), the labels of spinning records (in *The Buddy Holly Story* [1978] or *La Môme*, aka *La Vie en Rose* [2007]), sheet music (*Yankee Doodle Dandy* [1942]), or theater marquees (*Yankee Doodle Dandy*) are among the allusions to other media that the biopic makes its own. While Fosse avoids most of these, it is the form of *Lenny* itself that draws from various media. Fosse, working with the cinematographer Bruce Surtees, uses three discrete modes of black-and-white photography. If it is possible to discuss various forms of photography as media, then *Lenny* suggests intermediality in its montage organized around three different modes of black-and-white filming. These are the present, with the interview subjects in Fosse's film shot in the gray, low-contrast documentary look of pre-color television news, circa 1950–1966 – when all of *Lenny* takes place; the past, in the shadowy look of forties and fifties *film noir*; and 'show-biz' (the stage, with brightly lit foreground figures surrounded in high-contrast by an inky black background). Moreover, the editing rhythms of *Lenny* draw from other media, many of which Fosse brings to filmmaking with him.

2 The Intermedial Bob Fosse

Just before Bob Fosse filmed *Lenny,* his first imprint on the biopic, he became the only person to win, or even to be nominated for, the 'Triple Crown,' as Fosse referred to it, that is, the Broadway theater's Tony (for *Pippin*), the Hollywood film industry's Academy Award (for *Cabaret*), and television's Emmy (for *Liza with a Z*), all in the same season (1972–1973) (Wasson 2013: 344). Fosse was a dazzlingly intermedial director, ranking with very few others, such as Elia Kazan, Ingmar Bergman, Franco Zeffirelli, Julie Taymor, and Sam Mendes, as an artist who moved from stage to screen (of both kinds, in Fosse's case) with great facility. Moreover, Fosse was a dancer-turned-choreographer-turned-stage-and-then-movie director. Although few directors before or since have done as much as Fosse with the connections between dance and film editing, rhythm is the foundation of both. Thus it probably was inevitable that in the first film in which he had full artistic control, thanks to the 'Triple Crown,' this dancer-choreographer-director would design and execute a film with montage virtuosity.

Editing, the cinematic element that is unique to film, and the only element that had not existed in painting, theater, ballet, fiction, or poetry, nevertheless can enable cinema to take on the movement, the form, the sequentiality, and juxtaposition of other media. When Sergei Eisenstein in 1944 wrote of "Walt Whitman's huge montage conception" and "the Whitman *montage tradition,*" he was speaking in terms that readers of Whitman's own time probably would not have comprehended (Eisenstein 1949: 231). However, Eisenstein recognizes that in the long catalogues in "Song of Myself" the poet audaciously juxtaposes dozens of types of people in America, some respectable and revered, others barely or rarely acknowledged in polite society.[1] Moreover, research by film scholar Ben Singer found that Dziga Vertov, who started as a poet of the Futurist school, originally designed *Chelovek s kinoapparatom* (*The Man with a Movie Camera* [1929]) as a Soviet "Song of Myself," celebrating for the cinema all the claims that Whitman made for American poetry. Therefore, like the Soviet montage filmmakers, although without their ideological agenda, Fosse sought to liberate cinematic form from the cause-and-effect temporality of narrative moviemaking. In recent years, his efforts have been recognized. In 2012, when the Motion Picture Editors Guild asked its members to vote for the 75 best-edited films of all time, *All That Jazz* ranked fourth. *Cabaret* came in 30th. Although *Lenny* did not rank on this list, the experiments in life-writing form that Fosse undertakes in his first biopic are important to an understanding of the development of the biopic into its mod-

---

[1] For example, see Whitman, "Song of Myself," section 15.

ernist, investigatory, and finally, the neo-classical form in which it resides at present (Bingham 2010: 17–18).

When we discuss editing we move, almost involuntarily, to terminology that comes from music – rhythm, tempo, tone, overtone: the terms that Eisenstein applied in identifying the various types of editing (Eisenstein 1949: 72–81). Editing of silent Soviet Montage was conceived in opposition to the linear continuity editing that had been developed in America by D.W. Griffith and others for storytelling (Eisenstein 1949: 200–201). Thus Fossean editing seemingly owes more to dance and to the musical concepts Eisenstein and Vertov used in the Soviet Union in the 1920s than to Western continuity editing. It works on theme and variation, on psychological editing (another concept of Eisenstein's), counterpoint, contradiction, and collision, rather than on the linear continuity editing of the Classical Hollywood Cinema.

3 Cut (to) the Comedy

Fosse finds rhythm, contrast, and variety in the monologues of a stand-up comedian. The corrosive and profane beatnik comic Lenny Bruce was an object of fascination in the 1970s. The years from roughly 1956 to 1965, when Bruce, the fearless, disturbing night club comedian, plied his trade, already looked in the mid-1970s like a distant age – and a Dark Age, at that. The monologues that Bruce (played by Dustin Hoffman) performs in Fosse's film give the film spectator a sampling of the language and the irreverent wit that got the actual comedian arrested for obscenity multiple times. It was not only American authorities who considered Bruce objectionable; he was banned from Australia in 1962 and turned back from Heathrow Airport in London in 1963. Bruce died at the age of 40, found naked in the bathroom of his foreclosed-upon Hollywood mansion on August 3, 1966, one of the first of many counterculture celebrity drug overdoses in years to come. Bruce, all the rage in the hip culture of the Beat Generation, to which Bob Fosse also belonged, burned out after fewer than five years of white-hot night club and concert fame; Bruce was far past his peak at the time of his demise. He went from on-fire to untouchable after losing a months-long New York obscenity trial in 1964. Ten months before his death, he was declared legally bankrupt, a pauper. During the last two years of his life, he played all of two nightclub engagements (Goldman 1991; Collins and Skover 2002).

Bruce was both a victim of the speed of change that marked the era and a visionary who helped make the change happen. *Lenny*, Pauline Kael's review begins, "is conceived for well-meaning innocents who never saw Lenny Bruce and who can listen to Dustin Hoffman delivering bits of Bruce's routines and think, 'people just didn't understand him then – he isn't shocking at all'" (1976: 371). Shock is a relative notion. Some of Bruce's jokes, especially those about gay people, are much more offensive now than they were in the 1970s, much less in the early 1960s when the comedian made them. The issue of what one era finds "shocking" and why can be an instructive one to confront. Bruce launched the practice by comedians of riding the third rails of a culture, of unmasking its prejudices and exposing its hypocrisies. "Irony, irony, all is irony," wrote Clive Barnes, paraphrasing the Book of Ecclesiastes in the Old Testament, in his May 1971 review of Julian Barry's play on which the film is based. "What Bruce got busted for in private nightclubs is here being displayed in Broadway theater just five years after his death" (Barnes 1971).

Lenny Bruce was a seminal figure. As I found with Woody Guthrie, another pioneering folk hero with a New Hollywood biopic, *Bound for Glory* (Hal Ashby 1976), the media that might have carried his work to the public in his time did not exactly exist yet. Bruce's true medium was the nightclub stage; the only way to hear what he was like in performance is in uncensored recordings that were made of Bruce 'in concert,' itself a novel application of a term from high culture to show-business entertainment. These were not released until years after his death.[2] The albums made of Bruce's act in his lifetime were sanitized; his very few appearances on highly regulated late-fifties television only hint at his freeform brilliance (see *Lenny Bruce Without Tears*).

Fosse's specific medium was the 'New Freedom of the Screen' in the New Hollywood cinema that had just overcome its own highly censorial limits six years earlier, in 1968, when the Production Code was at long last replaced by the still-extant Motion Picture Rating System. The portable though bulky reel-to-reel tape recorders that take down the interviews in Fosse's film are similar to the instruments that intrigued Bruce, as the untutored though brilliantly verbal comic unwisely undertook his own legal defense, confident the laws of show business and his popularity with his small but fervent fan base would carry the day for him in court. Fosse well understood such laws. Lowdown dives, strip joints, dance hall parlors – the underside of showbiz – lured him again and again as the settings of his shows and films. Fosse's film stages and examines Bruce's life as if it were an artifact of an extinct civilization. Fosse makes scenes of Bruce's life and routines dance through his movie, while Surtees's coldly beau-

---

[2] See or, more correctly, hear: *Lenny Bruce Live at the Curran Theater.* 1971. Liner Notes by Ralph J. Gleason. Recorded live on 19 November 1961. Berkeley, Calif.: Fantasy Records, 1999. CD; *Lenny Bruce – The Carnegie Hall Concert.* 1972. Liner Notes by Albert Goldman. Recorded live on 4 February 1961. Hollywood, Calif: Capitol Records, 1995. CD.

tiful cinematography makes the late-1950s/early-1960s world of strip joints and night clubs vibrate with pastness.

Fosse's film aesthetic pushes against cinema's drive toward chronological, sequential time. His own film production team referred to this approach to cinematic temporality as "Fosse Time," with editing that is thematic and motif-driven, more like music and dance than cause-and-effect narrative (Wasson 2013: 374). For these reasons, *Lenny* cannot be fully understood in any of the conventional definitions of the biopic.

4 New Hollywood/Biopic: 'Warts and All' at an Impasse

I have written elsewhere of how the 1970s, the Hollywood Renaissance, was the most fallow of all decades for the biopic (Bingham 2011). The biopic missed out on the revisionism that transformed genres such as the western, *film noir*, and the gangster film amid what has been called 'Hollywood's Last Golden Age' (Kirshner 2012). The biopic in the 1970s found few paths away from the psychological realism of 'warts and all,' which took over the biopic in the 1950s, as the genre moved predominantly from statesmen, scientists, and authors to entertainers, athletes, and controversial political and military figures. *Lenny* does not exactly qualify for this subgenre, however.

Biopics in the 1950s balanced audience desire to know the private lives of famous people with the genre's enduring impulse to dramatize great accomplishments, the definition of which changed, as the Hollywood genre shifted from celebratory biopics to 'warts and all.' The former highlighted what Custen, citing Frankfurt School critic Leo Lowenthal, called "idols of production" (1992: 32–33). Such films were staples of the prewar and wartime years of the Studio Era and often depicted scientists, inventors, artists, and war heroes. After World War II, Custen found, the genre largely shifted to "idols of consumption," mostly entertainers and athletes. A number of factors, including a darker, more adult mood after the war, the influence of Italian Neo-Realism, the erosion of the Production Code self-censorship, and Hollywood's need to give audiences what they could not see at home on television, brought on the new biopics that purported to take an 'honest' look at the subject. These films set out to show the protagonist's bad qualities as well as the good, or 'warts and all,' a phrase traced to an instruction from Oliver Cromwell to his portrait painter (Kennedy 2013).

Warts-and-all biopics placed new emphasis on the private lives of famous people; the subjects chosen, moreover, tended to be those with dramatic, even sensational stories. Some of these films followed their protagonists down the road to alcoholism – and, after the 1956 liberalization of the Production Code permitted it – drug addiction. The subgenre also went along with the general drive in the 1950s toward realism, anti-heroes, and the new Method Acting style. It remained the dominant biopic mode through the 1960s and 1970s. The staleness of the mode by the 1970s partly accounts for the small number of biopics in that decade; it also moved Custen to claim that the biopic largely went to television after 1960 (1992: 214–232). The failure to innovate beyond 'warts and all' continued, although the uncompromising *Raging Bull* can be seen as its apotheosis, taking it to its most honest and even spiritual extreme. In the 1990s, revisionism, parody, and the investigatory mode finally hit the biopic, followed after 2000 by the neoclassical style, which unites all four earlier modes, in the 2000s and 2010s.

Molly Haskell titled her 1975 review of the film, "Lenny Sings the Blues," after the execrable 1972 biopic *Lady Sings the Blues*, which presented the great Billie Holiday (played by Diana Ross) as a pathetic junkie in need of salvation from her husband, Louis McKay (played by Billy Dee Williams), who survived to tell the tale and control the rights to it, and that is what *Lenny* could have become. There is, however, a competing Bruce biopic narrative: the Bruce who is brought down by a censorious Establishment, a culture war in its death throes. In this storyline, the one that Barry and Fosse adopt, drawing upon the mythology that had grown up around Bruce since his death, district attorneys and judges determine to put a stop to the 'declining morals' of the culture, and draw the line on obscenity and public decency at Lenny Bruce (Collins and Skover 2002: 192). At least by emphasizing Lenny Bruce the First Amendment prophet over Lenny Bruce the once-funny victim of his own excesses, the film shows what was significant about Lenny Bruce and why people listened to him.

5 Lenny Bruce: A Bob Fosse Film

Fosse's film juxtaposes documentary-style interviews with Bruce's nightclub monologues, as well as the pre-1967-style serious black-and-white movie with the *Cabaret* director's still-evolving montage-driven style. Alan Heim, his editor on *Lenny, All That Jazz,* and *Star 80,* has encouraged the notion that the non-linear structure of *Lenny* arose from a kind of re-choreographing of the shots and sound. After "an early, linear cut of *Lenny* played a tad sluggishly, Fosse encouraged Mr. Heim to dice the film into a collage, to compress the story and permit surprising juxtapositions" (Seitz 2009). This developing mythology was encouraged by Fosse's autobiographical film *All That Jazz* (1979), a movie that ironically has become much better known than *Lenny*. In it the theater-and-film director Joe Gideon (played by Roy Scheider in Fossean goatee and black garb) and his editor (Heim himself) are shown in an editing room where they endlessly cut and recut a soon-to-open film entitled "The Standup," about a comedian played by Cliff Gorman, who played Lenny in the original 1971 Broadway production. Despite the legend, *Lenny* hews mostly to the structure provided in the shooting script on file at the Library of Congress (Barry 1974).

Fosse turns passages of the script – Bruce's monologues, which are inserted into diegetic scenes in the comedian's life – into dialectical montage sequences. These were not necessarily cutting-room thunderbolts. A script's scenes have to be shot; they can be edited differently later. When a Hollywood film departs from the principles of temporal continuity and the editing begins to resemble Eisensteinian dialectical montage, what is the narrative destination? Bruce's art provides the dramatic conflict. The flashback frame common to many biopics – here, the interviews – is *Lenny*'s chief storytelling element. The classical straight-line narrative film is deprived of a conclusion. *Lenny*'s ending might seem rapid and abrupt. But then, Bruce's life, as shown in the film, appears that way, too. Fosse enfolds his curiosity – his sense of himself as an artist – into the film. The soft male voice of an interviewer amiably questions Bruce's ex-wife, Honey (played by Valerie Perrine); his mother, Sally Marr (played by Jan Miner); and his manager, Artie (played by Stanley Beck), a composite character who becomes a knowledgeable, sympathetic, but ultimately dispassionate participant in the twists and turns of Bruce's rise, decline, and legal travails. The interviewer is Fosse. His voice is heard addressing questions to the three people who knew Bruce well and who can give insight into him, or at least tell what they knew; this film suggests that insight might be too much to ask of our fellow human beings.

Fosse, in *Cabaret,* had proved himself adept as a montage director. In a montage sequence, the Tiller Girls perform a horrifying parody of goose-stepping Nazis; the Emcee in drag is cross-cut with the killing of the dog of a Jewish heiress by a gang of anti-Semitic goons. This was Soviet-style montage applied to the American musical, with Fosse manipulating footage like a Broadway/New Hollywood Eisenstein, using colliding 'attractions' (Eisenstein's term) to create a meaning that could not emerge from either image by itself, and thus to elicit both a psychological and physical/emotional response (see Bordwell 1993: 115–120). *Lenny* was shot in Florida during the winter season of 1974 to audiences recruited locally. Fosse reportedly hurled insults at audience members, with the camera on them, in order to capture shocked reactions that could be cut in anywhere, a modification of the Soviet Montage principle that editing creates reality (Wasson 2013: 362).

Because of the film's interview structure, reviewers have seen resemblances to *Citizen Kane* in *Lenny* (Ebert 1974; Westal 2007). As with *Kane*'s 'Rosebud' lips, the screen-filling lips of Honey Bruce are the first human feature we see in the film (figure 1). Indeed they are *Lenny*'s first image of any kind. "I'd say he was busted nine or ten times – three or four times for narcotics, and two or three times for obscenity," she says, but her three or four and two or three times do not add up to nine or ten. This suggests that the 'talking head' interviews in the film will be less than reliable. How can the interviewer learn anything, if what he is told is based on memory and subjectivity? As Fosse explained, journalist Lawrence Schiller conducted interviews in 1968 and 1969 with "people who knew Bruce, girl friends [sic], attorneys, other comics, etc." Schiller emerged as a major source of most of the works about Bruce that came out in the 1970s, including the play and film entitled *Lenny*, as well as Albert Goldman's massive book, *Ladies and Gentlemen, Lenny Bruce*, which was first published earlier in 1974 (Hornstein 1975: 31). *Lenny* sticks so scrupulously to the transcripts of these interviews that something as seemingly offhand as Honey crunching on a potato chip as she talks to the interviewer turns out to have come from Schiller. The spectator of *Lenny* does not know what the interviewer will do with all the impressions and memories he gathers. Fosse turns the film's spectator into *Citizen Kane*'s Mr. Thompson, the reporter who goes home at the end of the film not having made sense, he thinks, of all the information he has found.

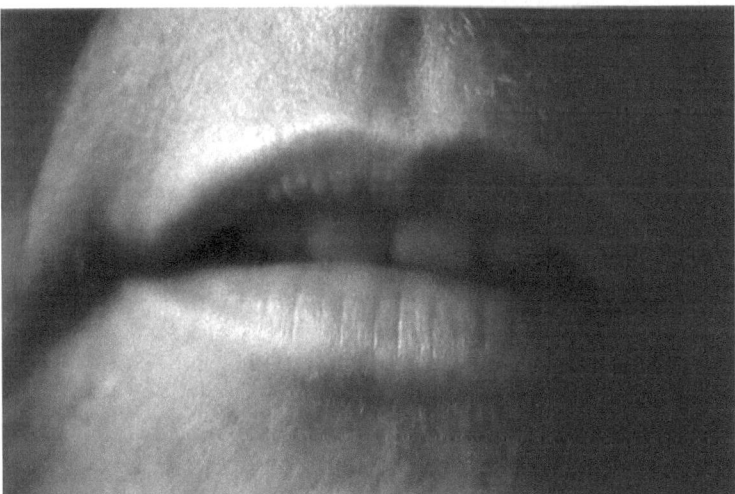

Figure 1: The gigantic mouth of the mundane middle-aged Honey, survivor of her life with Lenny. Digital frame enlargement. Source: *Lenny* 2002: 0:30:00.

Before we can see an establishing shot of the speaker beyond her gigantic lips, the film cuts as an off-screen announcer incants the then familiar phrase, "Ladies and gentlemen – Lenny Bruce!" The camera, from the upstage position, looks out onto a darkened nightclub. A slouching man leans on a microphone stand with one elbow and holds the mike with the other hand. The spotlight swings to the left, dramatically backlighting him. We can make out that he wears Levi's and a leather jacket, as if James Dean had come back to life as a hip comedian stand-up rebel, this one with a cause (figure 2).

Figure 2: In contrast, the mythological Lenny, literally larger than life, including his own. Digital frame enlargement. Source: *Lenny* 2002: 0:46:00.

Lenny does not present itself as the reenactment of times and places, with subtitles announcing cities and dates. The opening credit sequence sets out a thesis. As the opening credits run in white-on-black lettering, Hoffman-as-Bruce performs in voiceover a comedy monologue – *sans* audience laughter – attributing the spread of venereal disease to the fact that "nobody talks about it." Why? "Because talking about it" – as the credit "Directed by Bob Fosse" appears on the screen – "makes you the worst person in the community."

The film will show Bruce "talking about it" and getting ostracized as "the worst person" in "communities" from San Francisco to Chicago to New York. In other words, Bruce was shut down by 'us.' Bruce himself once told an audience, as police officers ringed the stage, poised to arrest him, "It's *your* fault I'm being busted [...] It's up to you to change the law" (Collins and Skover 2002: 135). In the shooting script of *Lenny* in the Bob Fosse and Gwen Verdon Collection at the Library of Congress, Lenny makes a similar speech (Barry 1974, scene 155, p. 102). It was possibly among the three minutes that, Alan Heim reported, were cut in the very last days of editing, when Fosse might just have taken too much out of his film (Wasson 2013: 386). Perhaps Fosse was concerned that his audience in the 1970s would feel that Lenny is speaking to them; indeed it is not so much that laws were changed but that they were reinterpreted, and that standards changed. Bruce, after all, was never charged with anything more serious than a misdemeanor.

An auteurist reading finds that like the Emcee in *Cabaret*, Lenny Bruce traffics in outrageous humor, standing on a stage saying the unsayable. The Emcee gets in no trouble for this (except in the revisionist Sam Mendes – Alan Cumming London and New York stage productions of 1993, 1998, and 2014). Lenny is destroyed for uttering on the stages of nightclubs, in 'mixed company,' the language of barracks, locker rooms, and factory floors. Bruce offends well-organized and powerful municipalities controlled by the very interests that Bruce mercilessly ridicules. These include white male patriarchy and organized religion, especially the Catholic Church. During Bruce's obscenity trial in Chicago, during which Ash Wednesday happened to fall in 1963, the judge and the entire jury came into the courtroom with ashes on their foreheads (Collins and Skover 2002: 168). This underlines the outsider status of the anti-assimilationist Bruce, one of whose hobby horses, as the film makes clear, was the mythology of America as a 'Christian nation.' In a period when a Bishop, Fulton J. Sheen, had a top-rated prime-time television show, and Cardinal Francis Spellman of New York could cripple the run of a film by an Academy Award–winning director (Elia Kazan's *Baby Doll* [1956]) by denouncing it from the pulpit, the Catholic Church saw it as its right and duty to help stamp out public indecency wherever it saw it. Not for nothing was a pamphlet of Bruce's collections of stories entitled "Stamp Help Out" (Goldman 1968: 46).

Among the facets of the conventional biopic that *Lenny* lacks is the *in medias res* opening, which the film takes up just before the revelation of events that make the subject significant and known to the public (Custen 1992: 51). Bruce's public ascent, on the other hand, begins approximately at the film's midway point. The first half, dominated by Honey's narration, has to do with their marriage, which ended before Bruce went on to stardom. This is why, with the divorce, the story is told by Bruce in his monologues, and by the interviews with Artie and Sally, who play the sidekick and mentor roles. Fosse omits some of the scenes in the script that show Bruce's characteristic bits. Thus again, while entertainer biopics usually place heavy stress on the creation of the works for which the subject is popularly known, Fosse does not weigh down the film with these, causing some reviewers to complain that the film omits most of Bruce's best-known bits (Kael 1976: 374). The 'ladder of success' images basic to idol-of-consumption entertainer stories are dealt with in a brief, punchy montage. A voiceover of Lenny's "I am totally corrupt" monologue – "Whatever they give, I'll grab" – provides the soundtrack for shots that present signs of Bruce's new wealth – Bruce's boxy house in the Hollywood Hills, his Filipino manservant, and his MG sports car.

In another example of Fosse's juxtapositions of private and public Lenny, Bruce sets up his wife in a *ménage-à-trois* with another woman, then afterwards reproaches her because "you didn't tell me you were gonna love it so much." Hoffman, at his most subtle, jealously but quietly unloads on Honey while insisting none of it bothers him. Although contemporary reviewers asserted that the film sanctified Lenny, scenes like this show him to be a passive-aggressive manipulator in his personal relationships. The *ménage* scene ends with Lenny half in light, half in shadow. This lighting strategy on Lenny continues in the aftermath scene. Lenny insists, "You obviously dig it [...] so that's cool," standing before us as a divided figure. In one shot, Lenny, from behind, momentarily catches a glimpse of himself in a mirror, knowing the torture he is inflicting on his wife, but steaming ahead with it. "You son of a bitch!" she screams after him. "Why do you have to be so fucking hip?" He wants to be "hip" and progressive, but cannot do it (figure 3).

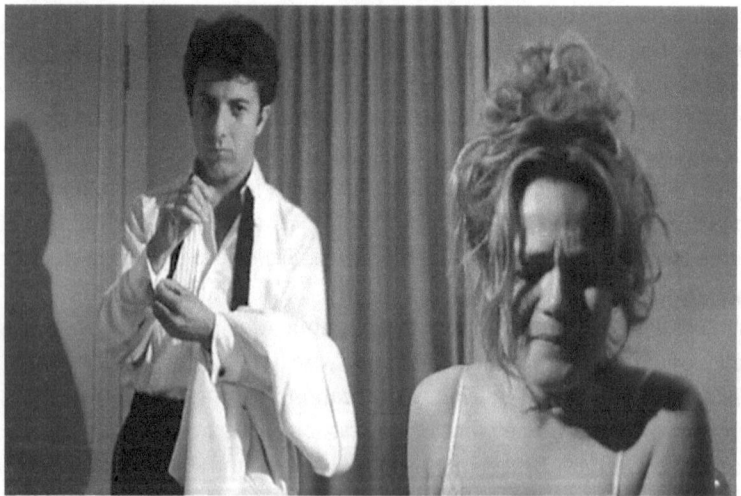

Figure 3: Half in shadow throughout the post-*ménage* scene with Honey. Fosse and Surtees compose and light the marital scenes like 1950s realistic *noir*, with a touch of Welles. Digital frame enlargement. Source: *Lenny* 2002: 0:44:53.

The after-scene is intercut with rhythmic bits of a long monologue:

INT: NIGHTCLUB – NIGHT
Lenny, bearded:
LENNY
(rather charmingly)
And now, a word about dikes.
I like dikes. That's what Will
Rogers once said, "I never met
a dike I didn't like." If you
notice, comics will do endless
fag jokes but never dike jokes
and the reason for that, I
figure, is that dikes'll really
punch the shit outta ya. Oh,
yeah. It's hard to spot dikes. *Why?*
'cause sometimes we're married
to them [...].
(Barry 1974: Scenes 82, 83, p. 47–48)

The script, for production logistics, has Lenny deliver this monologue *en bloc*. Fosse shoots the monologue rhythmically, with Hoffman sitting at the drum set, punctuating his routine like a jazz riff. The monologue is filmed in three different camera setups, with the punch line delivered as we look up at Lenny, from an extreme low angle. Then Fosse cuts from Lenny and Honey's dialogue to the "dikes" act five times, breaking the rhythm of Lenny's snappy monologue with the tawdry real-life scene, which concludes by contradicting it. Thus, this sequence shows Lenny in effect using his art to lie to himself, drawing a conclusion in his monologue that comes from his unfair treatment of Honey. The routine ends, "Sometimes we're married to 'em." But only in Lenny's fantasy (figure 4).

Wasson implicitly criticizes Fosse for imprinting his own preoccupations onto his subject (as if *auteur* directors were not celebrated for doing just that) (2013: 359). Fosse was also working through in *Lenny* his own fascinations. There is no evidence that Bruce was married to a "dike," and the film does not suggest that he was. Fosse uses the threesome as a metaphor for the 'hipness' to which Bruce aspired but was not ready for. Perhaps no one was. Making the film in the era of *Bob & Carol & Ted & Alice* (1969), when sexual liberality was referred to as 'open' rather than 'hip,' Fosse questions whether men and women can ever be 'cool' about non-monogamous relationships.

Figure 4: Contrast again, this time with "I like dikes." While the film displaces Bruce's drug habit onto Honey, Lenny in his nightclub act displaces his (fictional) desire for threesomes onto his wife, imagining that "sometimes, we're married to 'em." Digital frame enlargement. Source: *Lenny* 2002: 0:45:09.

6 Not Simply the Absence of Color

Lenny is not a 1970s biopic, like *Bound for Glory*, which defamiliarizes the past. The interview sequences defamiliarize the present in that, like all of *Lenny*, they are shot in black-and-white, a format which, Richard Misek asserts, was after 1966 used mainly to suggest the past (2010: 108). Fosse's post-1966 black-and-white is considerably more complex.

Similar to the way Fosse took the big sweeping choreography of Broadway and created movies that were small, downward, constricted, disciplined, and beautiful, in *Lenny* he evokes his protagonist with the absence of color. I remember how startling and breathtakingly vivid *Lenny*'s black-and-white cinematography, together with the rapid cutting, looked on the big screen when I first saw it in March 1975. It was backward-looking and forward-moving at once, a demonstration of Christian Metz's "imaginary signifier" (1982), cinema's capacity for simultaneously projecting absence – a world that does not exist as we look at it – and overwhelming presence. Accordingly, the interview sequences discuss a past that seems somewhat canceled out by the present. Honey and Sally have let themselves be forever defined by Lenny. The agent is the embodiment of show business insincerity, a Bob Fosse constant. With his silk shirt, tinted aviator glasses, and trendy early-1970s argot ("Right on, right on"), Artie emphasizes almost cruelly the swiftness with which his former client has been consigned to the past.

When Honey talks to the interviewer, everything about her and her environment is non-descript. The apparently clean former junkie lives in the past; her life with Lenny and her days as a great beauty are far behind her, but the memories of both appear to keep her going. The low-contrast lighting of Honey's interviews, the type of black-and-white that Wheeler Winston Dixon calls "drab," stands out from the 1950s melodramatic *noir* of her flashbacks to her day-to-day life with Lenny (2015: 18). Different yet again are the high-contrast eye-popping black blacks and white whites of Lenny's stage world, a world that Lenny appears to control, making him a fourth narrator, speaking for himself in his art.

Therefore, Fosse makes of the three distinct black-and-white registers in his film an intermedial heteroglossia, a much more subtle interplay of chromatic perception than if he used black-and-white and color to stand for separate states of being, as Wim Wenders did in *Der Himmel über Berlin* (*Wings of Desire* [1987]) to signify the point of view of eternity, in black-and-white, as distinct from the reality of the mortal world, filmed in color. *Cabaret* cut from a stage world to a real world, but here the real worlds divide into past (a realm of the interviewees' memories, which may not be reliable) and present. Moreover, the present here is confined to the places where Honey, Sally, and Artie speak to the interviewers, making the present a kind of stage. Only in the past do we see a cinematic narrative that moves with the action. Significantly, once we move with Lenny's progress as a big-name comic, his monologues become part of the story, which Artie mostly tells, not as counterpoint to interviews, mostly Honey's (figure 5).

Fosse cuts more from Honey's remembered scenes and her interviews to Lenny's stage routines because they provide the most telling contrasts among the three modes of black-and-white. As in *Cabaret,* the off-stage life of the characters takes place in the realm of cinematic realism. However, it is 1950s realism as defined in social problem dramas like *I Want to Live!* (1958) and *Anatomy of a Murder* (1959), with the starker *noir* cinematography of *Sweet Smell of Success* (1957) blended in.

The year of Bruce's death, 1966, was the final year in which the Academy Awards gave separate color and black-and-white awards for Cinematography, Art Direction, and Costume Design. American television converted to all-color in the fall of 1965, and the film industry followed. As in most of the very few films made in black and white after 1966, the use of black and white makes a statement. *Lenny*'s Oscar-nominated cinematography, in its exceptionalism, is practically a character in itself. Unlike other major black-and-white films made

Figure 5: One of the three visual modes: "Drab" black and white in present-day. Honey describes her marriage to the interviewer, played by Bob Fosse, his ever-present cigarette in hand. Digital frame enlargement. Source: *Lenny* 2002: 0:51:12.

in the early 1970s, *Lenny* does not quote specific film styles from Hollywood's past, as Peter Bogdanovich's *The Last Picture Show* (1971) and *Paper Moon* (1973) had, and as Mel Brooks's *Young Frankenstein* later in 1974 would. As it cuts from scenes in Lenny Bruce's life to interviews conducted in the present, it is clearly not out to evoke the past so much as it is to freeze Bruce within it.

7 Honey's Blues

Bruce's lingering ex-wife seems as much on the scene at the time of his death as she was before they were divorced in 1957. Fosse, however, valued a woman's perspective on his male protagonist. Almost alone among the Hollywood Renaissance directors, whose films tended to be male-oriented, he upheld the studio-era institution of the female star. Honey is far more important to the film than in Barry's play, however; indeed Valerie Perrine, who received a Best Actress Academy Award nomination for her performance, occupies as much screen time as Hoffman. Fosse considerably built up Honey's character, even after shooting began. For example, he gave her, rather than Lenny, as in the script, the answer to the repeated question from Aunt Mema (played by Rashel Novikoff) about how long Lenny and Honey knew each other before they got married, "About half an hour [...]," so that she keeps up with the two comics in the room, earning the mother's approval: "She's a terrific girl." The script's following line, "Look at that face," is dropped. Honey becomes more than a pretty face. Fosse magnifies the importance of Honey to Lenny's story beyond what it may have been in life. Also, "the fact that Fosse got along well with Perrine" clearly influenced his decision to cut numerous references in the script to her ignorance: "I wanted to win on the First Amendment," Lenny tells her. "Do you know what that is?" "No." Only the first sentence of that exchange is in the film (Barry 1974: scene 151, p. 94). Also gone are her infidelities and (in the diegetic scenes) the fact that she never accepted the divorce (Westal 2007). This Honey, pathetic junkie though she may have been, is granted her dignity, and not just because Fosse needed her permission to portray her (which Barry did not have for the play, in which she is named Rusty).

Despite all this, Honey's importance in the film is as a signifier of drug addiction; she is the stand-in for the overbearing drug habit that the film will not portray as Bruce's own. Sally blames Honey for the drugs. "He was just fine before you had to be schlepped back into it," Sally complains to Honey at a climactic moment. Because Fosse wanted to highlight the censorship Bruce suffered, the film greatly downplays his drug addiction. Sally asks Lenny about the pills he is popping, and he answers: "M & Ms." The line is tossed off, nearly inaudible. From the start of the second act, Lenny's drug addiction is mostly displaced onto Honey, another reason why she plays such a large part in the film. Fosse knew well that there was probably no way to portray the subject of a biopic as a drug addict without taking a moral position on the addiction, and causing it to become the point of the character and the film, as it had in *Lady Sings the Blues*. Moreover, from Goldman in the 1970s to Collins & Skover in the 2000s, Bruce's biographers portray him as having been brought down by a complex combination of the law's persecution, his own obsessive-compulsive responses, his refusal to be helped by a public campaign on his behalf, and the drugs.

After Lenny accepts an offer to work the 'hip' clubs for roughly eight times what he had been making, he announces to a strip club audience that "I'm leaving this toilet to go off and become a big star." Cut to a side close-up of a judge, with a giant wart on his neck, blowing his nose. As the film now threatens to become Dreyer's *The Passion of Joan of Arc* (1928), with its ugly inquisitors, we are introduced to the milieu of American courtrooms where the film will spend much of its final third. Instantly, Fosse makes the association between Bruce's stardom and his legal troubles; however, the judge actually presides over Honey's narcotics case in Hawaii. The home life with Honey is replaced, for contrast, with the sterile, unfeeling American courtroom. Most of the diegetic scenes with Honey take place in prison, making Lenny's relationships those with his audiences and with judges and lawyers.

One of the purposes of the interviews seems to be to slip the addiction out of the dramatic action and couch it in the interviewees' narration. "Lenny was really deep into drugs himself, wasn't he," the interviewer asks Honey, remarkably late in the film. "You're really cute, aren't you," she tells him. "You want me to say it." Of course, Fosse does not want her to say "it." In actuality Lenny was a virtuoso at managing his drug habit (Goldman 1991: 35–37). The film avoids the downward trajectory of the addiction narrative; it is not "Lenny Sings the Blues," after all.

Fosse wanted to avoid the clichés of the drug-addicted-celebrity biopic, but in so doing he gives the impression that the portrait of Bruce has been softened, whereas that might not even have been the intent. Furthermore, the last year of Lenny's life, which the film elides, was a sad anti-climax. The spark was gone; the old comic was gone. He turned forty, but he might as well have been a hundred. Whether the State destroyed Lenny or whether he destroyed himself, there was little of 'Lenny Bruce' left in the final year. In his "House on the Hill" (Goldman 1991: 315) in Laurel Canyon, Bruce dallied with girlfriends, imagined a comeback – in the legal system, not on the stage – and took drugs. He was a hipster-junkie Charles Foster Kane (albeit an impoverished one), dithering away his remaining time in his box-like Xanadu (Goldman 1991: 585).

Numerous critics of both Barry's play and the film found fault with *Lenny* for blaming Bruce's decline entirely on the puritanical 'establishment' and hardly at all on Bruce himself. In actuality, Bruce continued to fight an all-out war he could not win with a still censorious culture, bankrupted himself with attorneys' fees "when the American Civil Liberties Union was offering to handle his legal defense" and abused his body and mind on an epic scale with heroin (Collins and Skover 2002: 134–135). In Goldman's book, the index entries on "Bruce, Lenny: drugs used by" run to thirteen lines, far more than for any other item (1991: 650). Bruce himself refused to play the victim; "none of that wounded-bird stuff for me," he told an interviewer in 1963, "none of [those] Help Save Lenny Bruce Clubs that embarrass me" (Collins and Skover 2002: 135).

8 No Life after Death, Only Media Imagery

Lenny is, to my knowledge, the only biopic of any period or national cinema that offers no validation of the subject, no sense of his enduring legacy, and no sign that his significance transcends his mortal being. Nobody shows up to testify about how Bruce has influenced other comics or reinforced the value of the First Amendment. Missing is the sense that the subject leaves a legacy, that he transcends his body and subsequently lives on in the hearts of those he leaves behind. In *All That Jazz* the Lenny Bruce figure's monologue takes off on Elisabeth Kübler-Ross's five stages of grieving from her 1969 book, *On Death and Dying*: denial, anger, bargaining, depression, and acceptance. Survivors of Hoffman's *Lenny* never make it to even the first phase. Perhaps *Lenny* was made too close to Lenny Bruce's times for enough distance and perspective to have jelled. No one could know that Bruce would be pardoned by the governor of New York – in 2003 (Kifner 2003).

The film disregards validation in favor of intermedial iconography. For example, the Lenny of many of the nightclub monologues is bearded. The actual Bruce was first seen publicly in a beard less than six weeks before his death, on posters for the concerts put on at the Fillmore in San Francisco by rock promoter Phil Graham on 24 and 25 June 1966, which turned out to be Bruce's final gigs (Collins and Skover 2002: 337). Bruce had the beard when he died; thus these shots in Fosse's film represent Lenny in life less than they refer to images circulated after his death. Nearly all of Bruce's appearances were made clean-shaven; Fosse's Lenny appears bearded or clean-shaven seemingly without regard for temporality. In the 21 January script, eighteen separate 'scenes,' or excerpts from monologues, indicate that Lenny is "bearded" (Barry 1974). Other biopics would use changes in appearance to mark documented stages in the subject's life. Here the beard means that the scenes are from Bruce's period as a 'force,' a cultural icon. This makes Fosse's Lenny an intermedial one, the Lenny circulated in photos, posters, and on book and album covers, not the one experienced in actuality. This is the iconographic Lenny Bruce, the image disseminated in the years leading up to Fosse's film and after. Indeed a search in Google or Getty Images for 'Bearded Lenny Bruce' brings up many more shots of Dustin Hoffman in the film than of Bruce himself.

The film ends in a reenactment of the day Bruce was found dead, as his naked corpse, of which photographers snapped pictures when the Los Angeles Police allowed them in two at a time, appears on the screen from toe to head. Hoffman, in voiceover, mutters the last words anyone heard Bruce speak: "in the shithouse for good" (Goldman 1991: 641). *Lenny*'s ending makes for an abrupt and cruel way to conclude a biopic; Fosse refuses to digest, in any sense of that word, Lenny Bruce for the spectator.

9 Downward Trajectory in One Take

Avoiding the downward trajectory paradigm for biopics, especially those about victims and addicts, Fosse compresses Lenny's professional downfall into a five-minute-fifty-one-second take toward the film's end. Shot from the balcony of a theater, the scene takes the point of view of a nightclub patron watching a drug-zonked Lenny 'die' on stage. This shot represents more than a directorial stunt. By cutting to such a long, static take in a film whose average shot length (ASL) is 5.20 seconds, far below average for a Hollywood film in the mid-seventies, Fosse creates a mood of foreboding (Salt). In *Lenny*, cutting is a way of evading unpleasant reality, much as the characters do, and of confronting life with standup comedy, as Lenny does by turning his problems into art. A moving camera approaches something new, which in this film always feels dreadful, even deathly. The long take without movement is even worse, suggesting a fate from which there is no escape. Thus Fosse and Hoffman show a Lenny who has lost his timing, his spark, the spontaneity of the standup comic. From such a high angle, Lenny looks small and stranded. While the giant lips that open the film trap us in a character's subjective memory, Fosse employs open space, distance from his protagonist, and no-contrast, non-theatrical lighting – even though the setting is a stage – in order to show a Lenny who is small, stranded, and out of ideas. Bruce scrambles his greatest hits, as Fosse condenses the comedian's sad and pathetic final couple of years, in which he appeared before the few audiences whom he did entertain, disheveled and "not funny" (figure 6).

Figure 6: Fosse stops the show with a nearly six-minute take of Lenny in decline. The static shot makes Bruce's two-to-three-year downfall so sudden and drastic that it constitutes no less a compression than the rapid montage of most of the film. Digital frame enlargement. Source: *Lenny* 2002: 1:33:20.

This scene of a diminished-looking comic shows Bruce's decline, which was nearly as steep and abrupt as Lenny's sudden dissipation in the film. From 1963, when Bruce suffered his first conviction for obscenity, in the Gate of Horn case in Chicago, to December 1964, the opening of the New York Café-au-Go-Go trial, which took over six months from start to final sentencing, Bruce went to rack and ruin as a comedian, as a person, and as a professional performer. By the end of the New York case, he was overweight and unkempt. A comic who once did his act in sharp black suits and Italian shoes now often appeared on stage in an outlet store car coat. The 5¾-minute shot ends with the line, delivered in a dejected tone, "I'm not funny. I'm not a comedian."

In actuality, however, when Bruce's court appearances became more frequent than his nightclub acts, he did not drop this line on stage but instead rounded it out: "I'm not a comedian. I'm Lenny Bruce" (Goldman 1991: 383). In the script the long take ends this way (Barry 1974: scene 178, p. 119). The full statement, however, is not heard in the film. Could Fosse be trying to insist that Bruce is being silenced, as in his last courtroom scene when he pleads with the judge, "Don't take away my words"? Ironically, Fosse does the same thing; like a judge, he disallows Bruce's speech when it is out of order. "I'm not a comedian. I'm Lenny Bruce" is the statement of an artist who comes to see himself as more of an ongoing legal battle – the cause he refused to allow others to make of him – than an entertainer.

The apparent cold feet that caused Fosse to cut one of the script's most definitive lines, as well as its very climax, show that the biopic was not ready to evolve into the multi-faceted investigative genre it took another twenty years and films such as *An Angel at My Table* (1990), *32 Short Films About Glenn Gould* (1993), *Nixon* (1995), *I'm Not There* (2007), and *The Social Network* (2010) to become. Roger Ebert charged that the film had copied *Citizen Kane*, but the irony is that Fosse had not followed its example enough. *Kane* dares to expose its subject as a truly contradictory and self-defeating figure. Indeed *Kane* is a fully intermedial work, bringing in Welles's experience in radio and theater, cultural forms such as the rags-to-riches Horatio Alger novel and the Dickensian *Bildungsroman* about a young man's progress in the world, along with discrete film forms such as the newsreel, the newspaper saga, and the biopic itself (Bingham 2010: 50–71).

Lenny brings together Eisensteinian juxtaposition, Fossean dance, and interviews familiar from documentary forms of the 1950s and early 1960s, such as Edward R. Murrow's *See It Now* series. Fosse also dramatizes Schiller's interviews, which were used by Goldman's biography and Barry's play. More exactly, Fosse has made a film version of the interviews, intercutting them to Bruce's own comedy. This is a truly innovative approach, and one that no one else in the past forty years has tried. Fosse could have based a dramatic narrative film on Schiller's material. Goldman, who wrote his Bruce biography from the same interviews, bills them as 'journalism.' Again, like *Citizen Kane,* which followed a heard but not seen journalist as he interviewed those who knew Kane, *Lenny* mixes media. The difference is that *Lenny* is about a performer who delivers his medium, standup comedy, to us, often in dialectical opposition to what is being said about him. The montage of three divergent black-and-white media – the dazzling show business night club stage; the drab, gray style of black-and-white television news in the period coinciding with Bruce's performing career; and the high-contrast *films noirs* of the 1940s and 1950s – combines with Fosse's own intermediality to create a biopic that is mostly independent of narrative temporality.

Works Cited

Barnes, Clive. 1971. "*Lenny* Evokes Memory of an Angry Man Portrait of Comedian at Brooks Atkinson. Bruce Becomes Symbol of Political Dissent". *The New York Times* 27 May 1971. Reprinted in *Tom O'Horgan: Pre- and Post-Hair.* <http://www.orlok.com/hair/holding/prepost/tom/NYT5-27-71.html.> [accessed 24 October 2014].

Barry, Julian. 1974. "Bob Fosse's Final Script: *Lenny*". 5 January. Revision 21 January. *Lenny* Box 21C. Bob Fosse and Gwen Verdon Collection, Library of Congress. Washington, DC.

Bingham, Dennis. 2010. *Whose Lives Are They Anyway? The Biopic as Contemporary Film Genre.* New Brunswick, NJ: Rutgers University Press.

Bingham, Dennis. 2011. "Woody Guthrie, Warts-and-All: The Biopic in the New American Cinema of the 1970s". *a/b: Auto/Biography Studies* 26 (1): 68–90.

Bordwell, David. 1993. *The Cinema of Eisenstein.* Cambridge, MA: Harvard University Press.

Brevet, Brad. "Editors Guild Selects 75 Best Edited Films of All Time". 4 February 2015. <ComingSoon.net.> [accessed 15 May 2017].

Canby, Vincent. 1974. "*Lenny,* with Dustin Hoffman, Is One-Fourth Brilliant". *The New York Times* 11 November. <http://www.nytimes.com/movie/review?res=9404E4D9133BE63BBC4952DFB767838F669EDE> [accessed 15 January 2018].

Collins, Ronald K.L. and David M. Skover. 2002. *The Trials of Lenny Bruce: The Fall and Rise of an American Icon.* Naperville, IL: Sourcebooks.

Custen, George F. 1992. *Bio/Pics: How Hollywood Constructed Public History.* New Brunswick, NJ: Rutgers University Press.

Dixon, Wheeler Winston. 2015. *Black & White Cinema: A Short History.* London: I.B. Tauris.

Ebert, Roger. "*Lenny*". 10 November 1974. <http://www.rogerebert.com/reviews/lenny-1974> [accessed 23 July 2016].

Eisenstein, Sergei. 1969 [1949]. *Film Form: Essays in Film Theory.* Translated by Jay Leyda. New York: Harcourt Brace.

Goldman, Albert. 1968. "The Electric Resurrection of Lenny Bruce". *New York* May 20: 43–48.

Goldman, Albert (From the journalism of Lawrence Schiller). 1991 [1974]. *Ladies and Gentlemen – Lenny Bruce!!* New York: Penguin.

Gottfried, Martin. 2003 [1990]. *All His Jazz: The Life and Death of Bob Fosse*. New York: Da Capo.
Haskell, Molly. 1975. "Lenny Sings the Blues". *Viva* March: 39.
Hornstein, Scott. 1975. "The Making of *Lenny*: An Interview with Bob Fosse". *Filmmakers Newsletter* February: 30–34.
Kael, Pauline. 1976. "When the Saints Come Marching In". *Reeling*. Boston: Atlantic-Little, Brown. 371–377.
Kennedy, Maev. "Cromwell's 'warts and all' portraitist gets first exhibition in 40 years". *The Guardian* 8 November 2013. <https://www.theguardian.com/artanddesign/2013/nov/08/cromwell-portraitist-samuel-cooper-exhibition> [accessed 13 March 2017].
Kifner, John. "No Joke! 37 Years After Death Lenny Bruce Receives Pardon". *The New York Times* 24 December 2003. <http://www.nytimes.com/2003/12/24/nyregion/no-joke-37-years-after-death-lenny-bruce-receives-pardon.html?pagewanted=all> [accessed 30 July 2016].
Kirshner, Jonathan. 2012. *Hollywood's Last Golden Age: Politics, Society, and the Seventies Film in America*. Ithaca, NY: Cornell University Press.
Lenny Bruce Performance Film, The. 2005 [1967]. Directed by John Magnuson. Koch Vision. DVD.
Lenny Bruce Without Tears. 2005 [1972]. Directed by Fred Baker, produced, researched, and written by Fred & Barbara Baker. First Run Features. DVD.
Lenny. 1971. Original Broadway Cast Recording. Beverly Hills, CA: Blue Thumb Records. LP.
Lenny. 2002. Santa Monica, CA: MGM Home Entertainment. DVD.
Metz, Christian. 1982. *The Imaginary Signifier: Psychoanalysis and the Cinema*. Translated by Celia Britton, Annwyl Williams, Ben Brewster, and Alfred Guzzetti. Bloomington: Indiana University Press.
Nisek, Richard. 2010. *Chromatic Cinema*. Malden, Mass.: Wiley-Blackwell.
Salt, Barry. "Barry Salt's Database: Average Shot Length Data". *Cinemetrics*. <http://www.cinemetrics.lv/satltdb.php#asl> [accessed 13 March 2017].
Schickel, Richard. 1974. "Black-and-Blue Comic". *Time* November 25: 11.
Seitz, Matt Zoller. "All That Fosse: All Those Echoes of *All That Jazz*". *The New York Times* 27 December 2009. <http://www.nytimes.com/2009/12/27/movies/27jazz.html?_r=0> [accessed 5 May 2010].
Singer, Ben. 1987. "Connoisseurs of Chaos: Whitman, Vertov, and the 'Poetic Survey'". *Literature/Film Quarterly* 15 (4): 247–258.
Wasson, Sam. 2013. *Fosse*. New York: Houghton Mifflin Harcourt.
Westal, Bob. "*Lenny* and the Price of Freedom". *The House Next Door. Slant.com* 28 December 2007. <http://www.slantmagazine.com/house/article/lenny-and-the-price-of-freedom> [accessed 17 July 2016].
Whitman, Walt. 1892. "Song of Myself". *Poetry Foundation*. <https://www.poetryfoundation.org/poems/45477/song-of-myself-1892-version> [accessed 27 August 2017].

Ina Bergmann
The Remediation of Little Edie: From It-Girl to Loony Cat Lady to Cultural Icon

Abstract

The concept of remediation is a useful instrument in establishing a nexus between intermediality and life writing. Processes of creating media images of public personae or practices of 'iconizing' through various media changes can be unraveled and explained through remediation. A case study on cultural representations of Edith Bouvier Beale (1917–2002), also known as 'Little Edie,' a first cousin to Jackie Kennedy Onassis, will explicate this. From her earliest childhood until old age and then most notably after her death, Little Edie's public persona was largely created and continuously transformed by culturally specific remediations of her life story. The main focus here is on the shifts and changes in her public image brought about by three instances of remediating her life story: a documentary film (1975) by Albert and David Maysles; a Tony Award-winning Broadway musical (2006); and an HBO biopic (2009), all entitled *Grey Gardens*.

1 Life Writing, Intermediality, and Remediation

Sidonie Smith and Julia Watson define life writing "as a general term for writing that takes a life, one's or another's, as its subject. Such writing can be biographical, novelistic, historical, or explicitly self-referential and therefore autobiographical" (2010: 4). The Oxford Centre for Life Writing outlines a similarly broad approach on their website: "Life writing includes autobiography, memoirs, letters, diaries, journals (written and documentary), anthropological data, oral testimony, and eye-witness accounts" ("What Is Life-Writing?" 2015–2017).

Yet, there are differences between "self life writing" (Smith and Watson 2010: 1) and biography. The point of view in biography is "external to the subject" (5); therefore, "the events the subject becomes renowned for determine what the biographer selects to interpret as formative" (6). Consequently, "biographies offering different interpretations of particular historical figures may appear periodically over many centuries" (6). The terms biography or biographical narrative comprise all modes of biographical narration in whichever form or medium. They include "biofiction" (Middeke 1999), the "new biography" as well as "biographies on television" and the "biopic" (Smith and Watson 2010: 8–9).

https://doi.org/10.1515/9783110579253-007

The observation that "[m]ost biographers incorporate multiple forms of evidence, including historical documents, interviews, and family archives" (Smith and Watson 2010: 6–7), offers a potential link between biographical narratives and practices of intermediality. If the "evidence" is openly incorporated into the final cultural product, the biographer applies an intermedial technique.

According to Irina O. Rajewsky, intermediality "in a broad sense" is "a generic term for all those phenomena that [...] in some way take place *between* media" (2005: 46). While intermediality has developed into one of the most stimulating concepts in media studies, it has also become a "highly controversial term depending on the assumptions regarding the nature of mediality itself, with no shortage of various taxonomies and definitions concerning the types and categories of intermediality" (Pethö 2011: 1). Nassim Winnie Balestrini outlines at least "three basic variants" (2017: 70) of intermediality and Ágnes Pethö suggests to use the plural form, "intermedialities," when referring to "phenomena involving media relations," thereby "admitting that they can be approached from various points of view" (2011: 20).

One of those approaches to intermediality is remediation. Originally, the term "[r]emediation" meant "the act or process of remedying" (*Merriam-Webster* 2017), "used by educators as a euphemism for the task of bringing lagging students up to an expected level of performance and by environmental engineers for 'restoring' a damaged ecosystem" (Bolter and Grusin 2000: 59). The word derives from the Latin *remediare*, which means "to heal, to cure" (*Oxford Dictionaries* 2017). Drawing attention to the fact that the words 'media' or 'mediation' are incorporated in the term 'remediation,' Jay David Bolter and Richard Grusin adapt the latter term for media studies in their *Remediation: Understanding New Media* (2000).

According to Bolter and Grusin, "the representation of one medium in another" constitutes a "remediation" (2000: 45). They use the word "to express the way in which one medium is seen by our culture as reforming or improving upon another" (59). Remediation thus must be understood as the practice of appropriating, repurposing, and refashioning of the "property" (45) of one medium into another. The practice of remediation operates through the "double logic" or contradictory imperatives of immediacy and hypermediacy, as "our culture wants both to multiply its media and to erase all traces of mediation" (5). Bolter and Grusin explain that "[t]he logic of immediacy leads to erasing or rendering automatic the act of representation, the logic of hypermediacy acknowledges multiple acts of representation and makes them visible" (34). Astrid Erll and Ann Rigney argue that "memorial media" especially strive for immediacy, aiming at providing a "seemingly transparent window on the past," so that the recipient forgets about the presence of the medium and is seemingly presented with an "'unmediated memory'" (2009: 4). In this respect, "while 'immediacy' creates the experience of the presence of the past, 'hypermediacy', which reminds the viewer of the medium, points to the potential self-reflexivity of all memorial media" (Erll and Rigney 2009: 4). This effect is achieved by practices of recycling and by the multiplication of media (Erll and Rigney 2009: 4).

The function of "remediation as reform," highlighted by Bolter and Grusin (2000: ix), is especially interesting. They assert that it is "[t]he goal of remediation [...] to refashion or rehabilitate other media," proceeding from the ambiguous motives of homage and rivalry (49). Furthermore, because all mediations are both real and mediations of the real, remediation can also be understood as a process of reforming reality (55–56).

I will choose a dynamic approach here and study remediation as a constantly ongoing process in which the public image of a person is continually evolving, furthered by a refashioning of his/her life story in different media and genres. Whether remediations are always improvements, as Bolter and Grusin insinuate, is debatable. I aim at reconstructing a "genealogy of remediation" (Erll and Rigney 2009: 5) by focusing on repeated, culturally specific representations over time. I will approach remediation as a form of "diachronic intermediality" (Erll and Rigney 2009: 9). The notion that "remediation is concerned with the ways in which the same story is recalled in new media at a later point in time and hence given a new lease of cultural life" (Erll and Rigney 2009: 8) will be central to my discussion. The remediations of Little Edie are ideal examples for this debate, as every new remediation of her life story tapped into new audiences.

2 Edith Bouvier Beale's Life

Edith Bouvier Beale, the daughter of Edith Ewing Bouvier Beale and Phelan Beale was born in 1917. She was known as 'Little Edie' to distinguish her from her mother, 'Big Edie.' She was Jacqueline Lee Bouvier's first cousin, who was better known as Jackie Kennedy Onassis, once the First Lady of the United States.

Little Edie enjoyed a highly privileged upbringing in New York City's Upper East Side. She first attracted media attention when her introduction to society at a debutante ball at Pierre Hotel was reported on by *The New York Times* ("Beautiful Deb Writes Poetry" n. d.). Despite early aspirations of becoming a poet, the young socialite, then known as "Body Beautiful Beale" (*Grey Gardens Official* 2017), became a fashion model. She is said to have turned down marriage proposals by the most promising young men of her time, such as Joe Kennedy, Jr. – JFK's older brother –, J. Paul Getty, and Howard Hughes. One of the first it-girls of the twentieth century, she did not aspire to become a privileged wife. Living in New York City during the 1940s, she unsuccessfully tried to pursue a career as an actress and dancer.

In 1952, aged 35, Little Edie moved back in with her mother, Big Edie, who now lived permanently at the family's East Hampton summer estate, Grey Gardens, because Edie's father had abandoned her. She stayed with and took care of her mother for the next 25 years, until Big Edie's death. Their finances eroding, the two women drifted into poverty and isolation. The once grand Grey Gardens became a dilapidated house, infested with raccoons. The living conditions were miserable, not furthered by the myriads of cats the two Beales kept. The fact that these society ladies, used to servants, had never learned to keep house and also did not care to do so, gradually turned them into compulsive hoarders. In 1972, the Suffolk Health Department, alarmed by neighbors, threatened to evict them from Grey Gardens unless the house was cleaned. Little Edie thus hit the magazines again, now as a loony cat lady (Carpozi 1971). When the issue evolved into a national scandal, Jackie Kennedy Onassis footed the bill for the cleaning and some renovations of the house.

The same year, Albert and David Maysles, known for their Rolling Stones documentary *Gimme Shelter* (1970), were engaged by Lee Radziwill, Jackie's sister, to do a filmic photo album of her family. They also arranged to visit her aunt and cousin in the Hamptons. But once the two Maysles had met the two Beales, they soon abandoned the original project and decided to do a film solely about Little and Big Edie. They captured their aberrant lifestyle in a documentary film called *Grey Gardens*, which was filmed in 1973 and released in 1975.

After her mother's death in 1977, Little Edie tried to kick-start a career as an entertainer, at the age of 60, and indeed secured an engagement at Reno Sweeney, a Manhattan night spot, for eight cabaret performances. After many bad, in fact devastating, reviews – despite the fact that Andy Warhol seems to have been a fan who even attended repeatedly – she returned to Grey Gardens for a while and later sold the estate. Mostly forgotten by the general public, Edie died in 2002 at the age of 84 from a heart attack in her apartment in Florida. Her body was only found days after her death (Adair and Boyd 2013; "Edith Bouvier Beale" 2015; *Grey Gardens Online* 2009; Kaplan 1976; Martin 2002; Rakoff 2002; Rhodes 2006; Sheehy 1972 and 2007; Jennifer Wright 2012).

3 Little Edie's Afterlife

The "rich extra-textual life" (Anderson 2012: 295) of Little Edie originates mainly with the Maysles's documentary. At first, it seems to have especially appealed to gay men, whose enthusiasm launched Edie's cultural career as a camp icon (Colman 2009). This "underground fame" was amplified by the theatrical re-release of the documentary in 1996 (Anderson 2012: 295). Early on deemed a classic by Little Edie herself, the Maysles's film has today reached a status seldom achieved by documentaries (Anderson 2012: 295; Rhodes 2006: 83).

Since Little Edie's death, her iconic figure has been in the media limelight to a degree surpassing the public attention she received during her lifetime (McElhaney 2009: 97). Little Edie's life and her self-stylization serve as inspiration for all kinds of cultural products (McElhaney 2009: 96) and have ignited a veritable 'Bealemania.' The demand is met by the cultural market: Little Edie's private pictures, her letters, and her diaries have been published (Beale 2009 and 2010; Newkirk 2009) and former acquaintances have written memoirs in which they feature recollections of her (Lois Wright 2007; Newkirk 2008). Her life story has been turned into the novel *Gristmill* (1975) by George S. Caldwell, a "thinly disguised exploitation piece" (Adair and Boyd 2013: 32); into a Broadway musical, *Grey Gardens* (2006); and into an HBO biopic, *Grey Gardens* (2009). Albert Maysles released *The Beales of Grey Gardens* (2006), using hitherto undisclosed original footage. Singer-songwriter Rufus wrote and recorded a song called "Grey Gardens" for his album "Poses" (2001) (Pincus-Roth 2006: n. pag.). Furthermore, there is Grey Gardens retail (*Grey Gardens Official* 2017) and a comprehensive website (*Grey Gardens Online* 2009). Fans create all kinds of cultural products paying homage to Little Edie, among them paintings, dolls, and shirts (*Etsy* 2017). The current owner of Grey Gardens, Sally Quinn, who, together with her husband, *Washington Post* executive editor Ben Bradlee, had bought the house in 1979 from Little Edie, is also about to cash in on the publicity. She plans to publish a memoir, *Finding Magic*, and sell the house and the Beales' furniture for a price that is a hundred times the amount she and her husband originally paid (Dangremond 2017; Rogers 2017). Kent Bartram is on the verge of publishing a biography of Little Edie under the title *Staunch Character* (Colman 2009; Bartram 2018).

Particular aspects of Little Edie's life have been met with remarkable cultural resonance. Most notably, her individual style of clothing has affirmed Little Edie's position as a fashion icon (Adair and Boyd 2013; McElhaney 2009: 104) of an extraordinary kind. It is "Edie's outrageous and totally singular approach to wardrobe" (McElhaney 2009: 104) which appeals to a twenty-first-century set of imitators repeatedly struck by economic crisis. Little Edie's reinvention of old clothes and her turning of household textiles into outfits has earned her the title of a "recessionista" (Stein 2008; Tinkcom 2011: 58). Young women celebrate her signature style in blogs (for example Vaskeviciute n. d.), and imitations of her outfits range among the most popular Halloween costumes (for example Stilwell

2013). The textile, entertainment, and music industries have also discovered her style. Little Edie signature brooches and turbans are sold online (*Grey Gardens Official* 2017), and fashion designers such as Marc Jacobs, Todd Oldham, Calvin Klein, Isaac Mizrahi, and John Bartlett claim to have been inspired by her (Ingrassia 2006; Muther 2009; Stein 2008; Wilson 2009). There have been Little Edie fashion features on television ("Christine Ebersole Models Little Edie Fashion on Today Show" 2007) and spreads in magazines like *Vogue* and *Harper's Bazaar* (Martin 2002; Stein 2008). For the portrayal of Sarah Jessica Parker's character Carrie Bradshaw in the TV-series *Sex and the City* (1998–2004) and the two feature films (2008, 2010), costume designer Patricia Field adapted Little Edie's eclectic style. Especially one very memorable scene from the first movie, when Carrie is wearing a vintage sequin beanie hat, pajama pants, and a fur coat on New Year's Eve ("New Year's Eve on SATC" 2010), obviously cites an image of Little Edie in a headdress and a fur coat which was used on the publicity poster for the Maysles's documentary. In her music video "Applause" (2013), Lady Gaga also donned an outfit inspired by Little Edie, which specifically adapted Edie's signature headdress as well as her appreciation of close-fitting body or bathing suits ("Lady Gaga – Applause (Official)" 2013).

4 The Remediation of Little Edie

An examination and comparison of scenes from the Maysles's documentary and its remediations into a Broadway musical, *Grey Gardens* (2006), and an HBO biopic, *Grey Gardens* (2009), reveal in which ways the perception and reception of Little Edie's aberrant behavior changed over the course of time or, rather, how her image was refashioned by these culturally and historically specific representations. One particular scene that is (re-)mediated in all three cultural products concerns the central issue of fashion as a metaphor for nonconformity and has become a favorite among 'Bealemaniacs.' It will serve as a template for the discussion of the remediations.

Although the Maysles are icons of the so-called "direct cinema," *Grey Gardens* (1975) is a particular kind of documentary which has rightfully been described as "[a] compelling combination of fly-on-the-wall observation and more overt 'participatory' techniques by the Maysles, where they directly interact with the subjects of their film" (Ward 2007: 185; see also Prehn 2009: 158). The Maysles never aim at immediacy and unobtrusive observation (Ward 2007: 184; Vogels 2005: 128, 135), which would seem to be the intention of a documentary. Rather, the film self-reflexively lays open its hovering between fact and fiction, and between authenticity and performance (Vogels 2005: 128, 150–151; Prehn

2009: 158). Interestingly, the film conveys the representation of Edie as she wanted to be represented (Sterritt qtd. in McElhaney 2009: 96). The Beale women were aware of their 'roles' in the film (Singer 2015: n. pag.) and, contrary to what one may suspect, maintained a fair amount of agency in the process.

After the shooting, the documentary underwent a two-year editing process. It is by no means a chronological and unedited account of the Beale women's lives (Rhodes 2006: 94). It is rather a mix of biographical and documentary reading (Prehn 2009: 165). This genre hybridity of *Grey Gardens* opens it up "to multiple points of entry and to diverse possibilities for citation and appropriation" (McElhaney 2009: 103). It has, for example, been claimed that "the film is fully available to be read in relation to feminist discourses" (McElhaney 2009: 95; see also Vogels 2005: 153; McElhaney 2009: 155). Indeed, it follows an 'invented' feminist script (Tinkcom 2011: 20). Feminist issues were most probably on the agenda of the film's editors Susan Froemke, Ellen Hovde, and Muffie Meyer, all female, when they worked on it in the 1970s. But the documentary still does not create a biographic illusion in Bourdieu's sense. It is far from a teleological construction of a life.

The second scene of the documentary bears the chapter heading "The Best Costume for Today." Given its broad cultural resonance, it may very well be the most popular scene of the documentary:

> BACK YARD in field of clematis
> David Maysles: Edie, you look fantastic.
> Edie: David, you look absolutely terrific, honestly. You've got light, you've got light blue on. Well, Al, you're still, ah ... Mother says you're very conservative (laughs).
> Brooks, everything looks wonderful.
> Brooks: Thank you.
> Edie: Absolutely wonderful. This is the best thing to wear for today. You understand.
> Albert Maysles: Yeah.
> Edie: Because I don't like women in skirts, and the best thing is to wear pantyhose or some pants under a short skirt, I think. Then you have the pants under the skirt, and then you can pull the stockings up over the pants, underneath the skirt.
> Albert Maysles: Uh-huh ...
> Edie: And you can always take off the skirt and use it as a cape. So I think this is the best costume for the day.
> Albert Maysles: OK.
> Edie: (laughs) I have to think these things up, you know. Mother wanted me to come out in a kimono so we had quite a fight.
> [...]
> BROOKS EXITS. (Edie whispers) Do you think my costume looked all right for Brooks? I think he was a little amazed.
> David Maysles: He's probably seen it before.
> LAWN MOWER begins in background

> Edie: (whispers) No, no. This is the revolutionary costume. I never wear this in East Hampton. (gives a half laugh). (Sara and Rebekah Maysles 2010: n. pag.)

In this scene, Edie wears a worn brown sweater, an upside down, brown skirt, custom-fit by a knot in the waist and a fixing pin, with pantyhose and control briefs underneath. On her head she wears what looks like a black cardigan, adorned by her signature brooch. She obviously wears some eye makeup and lipstick. She declares that this odd ensemble of old, mixed, matched, and reinvented clothes is the "best costume for today" (Sara and Rebekah Maysles 2010: n. pag.). Further stressing the oddness of the scene, she declares in a somewhat embarrassed tone that she "has to think these things up," not disclosing whether an inner or an outer drive or force compels her to do so. When she refers to the fight with her mother, her behavior also comes across as strangely paranoid. Later in the scene, Edie feels ashamed of her attire when she comes face to face with the gardener Brooks. She then calls it "the revolutionary costume," something she would never dare to wear around town. In the first scene of the documentary, she indicates the object of her rebelliousness when she accuses East Hampton of being "republican" and declares punningly that there "they can get you for wearing red shoes on a Thursday" (Sara and Rebekah Maysles 2010: n. pag.).

On the one hand, Edie's improvised outfit, her living conditions, and her behavior are "outside the standard modes of social behavior" (McElhaney 2009: 130), and they are probably even appalling to the viewer, as the initially unfavorable response to the documentary may imply. Contemporary critics expressed discomfort or even disgust at the film (McElhaney 2009: 95; Vogels 2005: 140, 146). On the other hand, Edie herself offers another interpretation, that of celebrating nonconformity. And the viewer cannot help but be smitten with her charm and wit. But ultimately, the fascination with Little Edie remains at least ambiguous and can be linked to the fascination people today feel when they watch reality television. The Maysles's documentary is a forerunner of this format (Ward 2007: 185).

The first remediation of the documentary film to be examined here is the Tony Award-winning musical *Grey Gardens* (2006). Stacy Wolf correctly asserts that musicals are "[b]orn from a mélange of performance forms that included opera and operetta, vaudeville and burlesque, minstrelsy and jazz" (3). She states that "the form of the musical – the combination of music, dance, speech, and design – is paradoxical" (3). This ostensibly "paradoxical" quality to me exactly stresses the intermedial basis of the art form's strategies of meaning production. Wolf further argues that musicals have achieved "supreme artistry" and have strongly influenced culture "[i]n spite of their unapologetic commercialism" (3). Put differently, the very fact that musicals are highly popular and commercially successful makes their impact on culture so potentially significant and far-reaching. Their intermediality, which heightens their accessibility as it allows multiple points of interest, may be an important factor in this. It is true that "musicals have always sought to amuse more than instruct, and to make money more than make political change," yet they are also "[r]eflecting, refracting, and shaping U.S. culture" (Wolf 2011: 3).

The musical *Grey Gardens* takes a predominantly chronological approach within two time frames set three decades apart. It starts out with a prologue set in 1973, the time of the filming of the Maysles's documentary. The majority of the first act is then a flashback, set in 1941, whereas the second act returns to 1973. The first act of the musical is thus concerned with Little Edie's youth, while much of the dialogue of the second act is taken directly from the documentary. The first scene of the second act is called "The Revolutionary Costume for Today." It is certainly the highlight of the musical and central to this remediation of Edie, as it purposefully combines and extends significant scenes and themes from the documentary:

Scene 2-1: YARD
(Enter Little Edie Beale, now fifty-six. Over thirty years have passed since Act One. Edie is played by the same actress who played her mother, Edith, in Act One. Edie is in a highly eccentric ensemble of her own devising. Her face is framed by a black wimple-like snood held in place with an oversized gold brooch clasp. One wisp of grey hair protrudes. She wears heavy, Cleopatra-like eye makeup. Some garments of her outfit are worn "creatively," either upside down or safety-pinned or re-invented from generally unworn articles. She welcomes the audience directly.)
EDIE: Oh, hi! You look absolutely terrific, honestly.
(beat)
Mother wanted me to come out in a kimono, so we had *quite* a fight.
(Song: "THE REVOLUTIONARY COSTUME FOR TODAY")
The best kind of clothes
For a protest pose
Is this ensemble of pantyhose
Pulled over the shorts
Worn under the skirt
That doubles as a cape ...
(Unfastens her skirt and drapes it on her shoulders as she models Capri pants.)
... To reveal you in Capri pants
You fashion out of ski pants
In a jersey knit
Designed to fit
The contour of your shape ...
Then cinch it with the cord
From the drape.

And that's the revolutionary costume for today.
To show the polo riders
In khakis and topsiders
Just what a revolutionary costume has to say.
It can't be ordered from L.L. Bean.
There's more to living than Kelly green.
And that's the revolution I mean.
Da-da-da-da-dum ...
(Edie holds up a news clipping.)
Just listen to this!
(She reads it aloud using a magnifying glass.)
"*The Hamptons Bee*. July 1972. The elderly, bed-ridden aunt of former First Lady Jacqueline Kennedy, Mrs. Edith Bouvier Beale – "

(glances up at the audience)
My very own mother, can you imagine? –
(resumes reading)
"And her adult daughter, Miss Edie Beale, a former debutante once known as "Body Beautiful Beale" – they called me Body Beautiful Beale. It's true. That was my ... whaddayacallit ... sobriquet –
(back to the news clipping.)
"Are living on Long Island in a garbage-ridden, filthy, twenty-eight-room house with fifty-two cats, fleas, cobwebs, and virtually no plumbing. After vociferous complaints from neighbors, the Board of Health took legal action against the reclusive pair."
(waving the clipping aloft like a battle flag)
Why, it's the most disgusting, atrocious thing ever to happen in America!
You fight City Hall
With a Persian shawl
That used to hang on the bedroom wall
Pinned under the chin
Adorned with a pin
And pulled into a twist.
Reinvent the objet trouvé.
Make a "poncho" from a duvet.
Then you can be
With Cousin Lee
On Mister Blackwell's list.
(turning a cultured hand into a power fist)
Your full-length velvet glove
Hides the fist.
And that's the revolutionary costume for today.
Subvert the Cris–Craft boaters,
Those Nixon–Agnew voters.
Armies of conformity are headed right your way.
To make a statement you need to be
In Boston harbor upending tea.
And that's a revolution ... to me.

[...]
Honestly! They can get you in East Hampton for wearing red shoes on a Thursday and all that sort of thing. I don't know whether you know that. I mean, do you know that? They can get you for almost anything. It's a mean, nasty Republican town!
[...]
And that's the revolutionary costume pour de jour.
Ya' mix, ya' match, and presto:
A fashion manifesto.
That's why a revolutionary costume's de rigeur ...
(She glances around the yard through her magnifying glass.)
The rhododendrums are hiding spies.
The pussy willows have beady eyes
Binoculars in the privet hedge,
They peek at you through the window ledge
With guile ...!
We're in the revolution,
So win the revolution
With style!
Da-da-da-da-da ...
I have to think these things up, you know.
[...]
(Edie turns to see Brooks, Jr., the gardener, clipping overgrown privet hedges. He is the son of Brooks, Sr., the butler, played by the same actor.)
EDIE: Oh, Brooks! Is that you, Brooks?
BROOKS, JR.: Yes, ma'am.
EDIE: What a surprise. Everything looks wonderful, *absolutely* wonderful!
[...]
(to the audience, confidentially)
Do you think my costume looked all right for Brooks? I think he was a little amazed!
(Wright, Frankel, and Korie 2007: 83–88)

This scene offers a myriad of intriguing issues for analysis, yet the relevant points of discussion for the topic of remediation are musical Edie's appearance and persona, the musical's perspective and politics, and finally its reception. In this scene, Edie is not addressing the Maysles, as in the original scene from the documentary. The audience becomes the addressee (Adair and Boyd 2013: 32), and she breaks the fourth wall. The Maysles are not even part of the musical at all (McElhaney 2009: 97–98). The musical aims at immediacy, as it tries to erase the former medium in order to create a seemingly perfect window into the past.

In the Tony Award performance of 2007 by Christine Ebersole ("Grey Gardens 2007 Tony Performance" 2007), musical Edie's outfit is quite a good replica, in keeping with the style and colors of the original. What is significant, though, is, on the one hand, the emphasis that is put on the reversal of the skirt by prominently showing a button clasp above the knee, and, on the other hand, that the whole outfit indeed looks brand new. This similarly holds true for Ebersole's makeup during the Tony ceremony performance. There is a little too much of it, but it is all very neatly applied. Both, costume and makeup, are more of an exaggeration than an imitation. But there is nothing shabby, not to say appalling about the appearance of this version of Little Edie. Her outfit just looks very literally like a costume. Often, Broadway musicals will 'clean up' realities in order not to hurt the star appearance of the central performers. Here, the awkward effect of the film is removed by inserting an obvious performance by a fabulous-looking Broadway star.

When it comes to the lyrics, the nonconformity of the clothes is turned into a political statement. The dress assumes a certain meaning, it is a statement against the establishment, the upper class, from which Little Edie estranged herself, first by her artistic aspirations, and then by her aberrant lifestyle, gradually becoming an outsider (Prehn 2009: 160). The song includes lines from the first scene of the Maysles's documentary, when Edie talks about the raid and the conservative neighborhood:

> Edie: Yeah. We'll be raided again. We'll be raided again by the village of East Hampton. You know they can get you in East Hampton for wearing red shoes on a Thursday, and all that sort of thing. I don't know whether you know that. Do you know that? They can get you for almost anything. (Sara and Rebekah Maysles 2010: n. pag.)

Also, the musical refers to the intermedial introduction of the documentary, in which the Maysles filmed newspaper clippings of the time when the scandal surrounding the living conditions of the Beales hit the media. This is mimicked by Edie's reading out of a newspaper article in the musical. Musical Edie calls the legal action of the Board of Health against the Beales, prompted by their wealthy neighbors, "the most disgusting, atrocious thing ever to happen in America!" (Wright, Frankel, and Korie 2007: 84). By referring to the legal action in this way – not to the Beales' living conditions – Edie is turning society's argument upside down, just like her skirt.

Throughout, there are allusions to revolutionary events, such as the Boston Tea Party, to activist props, such as a "battle flag," and to revolutionary gestures, such as a "protest pose" (Wright, Frankel, and Korie 2007: 83–88). Finally, the song culminates in the definitive protest gesture, the power fist. The whole scene evokes Bertolt Brecht and Kurt Weill's *The Threepenny Opera* (1928) and its socio-political critique. It is strange, though, that a society dropout like Edie is here stylized as an underdog who fights the establishment in a working-class stance. Of course, the overall leftist drift of the musical scene gains certain topicality with regard to George W. Bush's presidency – consider the laughter during Ebersole's Tony performance, when she calls East Hampton "[a] mean, nasty Republican town!" (Wright, Frankel, and Korie 2007: 85; "Grey Gardens 2007 Tony Performance" 2007). By addressing the audience directly in this particular scene, Edie identifies herself as one of them, the culturally interested, democratic East Coast intelligentsia. This remediation of Little Edie thus meets the *Zeitgeist*. The squeaky voice of the performer and the overall quirky atmosphere turn musical Edie into a droll revolutionista, though by far a more socially acceptable (and assimilated) one than the original.

Loyal devotees of the documentary have, unsurprisingly, criticized exactly the elements of the musical that make Edie appear more conventional. They especially disapprove of scenes in which the dialogue from the Maysles's film was considerably extended for dramatic effect. "The Revolutionary Costume for Today" has in addition been rejected for turning Edie into a "cartoony" character, almost a "caricature" (Pincus-Roth 2006: n. pag.). Yet, the joy of being able to share the fascination with Little Edie with a wide audience instead of only a few people who are "in on the joke" has been described as "thrilling" (Pincus-Roth 2006: n. pag.).

The third and last cultural product to be examined here is the Emmy Award-winning HBO biopic *Grey Gardens* (2009), which was directed by Michael Sucsy and stars Drew Barrymore as Little Edie. Ellen Cheshire defines the "Bio-pic aka Biographical Picture" as "a film that depicts the life of a real person, past or present" (2014: 1). She differentiates between at least four types of biopics regarding the films' narrative structures. Cheshire's third type applies to *Grey Gardens*, namely films "that throw the viewer back and forward in time as events in the present trigger memories of the past" (12). The biopic covers Edie's life from her teenage years up to her Reno Sweeney performances, but its focal time is the period of the filming of the Maysles's documentary, from which flashbacks into various periods of the past ensue. The structure facilitates introducing the backstory of the two Edies, going back as far as the 1930s (Oppenheimer 2009: 16).

Dennis Bingham stresses general gender distinctions between biographical pictures about men and about women: "Films about men have gone from celebratory to warts-and-all to investigatory to post-modern to parodic. Biopics of women [...] are weighed down by myths of suffering, victimization, and failure" (2010: 10). Further, he distinguishes between the "female biopic" (11) which "dramatize[s] [...] the process of woman's degradation" (220), following a "downward trajectory" (222), and biopics which apply a "feminist point of view" (10). Bronwyn Polaschek introduces a third category, the "postfeminist biopic" (2013: 2), which has emerged since the 1980s. These films "actively address both traditional images of femininity, the alternatives offered by feminism and the critical responses to these feminist alternatives" (Eecke 2015: 396). On the cover of the DVD case, *Grey Gardens* bears the subtitle "True Glamour Never Fades," which already gives a hint at the direction this interpretation of Little Edie will take. Overall, the biopic is "much more conservative" (Tinkcom 2011: 89) than the original documentary and qualifies as a postfeminist biopic in line with Polaschek's categorization.

The costume scene in the biopic is very condensed, albeit extremely revelatory with regard to the intention of this remediation:

> David Maysles: Edie, you look fantastic.
> Adult Edie: David, you look absolutely terrific. Honestly. You've got light blue on. Well, Al, you're still, um – Mother says you're very conservative. This is the best thing to wear for today, you understand, because I don't like women in skirts. And the best thing is to wear pantyhose or some pants under a short skirt, I think. Then you have the pants under the skirt. And then you can pull the stockings up over the pants, underneath the skirt. And you can always take off the skirt and use it as a cape, so I think this is the best costume for the day.
> David Maysles: Okay.
> Adult Edie: I have to think these things up, you know? Mother wanted me to come out in a kimono, so we had quite a fight. (leaves for the garden) Al, was that good? You want me to do that again? (*Grey Gardens* 2009)

Biopic Edie's costume resembles the original Edie's, but it is a lot more stylish. The whole outfit has the appearance of a little black dress, with only a torn hemline. As with musical Edie, the clothes seem brand-new and flawless. The make-up is overdone and dominates all other visual features. It endows the outfit with the dramatic appearance of an evening gown, which seems out of place in bright daylight. Otherwise, biopic Edie is perfectly acceptable. She casts only one brief glance at the house when mentioning the fight with her mother that may strike viewers as peculiar.

The scene itself sticks largely to the original words from the documentary, although in a condensed form. But biopic Edie behaves much more like an actress on stage or a film star on a set, and she certainly looks and performs the part. She even enters and exits the stage, so to say, through the garden gate. The whole scene also puts more emphasis on the interaction between Edie and the Maysles, who are not only heard, as in the documentary, but also seen. Through the incorporation of the former medium, the hypermediacy of the film is stressed. The biopic Maysles laugh good-naturedly at Edie's oddness. They seem to be astonished, yet strangely fascinated by her. They thus resemble the contemporary fan followers and probably the film's viewers. Any kind of edges Little Edie did have in real life are smoothed out for the general public, the target audience of HBO movies. The only remnants of Edie's deviation from the norm in the scene discussed here are the overdone eye makeup and one brief weird glance. And since the whole setup affirms an interpretation of the scene as a performance, these remnants of oddness can also be explained away as part of Edie-the-star 'acting' Edie-the-oddball.

The idea behind the whole film follows a clichéd American Dream script, which trails Little Edie's ups and downs and casts her as a survivor. I believe the film's cinematographer Mike Eley's calling it "'a kind of love story' between two women" (Oppenheimer 2009: 16) falls short of what the film does. Biopic Edie is presented as a pitiable, though likeable, witty, and ultimately admirable character who gets to close the film with her Reno Sweeney performances, which contrary to reality function as climax and happy ending or, rather, from a different perspective, as "phony closure" (Nussbaum 2009). Edie's subsequent – or continued – demise is omitted. The movie creates a teleological construction of Edie's biography, a Bourdieuan 'biographical illusion.' It tells the story of an aspiring artist who exhibits – and is granted – some eccentric behavior and who – because she has never given up hope – finally comes into her own and fulfills her dream of becoming an entertainer at a late stage in her life.

5 Remediation, Sanitization, and Iconicity

With the HBO biopic, Little Edie is finally turned into a mainstream cultural icon. It is important to note that "mediation is linked to agenda-setting, iconization and publicity" (Erll and Rigney 2009: 6), while "agenda-setting organisations" include television (9). This means that remediations such as the HBO biopic are purposeful. With regard to Bolter and Grusin's theories, this means that the refashioning is not only historically and culturally specific; it also means that it often follows a certain trajectory. In the case of Little Edie, a niche celebrity is made not only acceptable but admirable to a broader audience.

Originally, the basic connotation of the term 'icon' refers to notions of visuality and sacred images (Leypoldt 2010: 5–6). Deriving from the Greek εἰκών, it describes "a usually pictorial representation," "an object of uncritical devotion," and more specifically "a conventional religious image typically painted on a small wooden panel and used in the devotions of Eastern Christians." Other than that, it can be "a sign (such as a word or graphic symbol) whose form suggests its meaning," for example "a graphic symbol on a computer display screen" (*Merriam-Webster* 2018). Klaus Rieser recognizes three groups of icons: "First, fictional as well as historic characters [...]; second, locales, monuments, or typical natural elements [...]; and third, logos, isotropes, and computer icons [...]" (2006: 7). Only the first group of icons are of concern for my investigation, namely icons in the sense of representative individuals as, for example, in Ralph Waldo Emerson's *Representative Men* (1850). The term 'icon' thus depicts a respected person, who is considered an exemplary symbol of a specific culture (Leypoldt 2010: 5–6). As Günter Leypoldt further argues, it is this meaning which "relates iconicity to the production of collective memory." Ultimately, "[t]o approach the study of cultural icons from a visuality-based viewpoint is to frame it as a kind of media study that engages with American icons primarily in terms of their function as disseminated images or simulacra." "[I]conic personhood" is created by the combination of the "abstract inscription [...] of collective identity" with a concrete example "of living practice" (2010: 5–7). The reception of icons or they themselves may change over time and mainstream icons may be appropriated by those from the margins and vice versa (Rieser 2006: 7–8). With the *Grey Gardens* biopic, the iconicity of Little Edie is changed from margin to mainstream.

Throughout her life, Little Edie's behavior developed from nonconformist to aberrant. The remediations of her life, a historical arch of public images, reverse this order. Tropes of individuation and the teleology reminiscent of the *Künstlerroman* are applied to reconstruct a fragmented self. The documentary shows a deviant character, presented as a feminist and attractive to an audience of social nonconformists critical of wealth-based categories of normative consumer behavior. The musical scene reinterprets Edie as a social revolutionary against the establishment – a characterization which appeals to a politically interested audience and meets the *Zeitgeist*, but the humor of the scene takes some of the edge out of her critical stance. Finally, Edie's marginalized fame hits the televised mainstream and its commercially viable codes when the biopic inscribes it with the narrative of a simplistic version of the American Dream. The biopic tells the story of an eccentric, but endearing, and ultimately successful artist. As a form of invented biography, it participates in perpetuating specific shapes and trajectories within cultural memory.

Countless identities have been culturally ascribed to Edith Bouvier Beale throughout her life and even more so after her death: the "beautiful deb" (*The New York Times* n. d.), the "body beautiful" ("Edith Bouvier Beale" 2015), the it-girl, the "socialite gone to seed" (Nussbaum 2009), the "crazy cat lad[y]" (Adair and Boyd 2013: 26), the self-declared "artist" (*Grey Gardens Online* 2009), the "drag-queen role model" (Nussbaum 2009), the proclaimed feminist, the "recessionista" (Stein 2008; Tinkcom 2011: 58), the "fashion innovator" (Adair and Boyd 2013: 37), the survivor, the revolutionista, and "the warning shot of reality television" (Nussbaum 2009). The discussion of three of the remediations of her life has shown how Little Edie's public persona was largely created and continuously transformed in culturally and historically specific ways. Little Edie's representation has over time visibly been sanitized. Recent remediations have turned her into an all-American heroine and broadly recognized cultural icon.

Works Cited

Adair, David and Annita, Boyd. 2013. "Returns From the Margins: Little Edie Beale and the Legacy of *Grey Gardens*". *Film, Fashion & Consumption* 2 (1): 25–42.

Anderson, Carolyn. 2012. "Book Review: Grey Gardens". *Historical Journal of Film, Radio and Television* 32 (2): 295–297.

Balestrini, Nassim Winnie. 2017. "Intermediality". In: Timo Müller (ed.). *Handbook of the American Novel of the Twentieth and Twenty-First Centuries*. Berlin: De Gruyter. 68–83.

Bartram, Kent. "Staunch Character: Edith Bouvier Beale, Jr. of Grey Gardens". *Facebook*. <https://www.facebook.com/StaunchCharacter/> [accessed 16 January 2018].

Beale, Eva Marie. 2009. *Edith Bouvier Beale of Grey Gardens: A Life in Pictures*. Paris: Verlhac.

Beale, Eva Marie (ed.). 2010. *I Only Mark the Hours That Shine: Little Edie's Diary 1929*. Mill Valley: Grey Gardens Collections.

"Beautiful Deb Writes Poetry". *The New York Times*, n.d. <https://wynstep.files.wordpress.com/2016/04/edie-beal-news-item.jpg> [accessed 9 November 2017].

Bingham, Dennis. 2010. *Whose Lives Are They Anyway? The Biopic as Contemporary Film Genre*. New Brunswick: Rutgers University Press.

Bolter, Jay David and Richard Grusin. 2000. *Remediation: Understanding New Media*. Cambridge: MIT Press.

Bourdieu, Pierre. 1990. "Die biographische Illusion". *BIOS – Zeitschrift für Biographieforschung – Oral History und Lebensverlaufsanalysen* 3 (1): 75–81.

Brecht, Bertolt. 2005. *The Threepenny Opera*. 1928. Translated by Jon Willett and Ralph Manheim. London: Methuen.

Caldwell, George S. 1975. *Gristmill*. New York: Stein and Day.

Carpozi, George Jr. 1971. "Jackie's Aunt Told: Clean up Mansion". *New York Post* October 22: 2.

Cheshire, Ellen. 2014. *Bio-pics: A Life in Pictures*. London: Wallflower.

Colman, David. 2009. "The Cult of Grey Gardens". *Advocate* 1025: 70–77. <https://www.advocate.com/arts-entertainment/television/2009/03/04/cult-grey-gardens> [accessed 16 January 2018].

"Christine Ebersole Models Little Edie Fashion on Today Show". GreyGardensBroadway. *YouTube*, 12 June 2007. <https://www.youtube.com/watch?v=QckKFuKwl0Q> [accessed 24 October 2017].

Dangremond, Sam. "Grey Gardens has Found a Buyer". *Town & Country*, 20 October 2017. <www.townandcountrymag.com/leisure/real-estate/news/a9532/grey-gardens-house-for-sale/> [accessed 24 October 2017].

Davis, John H. 1995. *The Bouviers: Portrait of an American Family*. Palo Alto: National Press.

"Edith Bouvier Beale". *Biography.com*, 2 October 2015. <https://www.biography.com/people/edith-bouvier-beale-435518> [accessed 7 November 2017].

Eecke, Christoph van. 2015. "Book Reviews: *The Postfeminist Biopic: Narrating the Lives of Plath, Kahlo, Woolf and Austen*". *Historical Journal of Film, Radio and Television* 35 (2): 396–397.

Emerson, Ralph Waldo. 1983 [1850]. "Representative Men". *Essays & Lectures*. New York: Library of America. 611–761.

Erll, Astrid and Ann Rigney. 2009. "Introduction: Cultural Memory and Its Dynamics". In: Astrid Erll and Ann Rigney (eds.). *Mediation, Remediation, and the Dynamics of Cultural Memory*. Berlin: Walter de Gruyter. 1–11.

Gimme Shelter. 2000 [1970]. Directed by David Maysles and Albert Maysles. Criterion. DVD.

"Grey Gardens 2007 Tony Performance". *YouTube*. Ryan Carroccino, 12 July 2007. <https://www.youtube.com/watch?v=gdh8EoYoAoM> [accessed 10 November 2017].

Grey Gardens Official. Eva Marie Beale, 2017. <https://greygardensofficial.com> [accessed 24 October 2017].

Grey Gardens Online. BJK, 2009. <http://greygardensonline.com> [last accessed 24 October 2017].

Grey Gardens. 2007 [1975]. Directed by David Maysles and Albert Maysles. Eureka Entertainment. DVD.

Grey Gardens. 2009. Directed by Michael Sucsy. HBO. DVD.

"Icon". *Merriam-Webster*. 2018. online. <https://www.merriam-webster.com/dictionary/icon> [accessed 16 January 2018].

Ingrassia, Michele. 2006. "Little Edie, Big Style: The Unlikely Fashion Icon Continues to Make Her Mark – On the Stage and the Runway". *New York Daily News*, 19 February 2006. <http://www.nydailynews.com/archives/nydn-features/edie-big-style-fashion-icon-continues-mark-stage-runway-article-1.605216> [last accessed 15 November 2017].

Kaplan, Seth. "An Andy Warhol Camelot: Grey Gardens Coming to Boston in Late April". *The Harvard Crimson*, 7 April 1976. <http://www.thecrimson.com/article/1976/4/7/an-andy-warhol-camelot-pbfbive-years/> [accessed 7 November 2017].

"Lady Gaga – Applause (Official)". LadyGagaVEVO. *YouTube*. 19 August 2013. <https://www.youtube.com/watch?v=pco91kroVgQ> [accessed 24 October 2017].

Leypoldt, Günter. 2010. "Introduction: Cultural Icons, Charismatic Heroes, Representative Lives". In: Günter Leypoldt and Bernd Engler (eds.). *American Cultural Icons: The Production of Representative Lives*. ZAA Monograph Series, vol. 11. Würzburg: Königshausen & Neumann. 5–28.

"little+edie". *Etsy*. 2017. <https://www.etsy.com/search?q=little%2Bedie> [accessed 24 October 2017].

Maysles, Sara and Rebekah Maysles. 2010. *Grey Gardens*. New York: Free News Projects.

Martin, Douglas. "Edith Bouvier Beale, 84, 'Little Edie,' Dies". *The New York Times*, 25 January 2002. <http://www.nytimes.com/2002/01/25/nyregion/edith-bouvier-beale-84-little-edie-dies.html> [accessed 15 November 2017].

McElhaney, Joe. 2009. *Albert Maysles*. Urbana: University of Illinois Press.

Middeke, Martin. 1999. "Introduction". In: Martin Middeke and Werner Huber (eds.). *Biofictions: The Rewriting of Romantic Lives in Contemporary Fiction and Drama*. Rochester: Camden House. 1–25.

Mittermayer, Manfred, Patric Blaser, Andrea B. Braidt, and Deborah Holmes. 2009. "Einleitung". In: Manfred Mittermayer, Patric Blaser, Andrea B. Braidt, and Deborah

Holmes (eds.). *Ikonen, Helden, Außenseiter: Film und Biographie*. Wien: Paul Zsolnay. 7–14.

Muther, Christopher. "Little Edie, Fashion Icon". *The Boston Globe*, 16 April 2009. <http://archive.boston.com/ae/movies/articles/2009/04/16/little_edie_fashion_icon/> [accessed 24 October 2017].

Newkirk, Walter (collect. and ed.). 2009. *Letters of Little Edie Beale: Grey Gardens and Beyond*. Bloomington: Author House.

Newkirk, Walter. 2008. *MemoraBEALEia: A Private Scrapbook About Edie Beale of Grey Gardens, First Cousin to First Lady Jacqueline Kennedy Onassis*. Bloomington: Author House.

"New Year's Eve on SATC". Amanda Raphael. *YouTube*. 31 December 2010. <https://www.youtube.com/watch?v=bACWtsuMd54> [accessed 24 October 2017].

Nussbaum, Emily. "Hampton Gothic". *New York Magazine*, 12 April 2009. <http://nymag.com/arts/tv/reviews/55972/> [accessed 15 November 2017].

Oppenheimer, Jean. 2009. "Production Slate: Ties That Bind: New York Eccentrics". *American Cinematographer – The International Journal of Film & Digital Production Techniques* 90 (5): 16, 18–19.

Pethö, Ágnes. 2011. *Cinema and Intermediality: The Passion for the In-Between*. Newcastle upon Tyne: Cambridge Scholars.

Pincus-Roth, Zachary. "Devoted Worshipers in a House of Glorious Decay". *The New York Times*, 22 October 2006. <http://www.nytimes.com/2006/10/22/theater/22roth.html> [accessed 16 November 2017].

Polaschek, Bronwyn. 2013. *The Postfeminist Biopic: Narrating the Lives of Plath, Kahlo, Woolf and Austen*. New York: Palgrave Macmillan.

Prehn, Ulrich. 2009. "'Embedded Stories': Dokumentarisch-biographische Annäherungen und (Selbst-)Inszenierungen in *Grey Gardens* (USA 1975)". In: Manfred Mittermayer, Patric Blaser, Andrea B. Braidt, and Deborah Holmes (eds.). *Ikonen, Helden, Außenselter: Film und Biographie*. Wien: Paul Zsolnay. 153–169.

Rajewsky, Irina O. 2005. "Intermediality, Intertextuality and Remediation: A Literary Perspective on Intermediality". *Intermédialités/Intermediality: Remédier/Remediation* 6: 43–64.

Rakoff, David. "The Lives They Lived; The Debutante's Staying-In Party". *The New York Times Magazine*, 29 December 2002. <http://www.nytimes.com/2002/12/29/magazine/the-lives-they-lived-the-debutante-s-staying-in-party.html> [15 November 2017].

"Remediation". *Merriam-Webster*. 2017. online. <https://www.merriam-webster.com/dictionary/remediation> [accessed 9 November 2017].

"Remediation". *Oxford Dictionaries*. English. 2017. online. Oxford: Oxford University Press. <https://en.oxforddictionaries.com/definition/remediation> [accessed 9 November 2017].

Rhodes, John David. 2006. "'Concentrated Ground': Grey Gardens and the Cinema of the Domestic". *Framework: The Journal of Cinema & Media* 47 (1): 83–105.

Rieser, Klaus. 2006. "Preface: Icons as Discursive Practice". In: Walter W. Hölbling, Klaus Rieser, and Susanne Rieser (eds.). *US Icons and Iconicity*. American Studies in Austria, vol. 4. Wien: LIT. 7–16.

Rogers, Katie. "Want to Live in Grey Gardens? It Can Be Yours for $20 Million". *The New York Times*, 2 March 2017. <https://www.nytimes.com/2017/03/02/fashion/news/grey-gardens-real-estate-sally-quinn-summer-home-sale.html> [accessed 15 November 2017].

Sheehy, Gail. "The Secret of Grey Gardens". *New York Magazine*, 10 January 1972. <http://nymag.com/news/features/56102/> [accessed 15 November 2017].

Sheehy, Gail. "A Return to Grey Gardens". *New York Magazine*, 28 May 2007. <http://nymag.com/arts/theater/features/23484/> [accessed 15 November 2017].

Singer, Olivia. "Lessons We Can Learn from Grey Gardens". *AnOther*, 10 April 2015. <http://www.anothermag.com/fashion-beauty/7264/lessons-we-can-learn-from-grey-gardens> [accessed 1 March 2017].

Smith, Sidonie and Julia Watson. 2010. *Reading Autobiography: A Guide for Interpreting Life Narratives*. Minneapolis: University of Minnesota Press.

Stein, Sadie. "Little Edie Beale: The Ultimate Recessionista". *Jezebel*, 11 October 2008. <https://jezebel.com/5082342/little-edie-beale-the-ultimate-recessionista> [accessed 24 October 2017].

Stilwell, Elizabeth. "Ethical Halloween Costume: Little Edie Beale". *The Note Passer*, 30 October 2013. <http://thenotepasser.com/blog/2013/10/30/ethical-halloween-costume-little-edie-beale> [accessed 9 November 2017].

Tinkcom, Matthew. 2011. *Grey Gardens*. New York: Palgrave Macmillan.

Vaskeviciute, Juste. "Inspired by Movies: Grey Gardens". *Pretty Ugly*. Blog, n. d. <http://www.prettyugly.eu/blog/inspired-by-movies-grey-gardens> [accessed 9 November 2017].

Vogels, Jonathan B. 2005. *The Direct Cinema of David and Albert Maysles*. Carbondale: Southern Illinois University Press.

Ward, Paul. 2007. "The Documentary Form". In: Jill Nelmes (ed.). *Introduction to Film Studies*. London: Routledge. 174–192.

"What Is Life-Writing?". *The Oxford Centre for Life-Writing*. Wolfson College, University of Oxford, 2015–2017. <https://www.wolfson.ox.ac.uk/what-life-writing> [accessed 15 November 2017].

Wilson, Eric. "Exploring the Style Behind 'Grey Gardens'". *The New York Times*, 15 April 2009. <http://www.nytimes.com/2009/04/16/fashion/16ROW.html> [accessed 15 November 2017].

Wolf, Stacy. 2011. "Introduction". In: Stacy Wolf (ed.). *The Oxford Handbook of the American Musical*. Oxford: Oxford University Press. 3–6.

Wright, Doug, Scott Frankel, and Michael Korie. 2007. *Grey Gardens – The Musical: The Complete Book and Lyrics of the Broadway Musical*. New York: Applause Theatre & Cinema Books.

Wright, Jennifer. "Shelved Dolls: Little Edie Beale – What Went Wrong?". *The Gloss*, 29 August 2012. <http://www.thegloss.com/beauty/little-edie-beale-grey-gardens-biography-shelved-dolls-827/> [accessed 15 November 2017].

Wright, Lois. 2007. *My Life at Grey Gardens: 13 Months and Beyond*. <https://www.amazon.com/My-Life-Grey-Gardens-Months/dp/0977746216> [accessed 16 January 2018].

Daniel Stein
Graphic Musical Biography: An Intermedial Case of Musico-Comical Life Writing

Abstract

This essay reads graphic biographies of popular musicians as a subgenre of intermedial life writing that does not adapt a specific source text into the comics medium but grapples with the visual-verbal adaptation of an intermedial life story instead. Foregrounding the specificity of graphic musical biography by distinguishing it from musical autobiography in comic form, I extend the common distinction between music in comics and comics as/like music to account for the ways in which graphic biographies of musicians such as Billie Holiday, Johnny Cash, Louis Armstrong, and John Coltrane not only represent and simulate but also contextualize and historicize the seminal sounds and musical practices they seek to approximate.

1 Comics and Intermedial Life Writing

Writing in the *Journal of the Royal Musical Association*, Tim Summers claims: "Comics have had a long-standing relationship with music" and are "a musically significant medium" whose "narrative apparatus" includes music (2015: 122, 123, 160). Why, then, has the musicality of comics garnered only little sustained scholarship, and why has it not inspired the systematic engagement we know from musico-literary intermedia studies that focus on the connections between music and literature (e.g., Wolf 1998; Wolf 1999; Rippl 2015; Wolf/Bernhart 2016)? To answer this question would mean to reassess the history of comics from their public reception since the late nineteenth century to their recent inclusion into mainstream academic research. It would also mean to provide a metacritical survey of intermedia studies to account for the relative absence of work on comics within this field, both of which I cannot offer here. What I can offer is a more modest proposal for an intermedial approach to one particular subgenre of life writing: biographies of popular musical figures narrated in the medium of comics, with a brief excursion into the graphic musical autobiography, both of which constitute intermedial life writing.¹ Graphic biography and graphic autobiography are examples of what I call musico-comical intermediality. As my analysis of Paquet's *Louis Armstrong* (2001), Camilo Sanin's "Louis Armstrong" (2003), and Paolo Parisi's *Coltrane* (2012 [2010]) shows, graphic biographies can further our understanding of intermedial life writing because they do not adapt a specific source text into the medium of comics but grapple with the visual-verbal adaptation of a previously existing intermedially constructed life story.²

2 Graphic Musical Biography vs. Graphic Musical Autobiography

Sidonie Smith and Julia Watson describe life writing "as a general term for writing of diverse kinds that takes a life, one's or another's, as its subject. Such writing can be biographical, novelistic, historical, or an explicit self-reference to the writer" (2010: 4). They emphasize essential differences between biography and autobiography:

> In biography, scholars of other people's lives document and interpret those lives from a point of view external to the subject. In [autobiographical] life writing, subjects write about their own lives [...] simultaneously from externalized and internal points of view. [...] Matters of time and timing also differentiate biography and [autobiographical] life writing. For a biographer, the death of the subject is not definitive. A biography can be written either during the life or after the death of the person being written about. [...] [T]he life narrator and biographer also engage in different kinds of evidence. Most biographers incorporate multiple forms of evidence, including historical documents, interviews, and family archives, which they evaluate for validity. [...] For life narrators, by contrast, personal memories are the primary archival source. (Smith and Watson 2010: 5–7)

Biographies generally narrate in the third person, autobiographies in the first person. In the context of the graphic musical biography, which adds a visual component to the notion of life writing, this difference can be illustrated by juxtaposing the Argentinian writer and artist team Muñoz and Sampayo's *Billie Holiday* (1990) with the German comics creator Mawil's *Die Band* (2008 [2004]).

---

1 Candida Rifkind defines graphic biographies as "books that tell the story of another person's (or people's) life in the form of comics" (2015: n. pag.).
2 Graphic biographies not considered here include Legg, McCarthy, and Flameboy 2003; Legg, McCarthy, and Flameboy 2004; Rausch 2005; Hiramoto 2005/2008; Monpierre 2006; McCarthy and Parkhouse 2012; Gille and Schröder 2014.

Muñoz and Sampayo's work foregrounds the fact that it is a third-person account of a person no longer alive by choosing the thirtieth anniversary of Holiday's death and a newspaper writer's attempts to pen a compelling tribute as its narrative occasion. In the first panel of page 37, we see the journalist at his typewriter as he is struggling with his assignment (figure 1). With the second panel, the scene changes to one of Holiday's performances recorded toward the end of her life for the *Sound of Jazz* television show (CBS, 8 Dec. 1957). The rest of the page shows Holiday singing in her frail voice (indicated by the scraggly lettering in the balloons) and interacting with the band, tenor sax player Lester Young in particular. The perspective is an external one, as the writer is not privy to the thought processes and emotions of the musicians. He consults external evidence, in this case a video of a television appearance that is remediated (Bolter and Grusin 1998) in comic form and through Muñoz's characteristic black-and-white style in order to compensate for this lack of internal insight.

The man at the typewriter is a character in the story who seems to serve as the narrator of Holiday's biography on the story level. He is, however, not the source of the visual-verbal discourse that constitutes the biographical narrative. This role belongs to the graphic enunciator (Baetens 2001). When we see Holiday in the third panel, the narrative perspective underscores this distinction as a predicament of biography. It emphasizes the need to simulate closeness to the biographical subject and to suggest access to the person's interiority despite the fact that the subject's interiority must remain opaque to the external observer and can only be experienced by the subject itself. Muñoz and Sampayo acknowledge this complex enunciatory position in the shift from the first to the second and third panels through a perspectival ambiguity: Do we see Holiday through the mental images of the newspaper writer? Are we entering a moment of focalization as we share the writer's gaze at the television images, which already appear as a remediated version of actual footage of the performance in the diegetic world? The television footage would then function as a first-order remediation of the actual performance, whereas the comic version would be a remediation of this remediation, or a second-order remediation. Or do we see a remediation of the television images through the perspective of the graphic enunciator, who uses the images of the performance as a source for the graphic representation of Holiday in his idiosyncratic drawing and narrating style?[3] The page invites us to ponder these questions as central concerns of graphic musical biography.

---

3 The issue of drawing style is significant because the goal of graphic biography cannot be to provide the most life-like image of the biographical subject but to find effective ways of combining an artist's personal style (whether specifically developed for the biography or not) with the visual source material. Kleist and Ackermann's *Elvis: Die illustrierte Biografie* (2007) assembles

Figure 1: Remediating Billie Holiday. Source: Muñoz and Sampayo 1990: 37. © Muñoz and Sampayo.

the work of different artists, each of whom illustrates and narrates a segment of Elvis's life and thus adds to an overall chronology of events as well as to a multiplicity of graphic styles and visual renditions of the musician. This foregrounds the constructedness of biography, acknowl-

The double splash page in the middle of Mawil's *Die Band* foregrounds the affordances of autobiographical storytelling (figure 2). The point of view is

Figure 2: A subjective account of performing live. Source: Mawil 2008: n. pag. © Mawil/Reprodukt.

through the eyes of the protagonist, the bass player Mawil, who is also the narrator of the panels and the writer-artist responsible for their existence. Readers share his view from the stage into the crowd, but they also gain access to the train of thought running through his head as he is playing the song. Mawil (the focalizing character) observes the audience, reflects on his appearance and its effects on those who are watching, and reminds himself to concentrate on the different parts of the song he is playing. Mawil (the artist) evokes music without reverting to conventional symbols (e. g., musical notation or sound words), with the exception of showing instruments and people playing music, including himself. More significantly, he has his graphic avatar narrate the different parts of the song (solo, break, bridge, chorus) and thereby offers

---

edging the diverging approaches, stances, and perspectives available to the biographer (Schmitz-Emans 2011: 203–206).

privileged access to the interiority of the narrating self so as to retroactively illustrate what playing this song must have felt like for an insecure teenager.[4]

As this splash page suggests, music is more than sound. At least when performed live, it involves musicians and their audience in a concrete place at a specific time in a particular cultural context. Mawil does not only evoke a past performance but also uses the page layout to make this point. Designed as a succession of panels separated by black gutters, the double page offers a structural analogy to the music that is naturally missing from the comic. The steady succession of panels recalls the steady rhythm of the song, whose different segments (intro, verse, chorus, bridge, etc.) are cued by the narration in the speech balloons.[5] This spatial arrangement creates a sense of temporal progression in the static medium of comics. Yet when taken in at a single glance, the double spread creates the sense that everything is happening at once, emphasizing the player's nervousness and tunnel vision at a moment of intense stage fright.

3 Toward a Model of Musico-Comical Intermediality

In contrast to a range of research on the "musicalization of fiction" (Wolf 1999) in intermedia studies, only few investigations of the relationship between comics and music exist that can serve as a foundation for the analysis of musico-comical intermediality in graphic musical biography.

Felix Giesa (2012: 73, 76) distinguishes between music in comics, i. e., depictions of musical sounds and practices on the level of content, and comics as/like music ("Comics wie Musik"), i. e., the mimicking of music on the level of form.[6]

---

[4] *Die Band* narrates the author's initiation into music and portrays high school kids forming a band, rehearsing, and performing. Mawil employs various techniques of visualizing music, including sound words ("Bumpadatschak"), generic notes to indicate unspecified music, musical notation of existing songs (Led Zeppelin's "Whole Lotta Love"), and chord patterns ("The House of the Rising Sun") (n. pag.).

[5] Replicating musical rhythm through page layout and panel construction is a frequent intermedial maneuver in comics. Groensteen (2012) views comics as inherently musical because they represent time spatially as well as sequentially, rhythm thus being a key structural element. Giesa (2012) cites Igort and Sampayo's *Fats Waller* (2005 [2004]) and *Bob Dylan Revisited* (2008) by various creators to underscore Groensteen's assumptions (74–76). See also Brown 2013.

[6] This matches Wolf's (1998: 133) distinction between the modes of telling ("thematization") and showing ("imitation") music in a literary text. In the showing mode, we find "a presence of music in the signification of a text which seems to stem from some kind of transformation

Giesa covers graphic biographies of and graphic autobiographies by musicians but groups them under the rubric of music in comics, which is not entirely convincing because both of these genres can depict and mimic music.[7]

By conceptualizing comics as a narrative form that uses "a mixed media code" (2011: 211), Monika Schmitz-Emans moves into the territory of intermedia studies. She notes that "comics actually do have an 'acoustic' dimension [...] [that is] graphically mediated" and adds that "[t]he history of comics is accompanied by the attempt to find sign language for sounds" (198). This sign language includes speech balloons, sound words, and onomatopoetic formulas that constitute a panoply of "visualized 'sound' representations" and "'translat[e]' [...] acoustic and somatic events into the code of pictures" (Schmitz-Emans 2011: 198).[8] Moving from representations of acoustic sound to the relation between comics and music, Schmitz-Emans distinguishes between music in comics and the "music-comic as equivalent of song-recordings" (199, 206). The latter category involves cases where the content and structures of song lyrics are transposed into comic form, creating "visual stories [...] [that] interpret the (song [...]) text according to their own set of aesthetic possibilities [and] inevitably develop individual interpretive approaches – and merge with the text into a media hybrid" (206).

Reinhard Kleist's *Cash: I See a Darkness* (2006) features this type of musicocomical intermediality. Kleist repeatedly takes the content of a famous Johnny Cash song and narrates it as a wordless comic. The pages that precede the first chapter retell the storyline of "Folsom Prison Blues" (1955), especially its signature line, "But I shot a man in Reno, just to watch him die" (figure 3). They depict Cash as the character whose actions the singer of the song confesses, registering the popular conflation of singer and song and the widespread practice of interpreting first-person song lyrics autobiographically. As the style of these visualizations is only slightly more cartoony than that of the biographical narrative, the reader must notice the subtle shift from biographical narrative to song lyrics, which foregrounds the porousness of the boundaries between fact and fiction,

---

of music into literature," and "we get the impression of experiencing music 'through' the text" (Wolf 1999: 51). The telling/showing terminology is problematic in the context of graphic biography because comics narrate by showing without necessarily imitating another medium.
7 Mahrt (2010) lists ways in which music can shape the form and content of comics.
8 Young and Lasky's graphic biography of the Carter family develops an innovative way of visualizing music. A.P. Carter encounters black musicians whose vocal delivery is so evocative of scenes and people that their singing bubbles are filled with drawn images rather than with written language or musical notes (2012: 90, 91, 93, 99).

Figure 3: Graphic musical biography as equivalent of song recordings. Source: Kleist 2006: 11–12. © Carlsen Verlag GmbH, Hamburg.

personal life and creative storytelling.[9] At the same time, this stylistic shift hardly eradicates the romantic notion that a convincing, i. e., emotionally resonating, vocal performance is only possible if the singer uses lived experience for inspiration. We can see this when Cash performs a song during his famous Folsom Prison concert that had been sent to him by the prison inmate Glen Sherley. Sherley is in the audience, and the verbal narration in the panels presents his thoughts (as does the opening of the biography's first chapter). While the song's authorship is thus explicitly acknowledged, it is also clear that Cash makes the song his own by singing, playing, and embodying it on stage and on recordings. We are, after all, reading a story about Cash, and Sherley's role in the narrative is relatively small, mainly adding credence to Cash's lyrical impersonation of down-and-out characters. Kleist's visualizations of Cash, especially his frequent iconic remediation of Cash's face and famous poses (including

---

9 Only the visual style of "The Ballad of Ira Hayes" (on *Bitter Tears* 1964) differs substantially from the rest of the narrative. The fact that Cash relates the story but that Hayes is the hero and that the text shifts from first-person to third-person narrative may explain the different drawing style.

the portrait gallery concluding the narrative), trigger musical recollection and retroactively add a comic dimension to Cash's music and iconography.

For the music in comics category, Schmitz-Emans (2011) names "the visual representation of rhythms and the sound of rhythm instruments" (199) as one way of translating acoustic rhythm into visual rhythm. Additional ways of incorporating musical elements are correlations among musical structures, styles, and genres and the "composition of the whole comic story" (including panel and page designs), "the use of graphic elements specially designed for the expression of music, such as notes and other signs of notation," and "the special design, form, and placing of 'singing bubbles'" (200).[10] Kleist's *Cash* reverts to 'singing bubbles' to evoke Cash's singing. These bubbles look different from regular speech balloons and afford the sung words a particular visual presence in the panel, suggesting an expressivity different from the spoken language captured in speech balloons. The singing bubbles are less contained, less clearly directed at a specific addressee, and less obviously attributed to the singer, creating a sense of sound emanating from the air. They float around Johnny Cash and his wife, June Carter Cash (figure 4), in their duet "Ring of Fire" at Folsom Prison while the tails of speech balloons in other panels point directly at Cash's mouth. His singing voice and the lyrics waft through the auditorium into the listening space of the audience in the final two panels of this double page. Music is not directly present here, but since we are witnessing the visual adaptation of a famous concert recording, the point may be not so much to emulate the music but to provide a sense of how this music connects musicians and audience.

As a final category beyond the music-in-comics and comics-as/like-music distinction, Schmitz-Emans (2011: 212) identifies an extratextual (cultural/contextual) dimension as a central element of musico-comical intermediality. This includes the depiction of musical scenes and subcultures that create specific associative connections, as well as portraits of musicians and their public visual extensions (album covers, photos, etc.), all of which may have "suggestive effects" (212) on the reader.

This extratextual dimension is crucial in the case of the graphic musical biography. It also figures in Tim Summers's tripartite model of musico-comical relations. Summers's first category is "musical citations," as in "instances of music in comics where the music is not directly depicted as sounding or performed in the comic, but is instead cited or referred to in other ways" (2015: 124, 125). Here, "musical (lyrical) intertextual sources that orbit [a comic] serve to situate the comic in a cultural context that places heavy emphasis on music and its ability

---

[10] See also Bachmann 2014: 10. An early study is Kalusche 1985.

Figure 4: Floating singing bubbles. Source: Kleist 2006: 170–171. © Carlsen Verlag GmbH, Hamburg.

to produce and transmit meanings" (126). The second category is "sounding music in comics," which refers to "situations in which music is shown to be performed or sounded" (124, 128). This includes "depictions of music that leave details of the musical content primarily to the reader's imagination; music that is explicitly defined by music or lyrics, but does not exist in the real world; and music identified as a piece that exists in the real world." The third category is "comics as musical performance" (124, 143) and entails the ways through which comics can simulate the sonic and structural properties of music.

How can these suggestions contribute to the development of an intermedial approach to graphic musical biography? Giesa's distinction between music in comics and comics as/like music is useful despite its overall lack of a cultural/contextual dimension.[11] In terms of music in comics, graphic musical biographies frequently depict existing musicians in the act of music-making, meaning that the references are usually specific. They also connect the narrative with images outside the biography, as well as with existing musical material that can

---

[11] This is also a weakness of musico-textual intermedia scholarship. I have suggested moving from a text-centered to a culture-oriented understanding of intermediality (Stein 2008).

either be cited, sounded, or performed through the narrative apparatus of comics. Moreover, graphic musical biographies thrive on the cultural and contextual suggestive effects that result from the relation between the visual and musical source material and its graphic remediation. In terms of comics as/like music, the narrative may strive to appear as an equivalent of music, symbolically depicting or mimicking the sonic and performative aspects of music through the choice of colors, drawing style, and layout. But comics can never become music. They can only approximate music through graphic means and are therefore predestined to mobilize intermedial strategies of representation, simulation (or emulation), adaptation, and remediation (Bachmann 2014: 19–20).[12] Most graphic musical biographies realize that narrating the musician's life story is as important as finding innovative ways of simulating his or her music on a formal or structural level. Indeed, the frame of reference must include the multiple media through which musicians become intermedially perceived public figures and through which their music gains a wider cultural resonance.

4 Musico-Comical Intermediality in Graphic Musical Biography: Case Studies

In their introduction to *Brilliant Corners* (2016), a special issue of *The Comics Grid*, Nicolas Pillai and Ernesto Priego encourage scholarship that views jazz and comics "as cultural and artistic practices within specific contexts and specific material conditions," and they call for analyses that "emphasi[ze] interconnection and the multimodal" (2–3). I take this as an incentive to focus an intermedial gaze on graphic musical biographies about two seminal American jazz musicians, Louis Armstrong and John Coltrane.[13]

---

[12] On intermediality and remediation, see Rajewsky 2005. Some graphic biographies include CDs so that the musical references they contain are specific and the reader/listener can create a co-presence of verbal-visual narrative and musical sound. The BD Jazz and BD Blues series by Éditions Nocturne offer biographical bandes dessinées as part of the CD package. The series includes Louis Armstrong, Billie Holiday, Dizzy Gillespie, Ella Fitzgerald, Charlie Parker, Django Reinhardt, Frank Sinatra, Count Basie, Charles Mingus, Fats Waller, Glenn Miller, Miles Davis, Thelonious Monk, Nina Simone, Bessie Smith, T. Bone Walker, and Muddy Waters.

[13] On comics and intermediality, see Hoppeler, Etter, and Rippl 2009; Becker 2011; Rippl and Etter 2013; Stein 2015. On multimodality, see Jacobs 2013.

4.1 Louis Armstrong

Louis Armstrong's life story has been narrated countless times, but Armstrong's active role in its creation has been less often noted (Stein 2012). Armstrong wrote many autobiographical narratives, communicated reminiscences in thousands of letters, and told his tale to a host of interviewers. We can approach this investment with his life story through Leigh Gilmore's notion of autobiographics. Gilmore maintains that "an exploration of a text's autobiographics allows us to recognize that the *I* is multiply coded in a range of discourses; it is the site of multiple solicitations, multiple markings of 'identity,' multiple figurations of agency" (1994: 45). As I argue elsewhere, we may push the implications of the graphics element in Gilmore's concept beyond the notion of verbal text and read it as a media-flexible mode of self-inscription that propels Armstrong's autobiographical storytelling into other genres and media, such as musical recordings, live performances, film, radio, and television appearances (Stein 2012: 13). These genres and media constitute a referential space that disperses the 'I' of Armstrong's life story across different discourses and media and thereby ascribes multiply coded identities to the musician. As such, they sanction intermedial expressions and extensions of life writing, and they serve as source material for biographical accounts of a life and its many remediations.

Graphic biographies of Armstrong enter the referential space of the musician's intermedial autobiographics through a particular genre (biography) and medium (comics). The Belgian illustrator Philip Paquet's *Louis Armstrong*, a genre hybrid that mixes autobiography and biography, is a case in point.[14] Paquet takes the verbal narration verbatim from Armstrong's second autobiography, *Satchmo: My Life in New Orleans* (1986 [1954]), and only adds a visual track. Paquet's illustrations function as a graphic adaptation of Armstrong's source text and as a biographical account that self-consciously enters the musician's autobiographics.

Paquet keeps Armstrong's words and his illustrations separate, alternating panels with black backgrounds that feature Armstrong's words in white handwriting with grayscale panels that visually interpret these words. In the resulting intermedial narrative, images and words comment reciprocally but seldom blend into one another. The illustrations alone would not suffice to carry the story, which means that Armstrong's words retain their original authority and are interpreted, but not overridden, by the illustrations. Paquet abridges the narrative of

---

[14] Less creatively ambitious Armstrong graphic biographies are O'Hern, Holland, Spay, and Campbell 2006; Collins and Pope 2013.

Satchmo but retains the self-image the source text promotes, creating a verbal storyline that could hold its own without the images but would be much less evocative of the specific settings and cultural practices of early jazz. Paquet adds his own take on Armstrong's life story and music through his visuals, for instance in a two-panel sequence about a tribute to his mentor King Oliver (figure 5b).

Figure 5a: Joe Oliver, unknown photographer, ca. 1915. Source: Wright 1987: 12.

The first panel offers a remediation of a King Oliver photograph (c. 1915), changing the print pattern of Oliver's tie to resemble a musical staff and adding a plume of smoke emanating from the cornetist's mouth. These changes constitute a subtle perspectival shift from biographical documentation to the graphic adaptation of autobiographical recollection. From a biographical perspective, a photograph of Oliver is evidence of his physical appearance. From the perspective of Paquet's adaptation of Armstrong's autobiographical recollection, the remediated photograph visualizes Armstrong's claim that "[n]o one in jazz has created as much music as he has" (symbolized by the tie pattern) and that "[n]o one had the fire and the endurance Joe had" (indexed by the smoke as the metaphorical fire that Armstrong felt in Oliver's music). The second panel, illustrating the sentence

Figure 5b: Joe Oliver and Louis Armstrong. Source: Paquet 2001: 3.

"I was just a little punk kid when I saw him," depicts a large Oliver and a small Armstrong. Each of them enunciates musical notes through a speech balloon, Oliver's two notes provoking Armstrong's single note in a call-and-response pattern that not only evokes early jazz but also foregrounds the communal aspects of African American music-making in early twentieth-century New Orleans. Little Armstrong is shadowed by a grown-up version of himself playing the trumpet, which illustrates Armstrong's self-professed dream of becoming a jazz musician and also reminds us that autobiography is an act of retroactive narration where an older self interprets a younger self, while Paquet's biography is an external account of another person's life that interprets the musician's self-interpretation.

Paquet uses photographs as evidence of Armstrong's life and as reminders of his commitment to historical veracity, even though he takes creative liberties in his depiction of specific scenes and characters.[15] When Armstrong begins to play jazz on Mississippi steamboats with the Fate Marable Band (1918–1921), Paquet remediates one such photograph to simultaneously historicize and person-

---

15 Igort and Sampayo's *Fats Waller* remediates images mainly to provide a historical setting for a story about Waller's life that is marked as fictionalized.

Figure 6a: Louis Armstrong with Fate Marable Band (c. 1919). Source: Hogan Jazz Archive, Tulane University.

alize his account (figures 6a and 6b).[16] Reinforcing Armstrong's assertions about the racial tensions between the black musicians and white audiences on these racially segregated entertainment boats, he moves the viewer farther away from the scene than in the original shot. The image now includes a number of dancing couples in the foreground. Their white skin color, stiff posture, and stern facial expressions contrast with those of the members of the Marable band in the background as well as with the more animated activities at black honky-tonks depicted elsewhere in the narrative. We encounter an intermedial mixture of photographic documentation of a musical performance, its remediation into graphic form, and Paquet's visual commentary on the racial context that shaped Armstrong's early life and gave contour and meaning to his music.

---

16 Paquet explained to me in a personal e-mail on Oct. 31, 2016: "I enjoy doing research but i [sic] also like to leave some space for personal interpretation."

Figure 6b: The Fate Marable Band. Source: Paquet 2001: 19.

Paquet further replicates Armstrong's tendency to forego detailed description of the music's technical aspects and instead portray the social and cultural environment in which black and Creole New Orleanians created jazz. Take Armstrong's depiction of the moments when he and other neighborhood boys peeked through cracks in the walls of the notorious Funky Butt Hall, where Buddy Bolden played to a rowdy audience of black locals (briefly in Armstrong 1986: 22–23; more extensively in Meryman 1971: 96).[17] Paquet's sequence (figure 7) evokes the content and style of Armstrong's autobiographical approach. The first image shows three kids peeking through a window into the honky-tonk, which emits a single speech balloon with two generic notes. The accompanying narrative notes that this is the place "where I first heard Buddy Bolden play his horn" (2011: 2). Thus, the generic musical reference in the speech bubble attains specific meaning, even though this meaning must remain unsounded because Bolden never recorded and the reader cannot replay any concrete music when perusing the page. The first two images on the next page (figure 5b) show Bolden in a medium close-up playing his trumpet and Armstrong's transfixed face in the window as he is overwhelmed by the music. Paquet evokes the sound of Bol-

---

[17] For further analysis, see Stein 2011; Stein 2012: ch. 1.

Figure 7: Louis Armstrong peeking into Funky Butt Hall. Source: Paquet 2001: 2–3.

den's cornet through circles that look like bubbles rising out of his horn, and he visually approximates Armstrong's claim that "Old Buddy Bolden […] blew too hard [and] finally went crazy" (2011: 2) (figure 5b). He does so through tiny ink splotches that spread out from Bolden's head beyond the panel frame and into the surrounding black gutter, suggesting a departure from the norm and a break with the conventions of perception reminiscent of Bolden's insanity and the rule-breaking innovations of early jazz.

The second panel on the bottom of the preceding page (figure 7) depicts the club from behind the bar from an ambiguous perspective that does not resolve whether we are sharing Armstrong's gaze through the cracks or have moved inside of the club by way of the graphic enunciator's imagination triggered by Armstrong's verbal narrative. It shows the band in the middle of performing and the members of the audience, some facing the stage, others facing the bar. The image features no obvious visual symbols for the music, but it would be impossible to read it as a silent scene. Judging from their postures and facial expressions, the musicians are playing their instruments. Armstrong's words and the music balloon in the image above the panel underscore this assumption.

Contextual knowledge tells us what kind of music would likely have been played in this type of environment, even though no audio evidence exists since the first jazz recordings were made more than a decade after this scene (which would have taken place around 1905). Finally, the smoke wafting through the place, the tough characters at the bar (note the thick scar across the man's face on the left), and the flashily-dressed, cigar-smoking, and Stetson-wearing character facing the viewer conjure up the environment of New Orleans jazz.

Rather than narrate Armstrong's life story chronologically, the Colombian Camilo Sanin's *bande dessinée* in the BD Jazz series by Éditions Nocturne uses the February 1926 recording of "Heebie Jeebies" and the myth that this performance birthed scat as the occasion for the narrative. Sanin splices bits and pieces of Armstrong's youth and early adulthood into this account through flashbacks that occur as Armstrong is recording the song, suggesting that personal memories drive musical improvisation. Sanin visualizes and verbalizes music, such as when Armstrong is portrayed with the trumpet in his hands and/or on his mouth, when he is singing into the studio microphone, and when the verbal narrative accompanying the images (there are no speech bubbles) spells out the structure of the song (2003: 6–9, 15, 18).

Yet this *bande dessinée* also emulates musical improvisation. Sanin employs a visual aesthetics that has much in common with Armstrong's musical (and autobiographical) approach and thus presents an intriguing case of musico-comical intermediality. Employing a collage form that juxtaposes snippets from existing photographs with thin-line drawings, Sanin pits his graphic interpretation against the (always already remediated) visual evidence of Armstrong's life and thus encourages the reader to unravel the amalgamation of factual evidence, intermedial presentation, and biographical interpretation. Sanin invests each page with an individual sense of color, space, and structure, abandoning the conventional narrative device of the panel grid by treating the page as the major narrative unit. Every page looks different, some being more crowded than others, some being swathed in dark red while others are tinged light-blue. Framed panels occur, but as fragments scattered over only a few pages, like scat singing uses fragments of language without assembling them into a comprehensible narrative. Much like scat syllables do not add up to actual words, Sanin fills the few existing framed panels with close-ups of body parts that fracture the music-making figure (figures 8a and 8b). Such divergence from conventional graphic narration recalls Armstrong's explanation for his alleged invention of scat: having dropped the lyrics sheet, he spontaneously made up his own language. Brent Edwards speaks of scat's capacity to produce "a shifting possibility of a multitude of meanings" and a "[d]eliberately 'false'" vocal production [...] [that is] supplementing the sayable" (2002: 624, 625). For

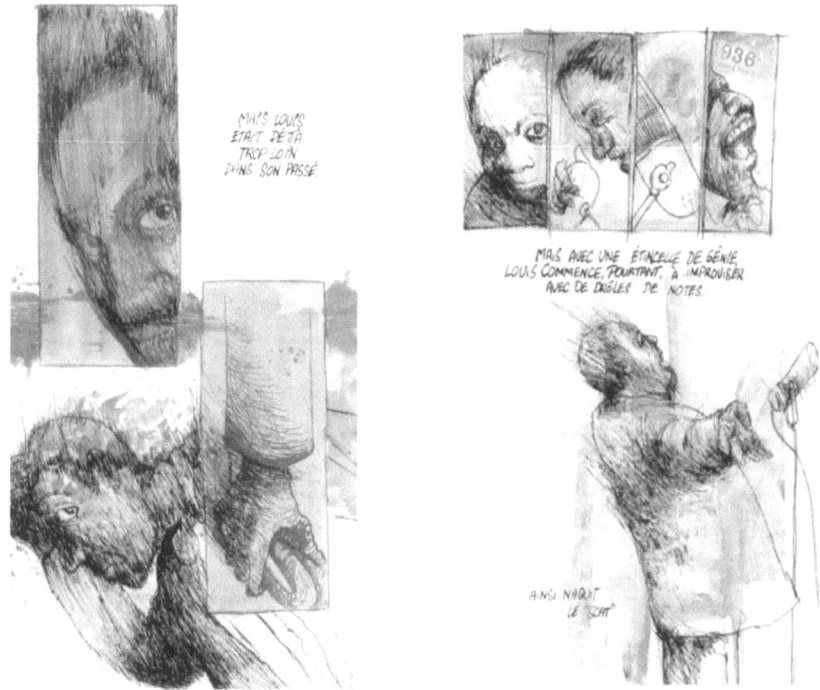

Figures 8a/b: Panel designs and layout suggestive of scat improvisation. Source: Sanin 2003: 16, 18.

Edwards, Armstrong's version of the story presents scat "as a fall, as a literal dropping of the words – as an unexpected loss of the lyrics that finally proves enabling" (621).[18] A similar dropping of established parameters of comic storytelling shapes Sanin's portrait, which questions the biographer's ability to paint a truthful picture of his subject but reaffirms his ability to create a compelling interpretation. Deliberately false forms of visual representation, such as drawings of Armstrong that do not resemble the musician's facial features and a dark undercurrent that visualizes Armstrong as a demonic figure, supplement and subvert the sayable of overly sanitized versions of his life story.[19]

---

18 See also Stein 2012: ch. 3.
19 Page 8 displays a drawing of Armstrong as a young boy with a mask-like, evil-looking face. Toward the end of the narrative (2003: 17), Sanin presents an eerie drawing of a bloated, whitish face of an old, nearly bald black man with thick lips and a bowtie covered in splotches of ink. Paquet writes in a personal e-mail on Oct. 31, 2016: "The person Armstrong intrigued me, he had

Sanin's choice of the collage form is apt because Armstrong was himself an "intermedia artist" (Veneciano 2004: 257) who reassembled scraps from newspapers, magazines, and photographs into collages. Armstrong invested these collages with a spontaneous and provisional quality that resembles his approach to music and self-narration, making the collages "autobiography by other means" (2004: 258–259). Sanin's cover illustration encapsulates these ideas (figure 9). It shows a pencil portrait of Armstrong playing his trumpet pointed to the

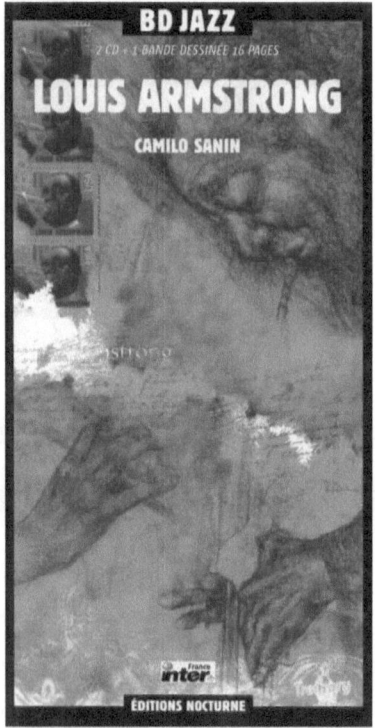

Figure 9: Cover of Sanin, "Louis Armstrong." Source: Sanin 2003.

floor, a white handkerchief in one hand, eyes closed in intense musical concentration. On the left side of the image, a third hand and another trumpet reach into view, suggesting that any graphic biography of the musician must contend with different versions of this intensely mediated figure. The Armstrong inside

---

this good guy vibe going but also a darker mood fueled by reefers and bad women, he wasn't the poster boy for jazz, as he was depicted later on." Paquet's illustrations register this darker mood through the voodoo spirit Gede (2001: 25) and through touches of the grotesque in renditions of black faces.

the story also takes on shifting guises, as he is rendered in different styles and with different drawing and painting techniques. On the cover, Sanin presents him as a serious artist rather than in the entertainer role for which he was also (and since the 1950s predominantly) known. In the upper left corner of the collage, Sanin pasted four commemorative 32-cent stamps (issued in 1995), acknowledging Armstrong's popularity in American culture but also self-reflexively marking his own contribution to the remediation of Armstrong's life and music as an intermedial performance. Finally, positioned in the middle of the image are snippets of Armstrong's handwriting that, like Paquet's use of Armstrong's words, point to the musician as an authoritative source for the graphic biographer. That Sanin includes cover images of Armstrong biographies later in the narrative (2003: 13, 19; e. g., Goffin 1947; Panassié 1947) underscores the competing agencies of autobiographical and biographical depiction within the larger space of Armstrong's autobiographics.

4.2 John Coltrane

Paolo Parisi's *Coltrane* opens with an image of a suspended gong and a mallet in front of it. A narrative box states, "In the beginning, there was sound" (2012: 3). The biblical reference to the story of Genesis, where light marks the beginning of the universe, and the visual reference to African and to East and Southeast Asian percussion recall jazz saxophonist John Coltrane's quest for musical and spiritual transcendence. Parisi's subtle yet powerful manipulation of the biblical reference topples the hierarchy of sense perceptions in Western culture, privileging sound over image as sound can be heard in the primordial darkness whereas vision depends on light. That he does so in a visual narrative about a jazz musician identifies the biography as a self-consciously intermedial tribute, where vision struggles to produce audible sound. The biblical reference introduces the central conundrum of graphic musical biography: the problem of suggesting the sonic and temporal dimensions of music in a silent, spatial medium. The book ends with an image that substitutes a saxophone and case for the gong (2012: 118), identifying the search for a solution to this problem as the frame for Parisi's inquiry into Coltrane's life and music and into the possibilities of graphic narrative. Another characteristic of this contrast is the juxtaposition of a non-Western folk music–related, religiously connoted, and ostensibly 'primitive' instrument with a more recent, industrially produced Western instrument, a contrast that portrays Coltrane's music as simultaneously universal and timeless as well as modern and American. This inquiry establishes a transmedial analogy to Coltrane's practice of exploring the expressive possibilities of music.[20]

Parisi replicates the four-part structure of Coltrane's *A Love Supreme* (1965) album, moving from "Acknowledgement" to "Resolution" to "Pursuance" to "Psalm" in a structural analogy between biography and album. Yet the cover image, a remediation of a photograph of Coltrane by Francis Wolff that shows him in a moment of musical reflection during the *Blue Train* recording sessions in Hackensack, New Jersey (September 15, 1957), complicates this analogy. Showing a musician holding but not playing his instrument, the image intimates that graphic biography can depict musicians in recognizable musical settings (recording studios, rehearsal rooms, music clubs, concert halls) but also acknowledges that it can only approximate the musical sounds and performative processes of composed and improvised jazz.

Parisi uses a minimalist black-and-white style that renders recognizable faces, postures, and gestures of famous musicians (Eric Dolphy, Miles Davis, Thelonious Monk, and others, in addition to Coltrane).[21] In combination with references to specific musical contexts, the likeness between comic characters and historical persons contributes to a sense of musical sound emanating from individual panels and panel sequences. A double page showing Coltrane's appearance with Monk at the Five Spot in 1957 exemplifies this impression (figure 10). The first panel shows Coltrane, Monk, and bassist Wilbur Ware in the middle of a performance, with Coltrane soloing and Monk comping on the piano. In the liner notes to *Soultrane* (1958), jazz critic Ira Gitler labeled Coltrane's fast arpeggios "sheets of sound" because they evoke a sense of layered notes rather than a horizontal progression.[22] Parisi transposes this approach into comic form by showing multiple note-filled music balloons that can be read as sounding at once (if we take the image as a momentary snapshot) or as following one after another at a rapid pace (if we allow it a temporal dimension). A tiny music balloon in front of Monk's mouth adds to the musicality of the scene by evoking Monk's idiosyncratic vocalization of his piano playing: the humming and muttering through which he habitually accompanied himself. Parisi also visualizes his idiosyncratic approach to playing the piano, especially the way in which his fingers hit the keyboard, and his habit of getting up and dancing

---

[20] Transmedial phenomena are not bound for their appearance to any specific medium but take on each medium's specific expressive form (Rajewsky 2002: 12–13).

[21] Parisi even creates a double-page spread with the faces of twelve musicians associated with the free jazz scene of the 1960s, including Archie Shepp, Albert Ayler, Pharoah Sanders, and Ornette Coleman (2012: 72–73).

[22] See "Trinkle, Tinkle" on *Thelonious Monk with John Coltrane* (1961 [1957]).

Graphic Musical Biography — 141

Figure 10: John Coltrane and Thelonious Monk at the Five Spot in 1957. Source: Parisi 2012: 40–41. The Random House Group Ltd. ©2012.

around stage during other players' solos. He mobilizes what I have labeled "Monkography" (Stein 2005: 609) to activate the reader's aural and visual memories of Monk's sound and performance antics as well as their public reception.[23]

There is more to Parisi's musicalization of the comics page than I can cover here. However, one double-page spread that connects Coltrane's music with the politics of the black civil rights movement must be mentioned because it shows that intermedial life writing is always culturally and historically specific by connecting not only the expressive content of the media involved but also their contextual configurations and associations (figure 11). On a superficial level, both pages feature a regular 3x2 grid of square panels. However, the content of these panels creates a different reading order suggestive of the interplay of horizontal and vertical logics in Coltrane's solos and the interplay of solo and chord

---

[23] I define Monkography as Monk's intermedial performances (musical, visual, verbal) and the discourses surrounding them: "Various forms of representation, including musical analyses, essayistic portrayals, record and concert reviews, television appearances and documentaries, as well as fictional or poetic celebrations, have competed, and continue to do so, in constructing Monk as an American icon with specific musical, social, and political meanings" (Stein 2005: 609).

Figure 11: Visualizing John Coltrane's "Alabama" (1964). Source: Parisi 2012: 94–95. The Random House Group Ltd. ©2012.

structure indicative of jazz. The preceding page states that Coltrane recorded his composition "Alabama" in response to the Ku Klux Klan bombing of the Sixteenth Street Baptist Church on September 15, 1963, so it is clear that we are dealing with a graphic depiction of this recording. Turning the page, we see a sequence of four images of the musicians (Coltrane on sax, Elvin Jones on drums, Jimmy Garrison on double bass, McCoy Tyner on piano) about to begin playing as they occupy the top-tier of panels, crossing from the first onto the second page. This arrangement forces an unusual reading sequence, signaling that this is neither a conventional composition nor a conventional comic. This effect increases through the similar arrangement of the second and third tiers. The second tier shows portraits of the four girls killed in the bombing (Cynthia Wesley, Carole Robertson, Denise McNair, Addie Mae Collins), expressing solidarity between the Coltrane quartet and the victims of the attack. The third and final tier follows the same structure but bifurcates the spread into images of white supremacy and racial violence (on the left) and of the peaceful civil rights movement (on the right), aligning Coltrane and his band members with the movement and ending the spread with a sense of hope for the future.

No actual music is involved here, but we still encounter a profound case of musico-comical intermediality, as we can relate the music in these drawings to the original recording. As Parisi notes in the acknowledgments, "the idea is to connect the reading to the listening" (2012: 120), and we are compelled by these images to consider Coltrane's sonic response to the bombing. The sequence highlights the fact that Coltrane's music must not be heard ahistorically: that it must be separated neither from his personal experiences nor from its broader cultural context. To listen to "Alabama" as merely a jazz piece would miss the point. It would ignore the fact that black jazz in the 1960s was an intensely political music that contributed to the fight for racial empowerment and released through its sonic structures an expressive power that connected the sounds, faces, and actions of jazz musicians with the civil rights movement.

5 Adapting Genre Iconographies

The purpose of my analysis in this essay was threefold. First, to illustrate that graphic musical biographies are a largely ignored form of life writing that facilitates thinking about the affordances and limitations of musico-comical intermediality and indicates the specific challenges of intermedial life writing. Second, to explore the specific ways in which these biographies extend the music-in-comics versus comics-as/like-music model by entering the referential space of a musician's intermedial autobiographics instead of merely adapting a single source text. Third, to conduct three case studies on the intermedial construction of the jazz lives of Louis Armstrong and John Coltrane that suggest that the aesthetics, style, and structure of these constructions are significantly impacted by the musical genre represented by the biographical subject. This is due in part to the fact that musical genres produce specific iconographies then adapted into graphic form and in part to the fact that each musical genre is characterized by particular sounds, structures, harmonies, melodies, and themes. In addition to the music's cultural and historical contexts, all of this provides the raw material for the graphic biographer's often innovative and highly suggestive approximations of music.

Works Cited

Armstrong, Louis. 1986 [1954]. *Satchmo: My Life in New Orleans*. New York: Da Capo.
Bachmann, Christian A. (ed.). 2014. *Bildlaute & laute Bilder: Zur 'Audio-Visualität' von Bilderzählungen*. Berlin: Bachmann.

Baetens, Jan. 2001. "Revealing Traces: A New Theory of Graphic Enunciation". In: Robin Varnum and Christina T. Gibbons (eds.). *The Language of Comics: Word and Image.* Jackson: University Press of Mississippi. 145–155.

Becker, Thomas (ed.). 2011. *Comic: Intermedialität und Legitimität eines popkulturellen Mediums.* Essen: Bachmann.

Bolter, Jay David and Richard Grusin. 1998. *Remediation: Understanding New Media.* Cambridge: MIT Press.

Brown, Kieron. 2013. "Musical Sequences in Comics". *The Comics Grid: Journal of Comics Scholarship* 3 (1): 1–6, 9.

Collins, Terry and Richie Pope. 2013. *Louis Armstrong: Jazz Legend.* North Mankato, MN: Capstone.

Edwards, Brent Hayes. 2002. "Louis Armstrong and the Syntax of Scat". *Critical Inquiry* 28 (3): 618–649.

Giesa, Felix. 2012. "Ein Bild, zwo, drei, vier: Comics und Musik, Musik und Comics". In: Caroline Roeder (ed.). *Blechtrommeln: Kinder- und Jugendliteratur & Musik.* München: Kopaed. 71–81.

Gille, Caroline and Niels Schröder. 2014. *I Got Rhythm: Das Leben der Jazzlegende Coco Schumann.* Berlin: Be.bra.

Gilmore, Leigh. 1994. *Autobiographics: A Feminist Theory of Women's Self-Representation.* Ithaca: Cornell University Press.

Gitler, Ira. 1958. Liner Notes. *Soultrane.* LP. Prestige.

Goffin, Robert. 1947. *Louis Armstrong: Le Roi du Jazz.* Paris: Seghers.

Groensteen, Thierry. 2012. "Die Rhythmen der Comics". In: Stephan Packard (ed.). *Bilder des Comics: Beiträge zur 5. Jahrestagung der Gesellschaft für Comicforschung 2010. Special Issue of Medienobservationen.* <http://www.medienobservationen.lmu.de/artikel/comics/comics_pdf/groenstein_comfor.pdf> [accessed 17 January 2018].

Hiramoto, Akra. 2008 [2005]. *Me and the Devil Blues.* Translated and adapted by David Ury. New York: Ballantine.

Hoppeler, Stephanie, Lukas Etter, and Gabriele Rippl. 2009. "Intermedialität in Comics: Neil Gaimans *The Sandman*". In: Stephan Ditschke, Katerina Kroucheva, and Daniel Stein (eds.). *Comics: Zur Geschichte und Theorie eines populärkulturellen Mediums.* Bielefeld: transcript. 53–79.

Igort and Carlos Sampayo. 2005 [2004]. *Fats Waller.* Translated by Ingrid Ickler. Bonn: Avant-Verlag.

Jacobs, Dale. 2013. *Graphic Encounters: Comics and the Sponsorship of Multimodal Literacy.* London: Bloomsbury.

Kalusche, Bernd G. 1985. *Musik im Comic: Funktion, Ästhetik, Ideologie. Massenmedien und Kommunikation* 29. Siegen: Forschungsschwerpunkt Massenmedien und Kommunikation an der Universität-Gesamthochschule-Siegen.

Kleist, Reinhard. 2006. *Johnny Cash: I See a Darkness.* Hamburg: Carlsen.

Kleist, Reinhard and Titus Ackermann. 2007. *Elvis: Die illustrierte Biografie.* Cologne: Egmont.

Legg, Barnaby, Jim McCarthy, and Flameboy. 2003. *Godspeed: The Kurt Cobain Graphic.* London: Omnibus.

Legg, Barnaby, Jim McCarthy, and Flameboy. 2004. *Eminem: In My Skin.* London: Omnibus.

Mahrt, Nina. 2010. "AWopBopaLooBopAlopBamBoom – Musik im Comic". In: Helga Arend (ed.). *"Und wer bist du, der mich betrachtet?" Populäre Literatur und Kultur als ästhetische Phänomene*. Bielefeld: Aisthesis. 219–230.
Mawil. 2008 [2004]. *Die Band*. Berlin: Reprodukt.
McCarthy, Jim and Steve Parkhouse. 2012. *Sex Pistols: The Graphic Novel*. London: Omnibus.
Meryman, Richard. 1971. *Louis Armstrong – A Self-Portrait: The Interview by Richard Meryman*. New York: Eakins.
Monpierre, Roland. 2006. *Bob Marley: La Légende des Wailers*. Paris: Michel.
Muñoz, José and Carlos Sampayo. 1990. *Billie Holiday*. Translated by Jörg Walker. Zürich: Edition Moderne.
O'Hern, Kerri, Gini Holland, Anthony Spay, and Alex Campbell. 2006. *Graphic Biographies: Louis Armstrong*. Pleasantville, NY: Stevens.
Panassié, Hugues. 1947. *Louis Armstrong*. Paris: Belvédère.
Paquet. 2001. *Louis Armstrong*. Antwerp: Bries.
Parisi, Paolo. 2012 [2010]. *Coltrane*. London: Cape.
Pillai, Nicolas and Ernesto Priego. 2016. "Brilliant Corners: Approaches to Jazz and Comics". Special issue of *The Comics Grid: Journal of Comics Scholarship* 6 (1): 1–7, 12.
Rajewsky, Irina O. 2002. *Intermedialität*. Tübingen: Francke.
Rajewsky, Irina O. 2005. "Intermediality, Intertextuality, and Remediation: A Literary Perspective on Intermediality". *Intermédialités* 6: 43–64.
Rausch, Andreas. 2005. *Zappaesk*. Berlin: Ehapa.
Rifkind, Candida. 2015. "What Is a Graphic Biography?" Project GraphicBio. <http://www.projectgraphicbio.com/blog/2015/4/22/what-is-a-graphic-biography> [accessed 15 January 2018].
Rippl, Gabriele (ed.). 2015. *Handbook of Intermediality: Literature – Image – Sound – Music*. Berlin: De Gruyter.
Rippl, Gabriele and Lukas Etter. 2013. "Intermediality, Transmediality, and Graphic Narrative". In: Daniel Stein and Jan-Noel Thon (eds.). *From Comic Strips to Graphic Novels: Contributions to the Theory and History of Graphic Narrative*. Berlin: De Gruyter. 191–217.
Sanin, Camilo. 2003. "Louis Armstrong". *Louis Armstrong: 2 CD + 1 Bande Dessinée 16 Pages*. Paris: Éditions Nocturne.
Schmitz-Emans, Monika. 2011. "The Languages of Music in Comics, Bandes dessinées and Fumetti". In: K. Alfons Knauth (ed.). *Translation & Multilingual Literature: Traduction & Littérature Multilingue*. Berlin: LIT. 195–213.
Smith, Sidonie and Julia Watson. 2010. *Reading Autobiography: A Guide for Interpreting Life Narratives*. 2nd rev. ed. Minneapolis: University of Minnesota Press.
Stein, Daniel. 2015. "Comics and Graphic Novels". In: Gabriele Rippl (ed.). *Handbook of Intermediality: Literature – Image – Sound – Music*. Berlin: De Gruyter. 420–438.
Stein, Daniel. 2012. *Music Is My Life: Louis Armstrong, Autobiography, and American Jazz*. Ann Arbor: University of Michigan Press.
Stein, Daniel. 2011. "Negotiating Primitive Modernisms: Louis Armstrong, Robert Goffin, and the Transatlantic Jazz Debate". *European Journal of American Studies* 2. <http://ejas.revues.org/9395> [accessed 15 January 2018].

Stein, Daniel. 2008. "From Text-Centered Intermediality to Cultural Intermediality; or, How to Make Musico-Textual Studies More Cultural". In: Frank Kelleter and Daniel Stein (eds.). *American Studies as Media Studies*. Heidelberg: Winter. 180–190.

Stein, Daniel. 2005. "Hearing, Seeing, and Writing Thelonious Monk: Toward a Theory of Changing Iconotexts". *Amerikastudien/American Studies* 50 (4): 603–627.

Summers, Tim. 2015. "'Sparks of Meaning': Comics, Music and Alan Moore". *Journal of the Royal Musical Association* 140 (1): 121–162.

Various. 2008. *Bob Dylan Revisited*. Paris: Delcourt.

Veneciano, Jorge Daniel. 2004. "Louis Armstrong, Bricolage, and the Aesthetics of Swing". In: Robert G. O'Meally, Brent Hayes Edwards, and Farah Jasmine Griffin (eds.). *Uptown Conversation: The New Jazz Studies*. New York: Columbia University Press. 256–277.

Wolf, Werner. 1998. "The Musicalization of Fiction: Versuche intermedialer Grenzüberschreitung zwischen Musik und Literatur im englischen Erzählen des 19. und 20. Jahrhunderts". In: Jörg Helbig (ed.). *Intermedialität: Theorie und Praxis eines interdisziplinären Forschungsgebiets*. Berlin: Schmidt. 133–164.

Wolf, Werner. 1999. *The Musicalization of Fiction: A Study in the Theory and History of Intermediality*. Amsterdam: Rodopi.

Wolf, Werner and Walter Bernhart (eds.). 2016. *Silence and Absence in Literature and Music*. Boston: Brill-Rodopi.

Wright, Laurie. 1987. *"King" Oliver*. Essex: Storyville Publications.

Young, Frank M. and David Lasky. 2012. *The Carter Family: Don't Forget This Song*. New York: Abrams ComicsArt.

Gabriele Rippl
Ekphrastic Encounters and Word–Photography Configurations in Contemporary Transcultural American Life Writing

Abstract

Autobiography and life-writing studies have recently undergone both a transcultural and an intermedial turn. Taking these developments into account, this contribution discusses autobiographical and autofictional texts by four contemporary American writers: Edward Said, Jamaica Kincaid, Teju Cole, and Aleksandar Hemon. Their highly self-reflexive intermedial aesthetic includes word–photography configurations as well as ekphrases of pictures, and raises generic, formal, ethical, and political questions. These questions address experiences of migration as well as peripatetic and transcultural lives in our globalized modernity. The following analysis of the writers' creative interventions brings to light an under-investigated quality of contemporary American life writing: the prominence of verbal–visual relations in transcultural texts which often touch upon topics such as the gaze, scopic regimes, and traveling images.

1 Transcultural Life Writing: Word–Photography Configurations and Ekphrasis[1]

Over the last 25 years, intermediality and ekphrasis research have become important fields in literary and cultural studies. At the same time, autobiography studies have undergone both a transcultural (Hornung 2009) and an intermedial turn (Rippl 2017). In the English language, the widening of the scope of self-expression, that is, of writing one's self and thinking about autobiographical modes of writing, is signaled by a new name, 'life writing' – an umbrella term which

---

[1] This text was written during my time as a fellow of the Center for Advanced Studies in the Humanities Morphomata at the University of Cologne. I would like to thank the Morphomata Center, Hanjo Berressem, and my co-fellows as well as the editors of this volume, Nassim Winnie Balestrini and Ina Bergmann, for their insightful comments on the first draft of my text.

https://doi.org/10.1515/9783110579253-009

covers a wide range of genres such as letters, journals, captivity and illness narratives, memoirs, biographies, blogs, and other evolving forms of self-representation in social media (Balestrini 2013, 2015; Hayes 2015). The term also covers other autobiographical narratives in forms such as the comic book and autobiographical fiction/autofiction (Zipfel 2009). Thus, when we speak of contemporary American life writing, we include not only differing conceptions of the self (Greedharry 2008; Moore-Gilbert 2009: xviii–xix) but also diverging modes of fictional and non-fictional writing styles, be they linear or non-linear, coherent, or fragmented, or be they written or presented in other inter/medial forms.[2] Today, autobiographies and autofiction often not only transcend the fiction/non-fiction boundary,[3] but they also showcase that they are doing so by questioning generic conventions and readers' genre-based expectations. As Tobias Döring points out, "[a]utobiography is a threshold genre. It traces and crosses boundaries between fact and fiction, memory and history, selves and others, images and texts – sometimes drawing these distinctions, but more often blurring them" (Döring 2006: 72). Contemporary life writing often not only blurs the boundaries of fact and fiction, but it also depicts culturally hybrid protagonists. This liminal generic and cultural state has its parallels in the intermedial quality of the texts. For the last three decades, many hyphenated Americans with transcultural identities have written autobiographical and autofictional texts which invent new, fascinating intermedial ways of telling a life. When we say 'transcultural,' we use the adjective the way Alfred Hornung introduced it to autobiography studies[4] and rely on Wolfgang Welsch's understanding of cultures as non-particularistic.[5] Edward Said, Jamaica Kincaid, Teju Cole, and Aleksandar Hemon are

---

[2] Cf. Dünne and Moser (2008a) and Moser (2017), who have introduced the term 'automediality' as an umbrella term for a range of multi-medial and hybrid modes of narrating a life.
[3] Since the 1980s, scholars such as Paul John Eakin (1985), Marlene Kadar (1992), Sidonie Smith and Julia Watson (1992, 1996, 1998, 2001) as well as Leigh Gilmore (2001) have broadened the notion of autobiographical writing by radically challenging the fiction/non-fiction dichotomy that still underlies narrow definitions of the term and by problematizing some of the claims to objectivity and truthfulness that build on that dichotomy (Saunders 2010: 7).
[4] Hornung uses the term "transcultural life writing" to differentiate among various types of life writing in connection with classic immigration countries like Australia, Canada, and the United States where "[w]aves of immigration since the end of the nineteenth century have challenged uniform national credos and transformed mainstream societies. The end to colonial rule in Third World countries and the appeal to free economic markets in the First World have created new patterns of global migration in the second half of the twentieth century" (Hornung 2009: 536).
[5] Welsch has contrasted transculturality with the classical separatory concept of single cultures and the more recent concepts of interculturality and multiculturality, which still originate in, and thus barely transcend, the traditional conception of cultural particularism. Welsch maintains, "the description of today's cultures as islands or spheres is factually incorrect and norma-

internationally renowned, prize-winning transcultural writers, whose highly self-reflexive intermedial autobiographies and autobiographical fiction include word–photography configurations as well as ekphrases of pictures. Their intermedial strategies help to express experiences of migration and to raise important generic, aesthetic, ethical, and political questions. Analyzing these writers' creative interventions epistemologically and understanding them as media constellations will reveal an under-investigated quality of life writing: the prominence of verbal–visual relations in transcultural texts which often touch upon topics such as visual power, the gaze, scopic regimes, and traveling images.

2 Approaching Word–Photography Configurations and Ekphrasis in Life Writing

As Liliane Louvel convincingly argues, literary scholars working in the field of word-and-image studies have focused more often on painting/text relations than on photography/text interfaces (Louvel 2008: 32). In our day and age in which digital new media and the internet facilitate combining verbal texts and images, contemporary autobiographies and autofiction may be said to be compelled to come in new intermedial shapes that attract contemporary readers or users (see Beckman and Weissberg 2013: xii–xiii). In order to establish how word and image relate in life writing, one has to remember that photography is

> a medium that is bound more firmly to the concrete object or process being recorded than any other media technology (with the possible exception of analogue sound recording). Following Peirce's concept of the index as a sign that signifies by means of causality, the photographic image is essentially understood, in a number of key positions in the theory of photography, as a trace of the real objects and processes which were in front of the camera at the moment of exposure. (Schröter 2013)

When investigating the links between photography and life writing, "[t]he commonsense view would be that photography operates as a visual supplement (illustration) and a corroboration (verification) of the text – that photography may help to establish, or at least reinforce, autobiography's referential dimension" (Adams 2000: xxi). Both photography and autobiographical writing have been understood as modes of representation that operate referentially, when in fact

---

tively deceptive. Cultures de facto no longer have the insinuated form of homogeneity and separateness. They have instead assumed a new form, which is to be called transcultural in so far as it passes through classical cultural boundaries" (1999: 197).

they can at best produce reality effects. That is to say, even in the digital age, photos – particularly in autobiographies, travelogues and news media – are frequently construed as documentation or evidence of an objectively verifiable reality. Added to an autobiographical text, pictures reinforce the message conveyed by words. But it is precisely this combination which is being subverted in, for instance, Cole's travelogue and Hemon's autofiction. Taking this phenomenon into account, Timothy Adams maintains that

> [i]n the wake of poststructuralism [...] the role of photography in autobiography is far from simple or one-dimensional. Both media are increasingly self-conscious, and combining them may intensify rather than reduce the complexity and ambiguity of each taken separately. [...] In my view, text and image complement, rather than supplement, each other; since reference is not secure in either, neither can compensate for lack of stability in the other. Because both media are located on the border between fact and fiction, they often undercut just as easily as they reinforce each other. (Adams 2000: xxi)

Adams finds in autobiographical writing a literary parallel "for two aspects of photography: its inescapable reference to the 'real world,' and its uncertain relation to the categories of fact and fiction" (Beckman and Weissberg 2013: xi).

One of the most prevalent relationships between images and words in texts are descriptions and verbal evocations of images, commonly called ekphrases.[6] Ekphrasis is, as James A. W. Heffernan puts it, "the verbal representation of visual representation" (1993: 2), and is commonly understood as 'intermedial reference' (see Rajewsky 2002, 2005; Wolf 2005; Rippl 2005). Since the late 1980s, ekphrasis has had a meteoric rise not only in literary studies but also in Anglophone literatures, where visual, ekphrastic, and intermedial aesthetics have played an increasingly crucial role – and this despite the fact that in the digital age pictures are ubiquitously available on the internet rather than being accessible only through verbal description. In contemporary writing, readers encounter a surprisingly high number of short and extended, concrete and

---

[6] Etymologically, ekphrasis is a Greek term meaning 'to speak out' or 'to show clearly and completely.' The *OED* records its first use in English in 1715. As a literary descriptive mode, ekphrasis is at least as old as Homer's depiction of Achilles's shield in Book 18 of the *Iliad*. Late antiquity already developed a 'theory' of description they called *ekphrasis* (in Greek) or *evidentia* (in Latin) (sometimes also *hypotyposis* or *descriptio*), which consisted of a set of rules about how to describe objects, people, place, and time properly (Webb 2009; Rippl 2005). Ekphrastic description was considered a mode of speaking which – by aiming at *enargeia* ('vividness' and 'clearness' in the visual sense) – was able to bring absent objects before the listeners' mental eyes, and served, according to Quintilian, to rouse their emotions by making them eyewitnesses. For ancient rhetoricians, the term ekphrasis referred to any description of persons, objects, places, or times that was 'enargetic.'

allusive ekphrases, which refer either to absent images or to images added to the text.[7]

Heffernan's influential definition of ekphrasis has been criticized due to its alliances with concepts of mimesis and referentiality (Rippl 2005) and its focus on the *paragone* (Kennedy 2012, 2015). In recent years, scholars critical of Heffernan's view have expanded the concept of ekphrasis considerably. This expansion includes the range of visual objects being described ekphrastically: accordingly, these objects are no longer exclusively works of art, but also include other visual representations such as TV and film stills, photographs, and comics. Furthermore, the genre and media of ekphrasis have become more comprehensive: language is no longer considered the only medium to deliver ekphrases; artistic forms like opera, drama, film, and graphic novels likewise do so (see Behluli and Rippl 2017). Also central in recent discussions is the question regarding the functions of ekphrasis (Rippl 2015), particularly because ekphrasis deals with the (medial/cultural) other (Mitchell 1992, 1994; Loizeaux 2008). This innovative focus on functionality will be crucial to the critical analysis in this essay.

3 Intermedial American Life Writing and Autofiction

Transnational mobility and transcultural negotiations represent the experiential core of extensive immigration to the United States in the twentieth and twenty-first centuries. Transcultural and transnational migratory movements trigger performative identity formation that specifically relates to immigrants' constructing of new identities and to finding novel forms of self-expression, among them intermedial strategies of life writing.[8] This holds true for Edward Said, Jamaica Kincaid, Teju Cole, and Aleksandar Hemon, that is, for 'hyphenated' American writers who were either born or grew up in the Middle East, the Caribbean, sub-Saharan Africa, or Europe, and who have lived – at least part-time – in the United States. Their autobiographies and autofiction tell the stories of lives

---

[7] Tamar Yacobi pointed out that "ekphrasis is remarkably variable in extent" (Yacobi 1997: 37) and can range from lengthy descriptions to abbreviated references and mere allusions to an ekphrastic model (Yacobi 1995).
[8] See Döring 2006: 71. The fictional and non-fictional texts of people on the move center on "a search for a sense of belonging or identity, a journey to find a home" and often tackle questions of "cultural identity pre- and post-migration, across place as well as down the generations" (Temple 2001: 601).

with multiple topographic settings and locations and of transnational as well as transcultural identities. The following set of questions will guide my analyses of ekphrastic encounters and word–photography figurations: How do these contemporary hyphenated American writers represent their transcultural lives? To what end do these transcultural writers include photographs, and how do these pictures relate to the respective text? Do they collaborate with the verbal narrative, or do they spark a struggle of representation – a *paragone?* What are the functions of the conspicuous ekphrastic references to and descriptions of images, and what do they tell us about epistemological set-ups and cultural hierarchies?

3.1 Edward Said's *Out of Place*

A classic of transcultural life writing dealing with issues of political recognition of Palestinians within the twentieth-century Middle-Eastern context, Palestinian diaspora, and exile is *Out of Place* (1999) by the Palestinian-American literary scholar Edward Said (1935–2003). *Out of Place* is a full-fledged autobiography about Said's life and his struggle for self-identification and recognition as a member of a marginalized Middle Eastern group, comprised of Palestinians and refugee Palestinians (see Sarkowsky 2012: 630). Said's autobiography presents his life retrospectively in a coherent narrative form, i. e., it adheres to a traditional Western pattern. It is intermedial in that it includes photographs and ekphrastically refers to some of the pictures he uses to illustrate his text. In the Vintage paperback edition, all photographs are placed after one third of the text; and while they interrupt the text at one point, they do not fragment it as is the case in Cole's and Hemon's works. Said's family photographs, which provide visual confirmation of what he writes about his middle-class family life in the Middle East in the 1930s and 1940s, also help to address the geopolitics of the Middle East, issues of place, of feeling out-of-place, and of diaspora.

Nonetheless there is an inherent tension between the visual documentation through pictures and the text that comes with them. The "surface self" produced through the narrative is eager to escape the controlling power exercised by the photographs and does this through fictionalization and the construction of "a second self" (Döring 2006: 74). However, the creation of two selves invites questions regarding the principles of (mis-)representation of a life. Said's 32 black-and-white photographs from his family album come with captions that indicate who is in the pictures and where they were taken. Some of them are reprinted on the cover from whose bottom right margin young Edward Said looks at us. This cover image appears with six additional photographic portraits on the book spine, depicting the autobiographer at various ages and locations, thus realizing autobiography as "auto-geography" (Döring 2006: 74). As Döring explains, many of these pictures were taken by Said's father who is depicted as a domineering parent who probably either remained unaware or did not know about his son's disconcerting experience of being photographed or filmed: "The camera was always there when we left the house for a walk or drive. It must always have been my father's way of capturing as well as confirming the ordered family domain he had created and now ruled" (Said 1999: 76). As ostensible documents depicting one version of 'Edward,' that is, Said's visual surface self, the images attest to the 'law of the father'; they are "a practice of control, a media technique to enforce authority and social regulation" (Döring 2006: 74). While photography is presented and used as a means of documentation of family life, pictures – like the images recorded by a film camera – also represent the father's "optical grid" (Said 1999: 76). As this is an autobiography by an intellectual intent on escaping a prescribed version of his identity, the 'Edward' in the pictures is on a quest for his true self and describes "the emergence of a second self buried for a very long time beneath a surface of often expertly acquired and wielded social characteristics belonging to the self my parents tried to construct" (Said 1999: 217). This second, 'real' self is carefully established against parental expectations and societal conventions (see Döring 2006: 72–73): through reading literature and eventually through writing his autobiography, i. e., his literary self-invention, 'Edward' is able to unearth his true self. The power of words[9] helps 'Edward' to escape and transcribe the parental and societal script of his visually realized surface self.

3.2 Jamaica Kincaid's *Lucy*

Thomas Michael Stein claims that "from the early stages of their literary production," writers from the Caribbean "have preferred to fictionalize personal experience and have launched a genre of its own," which Stein calls "fictional autobiography" (Stein 1998: 247). The Antiguan-American writer Jamaica Kincaid (b. 1949), who arrived in New York at the age of 17 to work as an *au pair*, is

---

9 "One of my recurrent fantasies, the subject of a school essay I wrote when I was twelve, was to be a book, whose fate I took to be happily free of unwelcome changes, distortions of its shape, criticism of its looks; print for me was made up of a rare combination of expression in its style and contents, absolute rigidity, and integrity in its looks. Passed from hand to hand, place to place, time to time, I could remain my own true self (as a book), despite being thrown out of a car and lost in the back drawer" (Said 1999: 76).

an ideal case in point. Her autobiographical novels *Annie John* (1983), *Lucy* (1990), *The Autobiography of My Mother* (1995), and *See Now Then* (2013) are clearly autofictional. In their chronological sequence, they add "volumes to a series" (Gilmore 1998: 214); and due to their references to other texts and to images, they are intertextual and intermedial experiments in postmodernist self-presentation. By presenting a subject-in-process and a serial postcolonial/transcultural identity, Kincaid's texts escape the fetters of colonial determination through a subtle aesthetic subversion of traditional autobiographical forms and Western regimes of vision. *Lucy*, which unlike the other three examples includes no reproductions of photographs in their usual medial form, turns to the rhetorical device of ekphrasis in order to negotiate the effects of cultural domination and the legacy of colonial education experienced by colonized subjects. However, she revises this device "counter-discursively" (Emery 1997: 262): Kincaid's/Lucy's ekphrases of several paintings and fictional photographs, amongst them the family photographs of the American family that employs her (see Kincaid 1990: 12, 79), offer alternative readings that deviate from common interpretations of photographic genres such as the family photograph. Lucy becomes an enthusiastic museumgoer while living in an American metropolis. Mariah, her employer, introduces her to the paintings of a Frenchman who had traveled the world and depicted people in far-away places. This painter is, of course, Paul Gauguin who painted women of the Southern Pacific region as exotic objects, displaying their bodies to the (male) Western gaze. While Lucy initially identifies with Gauguin and his feeling that home is an "unbearable prison" (Kincaid 1990: 95), she quickly comes to notice that, in his case, the romance of outsider status was facilitated by his gender and his fame, whereas her own agency as a young female is restricted. She was only able to leave the West Indies because she had accepted a job as an *au pair* in an upper-/middle-class white American family. In her first year in the United States, Lucy meets a painter called Paul (sic) whose lover she becomes. Like Gauguin, Paul paints people:

> Some of them women without their clothes on, some of them just faces. None of the paintings was straightforward; instead the people all looked like their reflections in a pool whose surface had just been disturbed. The colors were strange – not the colors any real person would be, but as if all the deep shades from a paintbox had been carefully mixed together in a way that still left them distinct. (Kincaid 1990: 97)

Again, a male painter paints unclad women who resemble their own mirror images as seen "in a pool whose surface had just been disturbed," that is, women whose visible contours are distorted and who are depicted in unrealistic hues, while Narcissus's mirror image, to which this passage refers, was a perfectly pleasing one. Lucy's use of ekphrasis allows her to de-naturalize the colonial male gaze on the colonized female body. While Gauguin did not 'distort' the women's shapes, he painted in deep gaudy colors used by cubist painters who aimed at dismantling the shape of the human body, and his paintings are intimately linked to the prejudiced and thus falsifying colonial gaze: his post-impressionist style simplified, idealized, and stripped the women he painted of their subjecthood.[10] Kincaid takes up an issue of gender politics here, particularly because most of Paul's party guests are male artists: "It seemed to be a position that allowed for irresponsibility, so perhaps it was much better suited for men – like the man whose paintings hung in the museum that I liked to visit" (Kincaid 1990: 98). When Paul visits Lucy in her new apartment after she left the family she had worked for, he gives her "a photograph he had taken of me standing over a boiling pot of food" in which she was "naked from the waist up; a piece of cloth, wrapped around me, covered me from the waist down" (Kincaid 1990: 155). In this short ekphrasis of the photo, in which Lucy "encounters a primitivized image of herself" (Emery 1997: 267), the obvious connection between gender and colonial aspects of possession links Paul's photo and behavior to Gauguin's paintings of his Tahitian girl-mistresses as exotic objects. But while Gauguin traveled to the exotic, Lucy's lover Paul merely appropriates and commands what traveled to him.

Lucy's sensitivity to discrimination based on gender and race becomes increasingly important in the course of the story, as it explores various meanings of post-colonial possession and dispossession (Emery 1997: 264). Ekphrases are Lucy's means to renegotiate the regime of male imperial visual culture and its representational strategies of photographic portraits. Becoming a photographer herself allows Kincaid's protagonist to claim "the power of the gaze" (Spurr 1993: 13) and "invent herself as a creator of images rather than a prisoner of them" (Emery 1997: 270). As a female photographer, Lucy becomes the maker of pictures rather than the depicted object. She ponders, "Why is a picture of something real eventually more exciting than the thing itself? I did not yet know the answer to that" (Kincaid 1990: 121). The answer to this question involves the issue of agency, of having the power to depict instead of being depicted. It is the power to define and invent oneself. After all, a picture – together with its inherent regimes of vision and epistemology – has the potential to survive. Towards the end of the text, Kincaid establishes the importance of books and writing for Lucy: "I had a camera and prints of the photographs I had taken, prints I had made myself. But mostly I had books – so many books, and they were mine; I would not have to part with them" (143). At the conclusion,

---

10 I would like to thank Edward Wright for sharing his ideas on Gauguin with me.

Kincaid proceeds from reading to writing, thus offering another medium for Lucy's self-invention. When Mariah gives Lucy a notebook as a present – a notebook with a leather cover dyed blood red and white pages "smooth like milk" (162) – Lucy comments, "my life stretche[s] out ahead of me like a book of *blank pages*" (163; emphasis added). Finding herself alone one night in the apartment she shares with her friend Peggy, she picks up the book and her fountain pen "full of beautiful blue ink," writes at the top of the page her full name, "Lucy Josephine Potter" (163), and then adds, "I wish I could love someone so much that I would die from it" (164), before feeling full of shame and weeping so hard "that the tears fell on the page and caused all the words to become one big blur" (164). The blurred writing, with which the text ends, invites us, as Emery claims, "to relinquish the gaze as our predominant and dominating means of access to knowledge" (1997: 271). But this last image of Lucy weeping hard and blurring her written words can also be read differently. It can be read as a critical assessment of logocentrism and a further prioritizing of the visual; after all, blurred words are no longer legible and therefore only appear as shapes. In its interpretative openness, this highly suggestive last scene of Kincaid's text asks each reader to determine its possible meanings, thus granting the reader the kind of agency Lucy herself desires.

3.3 Teju Cole's *Every Day Is for the Thief*

Teju Cole (b. 1975) is a Nigerian-American writer, photographer, and art historian whose 2007 travelogue *Every Day Is for the Thief* (first edition Nigeria 2007; second edition USA 2014) includes photographs. In this travelogue, Cole almost entirely ignores ekphrasis as an intermedial device, although it is a conspicuous feature of his first novel, *Open City* (2011). The male protagonist in *Every Day Is for the Thief* – the title is the first half of a Yoruba proverb, the second half of which reads "but one day is for the owner" – resembles the author in many ways: both are educated middle-class New York City dwellers of Nigerian descent who, after many years, return to Lagos for a visit. The trip allows the protagonist to fathom his own in-between identity: his gaze on Nigerian life is not exclusively a Western one; as a young man on a quest, he is contemplating the possibility of leaving New York City in order to start a new life in Lagos. He is clearly torn between bustling Lagos and a quiet life in the American metropolis which provides ample space to create art rather than being exhausted by "the hassle of a normal Lagos day" (Cole 2014: 68):

> There is a disconnect between the wealth of stories available here [in Lagos] and the rarity of creative refuge. [...] Writing is difficult, reading impossible. [...] The best I can manage is to take a few photographs. For the rest of the month, I neither read nor write. [...]
> I am not going to move back to Lagos. No way. I don't care if there are a million untold stories, I don't care if that, too, is a contribution to the atmosphere of surrender.
> I am going to move back to Lagos. I must. (Cole 2014: 68–69)

Various chapters of *Every Day Is for the Thief* are based on revised blog entries that Cole posted to a site he called *Modal Minority*; however, in 2007 "the site was deleted with no explanation" (Lewis-Kraus 2014: 61). Shortly after, a small publisher in Abuja, named Cassava Republic Press, issued their selections of postings with some of Cole's photographs in book form. The text (as published by Faber and Faber) is the protagonist's personal account of meeting family and friends in Lagos after years of absence and, at the same time, a political travelogue dealing with poverty, corruption, mismanagement, and communal violence in Nigerian cities. In spite of its many autobiographical (and autoethnographical[11]) features and its travelogue-like depiction of contemporary life in the highly intercultural and transnationalized metropolitan space of Lagos, Cole insists that *Every Day Is for the Thief* is a work of fiction (see Cole 2016: 79–80). Yet, the impression that the reader is actually dealing with a piece of life writing is not only supported by the black-and-white photographs taken by the author during a trip to Nigeria, but also by the intertextual references to another memoir (see Cole 2014 [2007]: 23, 41): to the Sri Lankan-Canadian writer Michael Ondaatje's *Running in the Family* (1982), which the protagonist-author admires for its "sensuous prose" and "intense visuality" (Cole 2014: 43). Ondaatje's formally innovative postmodernist and postcolonial work of intermedial life writing challenges traditions of autobiographical writing and traditional ideas of the autonomous self by presenting many voices (and hence projecting a relational self), intertextual traces, and different genres (such as biography, memoir, travel journal, and family saga). While the text plays with the fact/fiction boundary, it questions the reliability of memories and showcases the difficulties in reconnecting with the past (in 1978 and 1980 Ondaatje spent time in his native Sri Lanka which he had left at the age of eleven), while the featured family photographs produce effects of authenticity and immediacy (cf. Adams 2000: 40–56).

---

[11] Cf. Moser 2017 for a discussion of the term 'autoethnography,' which he describes as a genre of life writing which offers an analysis of the self in relation to culture and which breaks with the conventions of narrative linearity and teleology.

The 27 chapters of *Every Day Is for the Thief* read like a series of vignettes and fragments interspersed with nineteen captionless black-and-white photographs placed between chapters. Each photograph is demarcated by a thin black line which functions like a frame and an aesthetic allusion which will doubtlessly remind many readers of Robert Frank's famous photographic book *The Americans* (1985), namely the aesthetics of photographs shot with a handheld camera on Frank's road trip across the United States in 1955/1956. Since Cole's photos come without captions, there is much space for interpretation. Read as a documentary medium, analogue photography functions as a mode of registering reality that is close to traditional notions of autobiographical as well as travel writing. Thus, the inclusion of photographs could be understood as implying that they provide a supposedly palpable touch of immediate reality in a verbal text. But since Cole explicitly labeled his text as fiction, the ways words and photographs connect are far more complicated: they transcend the *paragone*, the 'illustration' paradigm, as well as naïve notions of photography as registering every single detail of reality. Perhaps the photographs are supposed to be read as an independent series, like a captionless photobook, without taking the interspersed words into account?[12] While the photographs offer "hazy glimpses into Nigerian worlds" (Neumann 2014: 318), by blurring the link between text and photo and by often disconnecting the photos from their rare and at best rudimentary ekphrastic descriptions, Cole leaves his readers puzzled, unable to relate word and photographic image in traditional ways.

In addition to the photo on the book cover, two more images invite the reader into the book: the first one is located on the title page, the second one directs the reader into the first chapter. These photos function as epigraphs for the book. The Faber and Faber cover picture, which is also the last photo in the text (cf. chapter 27: 163), shows a boat with two boys in a manner that, as the narrative voice suggests, evokes Charon's boat carrying recently deceased travelers to the other side of the river Styx. It thus depicts death as traversing or even transgressing a boundary, a topic relevant for an entire range of photographs included in the book. The little street of Lagos which provides the setting for this image is presented as a modern version of mythical Hades, as "an uncanny [...] dockyard of Charon's" (Cole 2014: 161). Continuing the theme of transitions, many photos depict a sub-Saharan country, in which men function as gatekeepers (Cole 2014:

---

[12] Cole explains the inclusion of the photos in *Every Day Is for the Thief* with the fact that he is a photographer as well as a writer and a blogger. He also refers to his attraction to writers and texts, e.g., Hemon's *The Lazarus Project*, where images have "imprecise connections to the text" (Cole 2016: 82).

2) and in which fences and gates signify separate spaces (e. g., Cole 2014: 104–105).

Photo 4 (12–13), which presents a view over the shoulder of a cab driver, exemplifies Cole's "extreme juxtapositions of foreground and background" and his employment of "mirrors and reflections to add a new dimension to an already complex image" (Zuckerman 2014). From a formal point of view, it is noteworthy that in this photo – as in several other blurry images – the field of vision is obstructed and a plain and clear view intercepted. Readers are not invited – in the sense of a 'readerly' image, to adapt Roland Barthes – into the pictures, which often veil rather than reveal the scenes they capture, thus drawing the reader's attention to that which is not visible. Viewers are prevented from entering the pictures and are hence urged to be content with an impenetrable surface and accept the denial of "voyeuristic appropriation and consumption" (Neumann 2014: 330). This impenetrability of the pictures is also a common feature of Cole's intermedial configurations, which leave the reader puzzled since s/he does not know how to link word and image.

While photographs in autobiographical texts commonly serve as illustrations and give an unobstructed view of people and objects represented in the picture (as, for example, in Said's text), Cole's intermedial, highly self-reflexive, and vignette-like autofiction plays with generic rules and widely accepted functions of photography by cutting the links between words and photographs and by reducing ekphrases to mere traces and allusions.[13] This complication of the readers' access to ideas and perceptions, however, is an effective way of appealing to readers to become involved co-producers of meaning, even though meaning remains inconclusive.

3.4 Aleksandar Hemon's *The Lazarus Project*

The Lazarus Project (2008) by the Sarajevo-born award-winning writer Aleksandar Hemon, who has been living in Chicago since 1992, serves as another example of transcultural American life writing in the form of intermedial autofiction which employs ekphrasis and includes 23 photographs (seven of which are historical ones, originally published in the Chicago *Daily News* between 1904 and 1919). This illustrated autobiographical novel focuses on immigration to the United States, U.S.-based value systems, as well as xenophobic and anti-Semitic anxieties around 1900 and 2000. It tells the story of three lives. First, there is

---

13 An exception can be found in ch. 20.

the life of the young Russian Jewish pogrom survivor and refugee immigrant Lazarus Averbuch. This immigrant shares his name with the biblical Lazarus who was restored to life by Jesus after his death. His name can also be read as a highly ironic reference to "The New Colossus" (1883), American poet Emma Lazarus's well-known sonnet which in 1903 was engraved on a bronze plaque for the pedestal of the Statue of Liberty, which symbolically welcomes immigrants on the cusp of arriving. Second, Hemon's *The Lazarus Project* blurs the fact/fiction boundary by juxtaposing Averbuch's story with that of the text's narrator-protagonist named Brik (the author's *alter ego*), who lives in Chicago a hundred years later, and his photographer-friend, Rora. Like Averbuch, Brik is an immigrant who struggles with constructing his transcultural identity.

The text starts with an event from 2 March 1908, when Averbuch tries to deliver a letter to the city's Chief of Police. He is shot dead in a time period when numerous Americans are obsessed with anarchism and harbor anti-Semitic sentiments. After the shooting, he is branded as an anarchist assassin and as an agent of foreign operatives who wanted to bring down the United States. From the start, *The Lazarus Project* vets America's past and present value systems as well as its attitude towards immigrants. Hemon blends the historical events in Chicago at the beginning of the twentieth century with contemporary immigration politics, value systems, patriotism, and anxieties in the USA today, for instance, when the protagonist Brik claims: "The war against anarchism was much like the current war on terror – funny how old habits never die" (Hemon 2008: 42). On the book's title page, directly below the title and author's name, it says: "With photographs by Velibor Božović and from the Chicago Historical Society" – but it is deliberately left unclear in this autofictional novel which photos are historical and which were taken by Božović (only the picture credits at the end of the text provide clarification). Some of the historical photographs have an illustrative and documentary function, as is the case with the photograph facing page 1 which depicts a historical house and has an address written on its top part, saying "The Shippy Residence 31 Lincoln Pl." The text reads: "Early in the morning, a scrawny young man rings the bell at 31 Lincoln Place, the residence of George Shippy, the redoubtable chief of Chicago police" (Hemon 2008: 1). Another example of the illustrative and documentary function of photographs added to the text occurs when a city skyline is shown (10), whereas the verbal text refers to the picture as "the Chicago skyline" (Hemon 2008: 13).

While these photos evoke an atmosphere of historical accuracy, a number of other cases subvert the commonsense view that photographs are documentary material which serves to illustrate and authenticate texts. This is the case with the photos taken during Brik's journey through Ukraine: like the historical photos, they are black-and-white with black borders, reminiscent of old photo albums (an impression supported by additional black pages in the book). This device underscores the photographs' artificiality. By "echoing the distinct Sebaldian foggy, mournful stylistics," Hemon creates an "eerie atmosphere [which] undercuts the documentary function" (Fjellestad 2015: 205). The photographs fragment the text because Hemon placed them between the chapters – a strategy which on the one hand parallels "the rupture of migration" (Weiner 2014: 215) and on the other demands that the reader actively link them to the text: "the reader is urged to braid images with the story" (Fjellestad 2015: 206). However, despite the ekphrases provided in the novel, the logical connection between text and photo is not always clear. According to Sonia Weiner, "Hemon purposefully allows his narrative to clash with the images" (2014: 226). This is, for instance, the case with the photo on page 24 and its ekphrastic description: "Assistant chief of police Schuettler [...] carefully steps over the carmine blood puddle, shaped like an obscure ocean on the light maple floor, to land on the carpet where the young man's body lays supine" (Hemon 2008: 25). Even though the quality of the photograph's reproduction is poor, one can spot white X marks characterizing the image as depicting a crime scene. But neither the pool of blood nor Averbuch's dead body are visible in the photograph. Hemon's autofictional text with its word–photography figurations and allusive, trace-like ekphrases engages in social and political discourse by telling the forgotten story of the unfortunate immigrant Lazarus Averbuch and of his fellow immigrant Brik, alias Hemon, 100 years later. Like Cole, Hemon uses ekphrasis to invite his readers to participate in meaning-making processes by contemplating possible links between words and photographs. At the same time, Hemon asks them to ponder commonly accepted views on these bi-medial figurations in order to contemplate the – more often than not – torn lives of immigrants specifically via the intermedial experiments of a text fragmented by photographs.

4 Life-Writing Experiments in Intermediality

All texts discussed in this chapter play with generic rules as well as semiotic and medial boundaries. They are of an experimental nature and serve as examples of conspicuously self-reflexive modes of contemporary life writing. The texts' intermedial quality must, on the one hand, be read as an inquiry into how a life can be expressed today. On the other hand, the intermedial devices adhere to political and ethical agendas aimed at social change. In Edward Said's *Out of Place*, Jamaica Kincaid's *Lucy*, Teju Cole's *Every Day is for the Thief*, and Aleksandar Hemon's *The Lazarus Project*, the ways text and photographs are connected vary considerably: Said follows a fairly traditional Western model of coherently narrating his life from hindsight. But while his autobiography, as so many others, includes family pictures to document life in the Middle East in the first half of the twentieth century, the relation between text and image is nonetheless full of tension. In Kincaid, ekphrasis is used as a full-fledged critical device that does cultural and political work and that functions as a transformative power, able to uncover epistemological hierarchies and to transcribe prescribed identity scripts. *Lucy*'s open ending introduces an image of blurred visual perception, inviting readers to contemplate the role of vision and writing in our culture. Finally, in Hemon's and Cole's autofictions, the photographs fragment the text and disrupt the flow of the narrative as well as the teleological linearity and continuity encountered in more traditional autobiographical modes. Both immigrant writers express the experience of migration via an intermedial aesthetic, thus "turning loss and rupture into a creative act" (Weiner 2014: 229). Because the connection between words and photos often remains unclear, they also impair indulgence into the traditionally naïve function of illustration: often the reader cannot see in the photograph what the text describes and is thus implicitly asked to participate in meaning-making processes. Said's, Kincaid's, Cole's, and Hemon's interest in intermedial experiments helps to problematize conceptions of the self, established autobiographical modes, and representation *per se*. They thus demonstrate the broad thematic, formal, and aesthetic range of contemporary life writing with its transcultural protagonists and settings.

Works Cited

Adams, Timothy Dow. 2000. *Light Writing and Life Writing: Photography in Autobiography*. Chapel Hill: The University of North Carolina Press.
Anderson, Linda. 2001. *Autobiography*. London: Routledge.
Baena, Rosalia (ed.). 2007. *Transculturing Auto/Biography: Forms of Life Writing*. London: Routledge.
Balestrini, Nassim Winnie. 2013. "Photography as Online Life Writing: Miranda July's and Harrell Fletcher's *Learning to Love You More* (2002–2009)". In: Alfred Hornung (ed.). *American Lives*. Heidelberg: Winter. 341–353.
Balestrini, Nassim Winnie. 2015. "Life Writing in the Internet Age: Miranda July and the Limits of Art as Social Practice". *Arbeiten aus Anglistik und Amerikanistik* 40 (1–2): 127–150.
Beckman, Karen and Liliane Weissberg (eds.). 2013. *On Writing with Photography*. Minneapolis: University of Minnesota Press.
Behluli, Sofie and Gabriele Rippl. 2017. "Ekphrasis in the Digital Age". In: Christina Hoffmann and Johanna Öttl (eds.). *Antikanon*. Vol. 2: *Digitalität und literarische Netz-Werke*. 131–176.
Cole, Teju. 2016. "A Conversation with Aleksandar Hemon". *Known and Strange Things: Essays*. New York: Random House. 78–92.

Cole, Teju. 2014 [2007]. *Every Day Is for the Thief*. London: Faber and Faber.
Cole, Teju. 2011. *Open City*. New York: Random House.
Dalziell, Rosamund (ed.). 2002. *Selves Crossing Cultures: Autobiography and Globalisation*. Kew, Vic.: Australian Scholarly Publishing.
Döring, Tobias. 2006. "Edward Said and the Fiction of Autobiography". *Wasafiri: The Transnational Journal of International Writing* 21 (2): 71–78.
Dünne, Jörg and Christian Moser (eds.). 2008. *Automedialität. Subjektkonstitution in Schrift, Bild und neuen Medien*. München: Fink.
Eakin, Paul John. 1985. *Fictions of Autobiography: Studies in the Art of Self-Invention*. Princeton: Princeton University Press.
Emery, Mary Lou. 1997. "Refiguring the Postcolonial Imagination: Tropes of Visuality in Writing by Rhys, Kincaid, and Cliff". *Tulsa Studies in Women's Literature* 16 (2): 259–280.
Emery, Mary Lou. 2007. *Modernism, the Visual, and Caribbean Literature*. Cambridge: Cambridge University Press.
Fjellestad, Danuta. 2015. "Nesting – Braiding – Weaving: Photographic Interventions in Three Contemporary American Novels". In: Gabriele Rippl (ed.). *Handbook of Intermediality*. Berlin: De Gruyter. 193–218.
Gilmore, Leigh. 2001. *The Limits of Autobiography: Trauma and Testimony*. Ithaca, NY: Cornell University Press.
Gilmore, Leigh. 1998. "Endless Autobiography? Jamaica Kincaid and Serial Autobiography". In: Alfred Hornung and Ernstpeter Ruhe (eds.). *Postcolonialism and Autobiography: Michelle Cliff, David Dabydeen, Opal Palmer Adisa*. Amsterdam: Rodopi. 211–231.
Greedharry, Mrinalini. 2008. *Postcolonial Theory and Psychoanalysis*. Basingstoke: Palgrave.
Hayes, Patrick. 2015. "Human 2.0? Life-Writing in the Digital Age". In: Leander Zachary (ed.). *On Life-Writing*. Oxford: Oxford University Press. 233–256.
Heffernan, James A. W. 1993. *The Museum of Words: The Poetics of Ekphrasis from Homer to Ashbery*. Chicago, IL: The University of Chicago Press.
Hemon, Aleksandar. 2008. *The Lazarus Project*. London: Picador.
Hornung, Alfred. 2009. "Transcultural Life-Writing". In: Coral Ann Howells (ed.). *The Cambridge History of Canadian Literature*. Cambridge: Cambridge University Press. 536–555.
Hornung, Alfred and Ernstpeter Ruhe (eds.). 1998. *Postcolonialism and Autobiography: Michelle Cliff, David Dabydeen, Opal Palmer Adisa*. Amsterdam: Rodopi.
Huddart, David. 2008. *Postcolonial Theory and Autobiography*. London: Routledge.
Jay, Paul. 2010. *Global Matters: The Transnational Turn in Literary Studies*. Ithaca, NY: Cornell University Press.
Kadar, Marlene. 1992. "Coming to Terms: Life Writing – From Genre to Critical Practice". In: Marlene Kadar (ed.). *Essays on Life Writing: From Genre to Critical Practice*. Toronto: University of Toronto Press. 3–16.
Kennedy, David. 2012. *The Ekphrastic Encounter in Contemporary British Poetry and Elsewhere*. Farnham: Ashgate.
Kennedy, David. 2015. "Ekphrasis and Poetry". In: Gabriele Rippl (ed.). *Handbook of Intermediality*. Berlin: De Gruyter. 82–91.
Kincaid, Jamaica. 1994 [1990]. *Lucy*. London: Picador.

Lewis-Kraus, Gideon. 2014. "Dragooned into Solidarity". *The New York Review of Books* LXI (12): 61–62.
Loizeaux, Elizabeth Bergman. 2008. *Twentieth-Century Poetry and the Visual Arts*. Cambridge: Cambridge University Press.
Louvel, Liliane. 2008. "Photography as Critical Idiom and Intermedial Criticism". *Poetics Today* 29 (1): 31–48.
Mitchell, W.J.T. 1992. "Ekphrasis and the Other". *South Atlantic Quarterly* 91 (3): 695–719.
Mitchell, W.J.T. 1994. *Picture Theory: Essays on Verbal and Visual Representation*. Chicago, IL: University of Chicago Press.
Moore-Gilbert, Bart. 2009. *Postcolonial Life-Writing: Culture, Politics and Self-Representation*. New York: Routledge.
Moser, Christian. 2018 (forthcoming). "Autoethnography". In: Martina Wagner-Egelhaaf (ed.). *Handbook of Autobiography/Autofiction*. 3 vols. Berlin: De Gruyter.
Neumann, Birgit. 2014. "Verbal-Visual Configurations in Teju Cole's *Every Day Is for the Thief* – Practices of Translation and Moments of Re-vision". *Literatur in Wissenschaft und Unterricht* 47: 317–334.
Perkins, Maureen, et al. 2007. "Mixed Race, Hybrid, Transnational: Writing Lives in National and Global Frames". *Life Writing* 4 (1): 1–151.
Rajewsky, Irina O. 2002. *Intermedialität*. Tübingen: Francke.
Rajewsky, Irina O. 2005. "Intermediality, Intertextuality, and Remediation: A Literary Perspective on Intermediality". *Intermédialités* 6: 43–64.
Rippl, Gabriele. 2018 (forthcoming). "Autobiography in the Globalized World". In: Martina Wagner-Egelhaaf (ed.). *Autobiography/Autofiction. An International and Interdisciplinary Handbook*. 3 vols. Berlin: De Gruyter.
Rippl, Gabriele, et al. (eds.). 2013. *Haunted Narratives: Life-Writing in an Age of Trauma*. Toronto: Toronto University Press.
Rippl, Gabriele. 2005. *Beschreibungskunst. Zur intermedialen Poetik angloamerikanischer Ikontexte (1880–2000)*. Munich: Fink.
Rugg, Linda Haverty. 1997. *Picturing Ourselves. Photography and Autobiography*. Chicago, IL: University of Chicago Press.
Sarkowsky, Katja. 2012. "Transcultural Autobiography and the Staging of (Mis)Recognition: Edward Said's Out of Place and Gerald Vizenor's Interior Landscapes: Autobiographical Myths and Metaphors". *Amerikastudien/American Studies* 57 (4): 627–642.
Saunders, Max. 2010. *Self Impression: Life-Writing, Autobiografiction, and the Forms of Modern Literature*. Oxford: Oxford University Press.
Schröter, Jens. 2013. "Photography and Fictionality". *Mediascape*. <http://tft.ucla.edu/mediascape/Winter2013_Photography> [accessed 7 January 2017].
Sedlmeier, Florian. 2015. *Rereading Form: Paratexts, Transpositions, and the Postethnic Literary*. Berlin: De Gruyter.
Smith, Sidonie and Julia Watson (eds.). 1992. *De/Colonizing the Subject: The Politics of Gender in Women's Autobiography*. Minneapolis: University of Minnesota Press.
Smith, Sidonie and Julia Watson (eds.). 1996. *Getting a Life: Everyday Uses of Autobiography*. Minneapolis: University of Minnesota Press.
Smith, Sidonie and Julia Watson. 1998. "Introduction". In: Sidonie Smith and Julia Watson (eds.). *Women, Autobiography, Theory: A Reader*. Madison: University of Wisconsin Press. 3–52.

Smith, Sidonie and Julia Watson. 2001. *Reading Autobiography: A Guide for Interpreting Life Narratives*. Minneapolis: University of Minnesota Press.
Spurr, David. 1993. *The Rhetoric of Empire: Colonial Discourse in Journalism, Travel Writing, and Imperial Administration*. Durham, NC: Duke University Press.
Stein, Thomas Michael. 1998. "Fictional Autobiography in the Caribbean: George Lamming's In the Castle of My Skin and Wilson Harris's The Infinite Rehearsal". In: Alfred Hornung and Ernstpeter Ruhe (eds.). *Postcolonialism and Autobiography: Michelle Cliff, David Dabydeen, Opal Palmer Adisa*. Amsterdam: Rodopi. 247–257.
Temple, Bogusia. 2001. "Migration, Diaspora, and Life Writing". In: Margaretta Jolly (ed.). *Encyclopedia of Life Writing: Autobiographical and Biographical Forms*. 2 vols. London: Fitzroy Dearborn. vol. 2: 601–602.
Webb, Ruth. 2009. *Ekphrasis, Imagination and Persuasion in Ancient Rhetorical Theory and Practice*. Farnham: Ashgate.
Weiner, Sonia. 2014. "Double Vision and Aesthetics of the Migratory in Aleksandar Hemon's The Lazarus Project". *Studies in the Novel* 46 (2): 215–235.
Welsch, Wolfgang. 1999. "Transculturality: The Puzzling Form of Cultures Today". In: Mike Featherstone and Scott Lash (eds.). *Spaces of Culture: City, Nation, World*. London: Sage. 194–213.
Wolf, Werner. 2005. "Intermediality". In: David Herman, Manfred Jahn, and Marie-Laure Ryan (eds.). *Routledge Encyclopedia of Narrative Theory*. London: Routledge. 252–256.
Yacobi, Tamar. 1995. "Pictorial Models and Narrative Ekphrasis". *Poetics Today* 16: 599–649.
Yacobi, Tamar. 1997. "Verbal Frames and Ekphrastic Figuration". In: Ulla-Britta Lagerroth, Hans Lund, and Erik Hedling (eds.). *Interart Poetics: Essays on the Interrelations of the Arts and Media*. Amsterdam: Rodopi. 35–46.
Zipfel, Frank. 2009. "Autofiktion. Zwischen den Grenzen von Faktualität, Fiktionalität und Literarität". In: Simone Winko, Fotis Jannidis, and Gerhard Lauer (eds.). *Grenzen der Literatur. Zu Begriff und Phänomen des Literarischen*. Berlin: De Gruyter. 285–314.
Zuckerman, Jeffrey. "Teju Cole's Every Day Is for the Thief". *Music and Literature*, 1 April 2014. <http://www.musicandliterature.org/reviews/2014/3/31/teju-coles-every-day-is-for-the-thief> [accessed 7 July 2016].

Danuta Fjellestad
"A Figment of Someone Else's Imagination": Intermedial Games in Paul Auster's *Report from the Interior*

Abstract

Some two decades ago Linda Haverty Rugg captured the intense critical interest in the function of photographs in self-writing in the question: "What (or how) do photographs mean in the context of an autobiography?" (1997: 1). In her discussion of the transformation of self-writing under the pressures of the medium of photography, Rugg, like other critics, assumes that the pictures are those of the writing subject and/or are related to his or her life. In his *Report from the Interior* (2013), Paul Auster systematically thwarts this assumption: his assemblage of over one hundred images in the book's fourth section, entitled "Album," does not include a single picture of himself or of his family. By provocatively substituting private images with public ones, Auster mischievously breaks what can be called the 'autophotographic pact' in self-writing. Above all, the images reference a broad variety of media (print, photography, film, TV, painting, book illustrations, etc.), creating a complex web of intermedial relations. Auster's pairing of his well-known narrative experimentation with his innovative use of images broadens Rugg's question to 'What (or how) do media mean in the context of an autobiography?'

1 'Troubling' Autobiographic Writing

Asked to define himself in seven words, Paul Auster (2012b) came up with the following list: American, New Yorker, wanderer, husband, father, writer, and troublemaker. To be a troublemaker, not to follow artistic conventions, Auster continued, was essential to his identity as a writer. Indeed, throughout his career Auster has 'troubled' fiction writing by bending, blending, and even breaking narrative conventions. Numerous critics have analyzed Auster's novels for their delightful, if at times bewildering, violation of ontological boundaries, their haunting intertextuality, metacommentary, self-referentiality, lack of closure, fragmentation, and exploration of identity and subjectivity – that is, for the narrative strategies that have put him on the Parnassus of postmodern writers (cf. Nealon 1996; Rubenstein 1998; Sorapure 2002; Martin 2008; Espejo 2014).

In a similar fashion, from the start of his career, Auster has experimented with the genre of autobiography in a broad sense. In his debut text, *The Invention of Solitude* (1982), Auster pairs two tales: in the first part, "Portrait of an Invisible Man," he pieces together a picture of his elusive father; in the second, "The Book of Memory," he chronicles his years of poverty and artistic struggle. While the first part is written in the first person, the second shifts to a third-person perspective of the narrator called A. Thirty years later, in *Winter Journal* (2012), Auster offers a collection of memories and musings about his body, its strengths and ailments, its appetites and failures. Here Auster employs a narrative mode of the second-person rather than the conventional first-person account. In *Report from the Interior* (2013), commonly regarded as a companion volume to *Winter Journal*, Auster shifts his attention from his physical body to his psychological development from childhood to early adulthood. Continuing the use of the second-person perspective, he 'troubles' the genre of autobiographical writing in yet another way, this time with unconventional word–image interactions.

It is Auster's visual-textual games that this essay attempts to unravel. In his innovative autobiographical project Auster weaves together a rich web of visual, acoustic, audiovisual, and mixed media to suggest that media configure not only perceptions of the external world but of one's interiority. Altogether, the volume can be read as an exploration of an always already intermedial nature of (auto-biographic) subjectivity.

As the introduction to this volume makes clear, the concepts of autobiography and intermediality have been subjects of intense deliberations. Previously marginalized (Gilmore 1994: 4), autobiographical practices have become central to critical thought in the wake of the (postmodern, poststructuralist) debates about the concepts of the self and of subjectivity. A plethora of new terms emerged to account for diverse practices of self-representation to encompass not only traditional autobiography, memoir, diary, or confession but also testimony, interviews, profiles, personal literary criticism, blogs, and web pages (cf. Adams 2000; Eakin 2004). Tags such as ego-literature, self-narration, self-writing, life writing, and auto/bio/graphics have been coined to capture the diversity of writing in the first person. And since one of the central challenges is the blurry boundary between what purports to be factual narrative and its cousin, fiction, terms such as pseudo-autobiography, auto-fiction, or auto-mytho-biography have been added to indicate the inevitable ingredient of self-fashioning even in most classical and traditional Western forms of autobiography. Today, then, staple texts such as *The Confessions of St. Augustine* (397–398) or *The Au-*

tobiography of Benjamin Franklin (1771–1790) find themselves in the company of Eve Kosofsky Sedgwick's *Dialogue on Love* (1999) or Linda Barry's *One Hundred Demons* (2002). But while any certainty about the genre seems to have been shredded by scholarly investigations and the time when autobiography and memoir were believed to be able to tell the truth about the extralinguistic subject in a (more or less) coherent way is long gone, the sheer evocation of the genre continues to activate some vestiges of an expectation of "referential aesthetic" (Eakin 1992) or of what Philippe Lejeune (1975) has called the "autobiographical pact." For the general reader, at least, an autobiography promises a disclosure of some (more or less) truthful details about the subject's life. Auster's *Report from the Interior*, like *Winter Journal*, "a book of autobiographical fragments" (a category suggested by Auster himself in an interview with Paul Holdengräber; 2012b), is an eccentric bedfellow of both traditional and experimental self-writing.[1]

Like autobiography, intermediality is a fraught area of investigation, the terminological proliferation a testament to both the vibrancy and turbulence of the field. My reading of *Report from the Interior* is informed by Irina O. Rajewsky's (2005) and Werner Wolf's (2011) conceptions of intermediality, since they are based in literary studies and are 'literature-friendly' (perhaps even 'literature-centric'). Particularly useful to my argument is Rajewsky's distinction between three subcategories of intermediality: medial transposition, media combination, and intermedial references (2005: 51–53). All three types of intermediality are pervasively present in Auster's text. Throughout *Report from the Interior* the reader encounters numerous mentions of film, photography, painting, sound, etc. Medial transposition organizes part two, "Two Blows to the Head," in which two American movies are transformed into verbal discourse through scene-by-scene summaries of the films' action as well as descriptions of camera work and accompanying music and sound. Finally, as verbal discourse is combined with a set of materially present images, this "overt" type of intermediality supplements the "covert" one, to use Wolf's terminology (1999: 37–44).[2]

---

[1] Taking a cue from Auster himself, I will be using the term autobiography (and at times memoir) when referring to Auster's *Invitation to Solitude*, *Winter Journal*, and *Report from the Interior*.
[2] It could be argued that, appealing to the eye, written language is primarily a visual medium. Yet as "a conventionally and culturally distinct means of communication" (Wolf 2011: 2), written language is regarded as a verbal mode, its organization different from that of the visual mode.

2 Photography–Autobiography Liaisons

The mere fact that Auster's "book of autobiographical fragments" includes 107 black-and-white photographs is in itself not particularly remarkable; after all there seems to be a "natural affinity" (Hughes and Noble 2003: 4) between life writing and the photographic image, an affinity predicated on the (conventionally assumed) indexicality of both.[3] As a manifestation of "that-has-been" of which Roland Barthes wrote so persuasively in *Camera Lucida* (1981), the photograph both aides and shapes personal and collective memory; it intersects in complex ways with the verbal self-fashioning of the autobiographical subject (cf. Hirsch 1997; Rugg 1997; Adams 2000). While there are of course many memoirs, autobiographies, or biographies that do not feature a single photographic image (cf. George Steiner's *Errata: An Examined Life* [1997]), it is *de rigueur* to deploy at least one photo-image of the author, often in a paratextual position (cf. Frank Lentricchia's photo on the flap end of the dust cover of *The Edge of Night* [1994]). Nor is it uncommon to encounter an insert with several photo-images, as is the case in Edward W. Said's memoir *Out of Place* (1999): halfway through the book the reader comes across sixteen pages filled with captioned photographs of Said himself as well as of his family members.[4] More rare are the cases of photographs interspersed throughout the narrative; one example of this type of placement of photographs is Nancy K. Miller's chronicle of the personal and the cultural in *But Enough about Me* (2002).

Auster too has included photographs in his autobiographical writing, but they have played a generative rather than illustrative role. In his first published text, *The Invention of Solitude* (1982), pictures figure as points of departure for his

---

[3] The foundational belief in the indexical character of autobiography and photography is highly contestable; both are "obviously artificial representations of lives," as Adams (2000: 5) points out. The tension between photographic images' mimetic and artful aspects has been registered by, for instance, Sontag (1977: 5–7), who writes at length about photographs, on the one hand, as passing for "incontrovertible proof that a given thing happened" and, on the other hand, as being "as much an interpretation of the world as paintings and drawings are." See Rugg (1997) and Adams (2000) as well as collections of essays edited by Hughes and Noble (2003) and Edwards, Hubbell, and Miller (2011) for particularly insightful discussions of liaisons between photography and life writing.

[4] Apart from the photo insert, the dust jacket of Said's memoir displays a well-known studio photograph of the mature critic on the back flap, a front-face photograph of him as a young boy, a back-face photo of a group of relatives at the family store, and a series of seven photographs of the author from various stages of his life on the spine of the book.

narrative (re)construction of family history.⁵ Having found hundreds of photographs stashed in envelopes and drawers in his late father's house, the narrator is spellbound:

> Back home, I pored over these pictures with a fascination bordering on mania. I found them irresistible, precious, the equivalent of holy relics. It seemed that they could tell me things I had never known before, reveal some precious hidden truth, and I studied each one intensely, absorbing the least detail, the most insignificant shadow, until all the images had become a part of me. I wanted nothing to be lost. (Auster 1982: 14)

Two of the photographs subjected to particularly close scrutiny turn out to be manipulated. One of them, apparently portraying five men sitting around a table "as if they have gathered there to conduct a seance" (31), is in fact an image of one and the same person – Auster's father – shot from five different angles. The other photograph shows the narrator's grandmother with her five children when Auster's father was about one year old. Studying closely the tear in the middle of the portrait, the narrator realizes that what at first appeared to be an accidentally torn and clumsily mended photograph is a family portrait from which the figure of his grandfather was purposefully cut out. An inquiry that follows reveals this expunged character to be a cipher of sorts of a family tragedy: the grandfather was shot and killed by Auster's grandmother in 1919. Acquitted of the murder, neither the grandmother nor any of her children ever spoke about this family secret. Both photographs are reproduced in *The Invention of Solitude*, albeit in paratextual spaces: the front cover features the trick photograph of his father, the frontispiece the doctored group portrait with the grandmother holding Auster's father as a baby in her lap, her four older children surrounding her, her husband scissored out.⁶ The presence of fabricated pictures simultaneously dismantles the idea of easily decipherable photographic documentation and sustains the 'autophotographic pact' that the photographic images included in a piece of life writing are personal and relevant to the author's unique life story.⁷

---

5 The first Penguin edition (1982), as far as I know, is the only one to feature the subtitle 'A Memoir' on the cover.
6 This placement of the two photographs, established by the first Sun and Moon edition of 1982, has been followed by most, but not all, subsequent publications. For instance, the trick photograph of Auster's father does not appear on the cover of the 2007 Penguin edition of *The Invention of Solitude*; instead, both pictures are inserted in close proximity to where they are discussed in the narrative.
7 For an analysis of photographs in *The Invention of Solitude* see, for instance, Barrett 2009.

In *Report from the Interior*, however, none of the 107 images is a private photograph; neither Auster himself nor any of his relatives figure in the pictures. Instead, the reader-turned-viewer can see numerous stills from a variety of films; photographs of actors, sportsmen, and writers; war photographs; reproductions of book illustrations and paintings; images of everyday things such as a can of Calumet baking powder or a radio; images of posters; pictures of buildings and street life, etc. The public character of these images is confirmed by the "Photo Credits" section: most of them come from the archives of agencies such as Everett, CORBIS, NASA, or the Library of Congress, or are acknowledged to have been taken by specific photographers such as Rolf Nussbaumer or Ron Saari.

What is the function of these non-personal images in a text whose title promises to focus on the interiority of the writing subject? How do the images intersect with the narrative? Why assemble them on sixty-four unnumbered pages in a separate section and call it "Album"? Does the assemblage of the pictures tell its own story? And if so, what kind of story is it? In addressing these and similar questions, I am primarily interested in the "overt" (Wolf 2011) type of intermediality; my focus is on the interactions between the first, titular part of the book and the images in part four that are linked to it.[8] Identifying a few clusters of thematic concerns in what appears to be but a random assembly of memories, I analyze Auster's ingenious – even sly – pairing of the verbal with the visual in his exploration of the voices and images that have configured his self.

3 Assembling Vestiges of Memory

The assemblage of photographs in the Album section is preceded by three narrative parts in which Auster gathers the memories of his early childhood, adolescence, and student days. But although the reader encounters the first picture only after having read some 270 pages, he/she "step[s] into the visual" (Pedri 2008: 169) right from the beginning, with the young Auster 'seeing' the objects that surround him: scissors, teapots, telephones, pens, coins, trees, and stones, all of which appear magical to him. Visual experiences are recorded in all their

---

[8] I would like to acknowledge the importance of intermedial references to sounds and music woven into the fabric of the verbal and visual narratives. The soundscapes which formed the young Auster are brought forth by several images: for instance, there is a drawing of the cat and the fiddle from *Mother Goose*; a picture of a Philco radio; photographs of Buddy Holly and the Everly Brothers singing and playing their guitars; images of microphones, a telephone, and supersonic jets. Such 'sonic visuality' deserves careful analysis of its own.

immediacy and enthrallment; they stir wonder as well as confusion and puzzlement. Yet this visual intimacy with mundane objects gradually recedes with the narrator turning his gaze onto himself, anxious about how he is perceived by others.

In the second part the narrator walks the reader through two movies, *The Incredible Shrinking Man* (1957, dir. Jack Arnold) and *I Am a Fugitive from a Chain Gang* (1932, dir. Mervyn LeRoy), which he saw at the age of ten and fourteen respectively. Having experienced a "cinematic earthquake" (135), the narrator saturates his rendition of what he sees with minute details, fully aware of how his vision is framed by camera work:

> A close shot of the face as it crumples up and disintegrates, as tears begin to gather in his eyes. His mouth twitches. His body shakes. He lowers himself onto the bed with clenched fists, no longer seeing anything, no longer a part of this world. Jabs his fists into the air. Feeble, spasmodic jabs – aimed at nothing, hitting nothing. The scene goes black. (171)

Here the narrator voices his recognition of the mediated character of the visual: filmic techniques manipulate and control both what is seen and how it is to be perceived.

The third part of the book, "Time Capsule," is the least 'visual' one. Consisting of annotated passages from Auster's letters to his college sweetheart and first wife, Lydia Davis, its focus is mostly on language. The narrator dwells at length on his writing of letters, poems, novels, and film scripts, on translating poems and plays, and on extensive reading of literary and critical texts, both his own (of the letters themselves, of his first poems and novels) and those by others (such as his girlfriend, poets, novelists, journalists, critics).

That the visual world of the young narrator gives way to a more word-oriented one as he grows up is underscored by the number of images relating to each section. Sixty-seven photographs can be linked to the first part of the book; twenty-six (mostly) film stills relate to part two; only fourteen photographic images are connected to part three. Of the fourteen, nine present half-desolate urban spaces and five depict scenes of violent confrontations between police and civilians. Gone is the bewitching variety of vivacious images; here the pictures emanate an eerie atmosphere of forlornness, reverberating with the narrator's increasing sense of solitude and his inward turn as he struggles to launch his writing career.

Sentences and phrases from the three narrative parts function as captions to the images in the "Album." The images are numbered, but since the captions are not accompanied by page references, it is not easy to identify the specific narrative contexts in which the phrases have first appeared. (The narrative itself does not signal the presence of reproductions of pictures at all.) The considerable physical and – from the perspective of the reading experience – temporal distance between the narratively embedded phrases and their repetition in captions creates an unnerving *echolalia:* the reader is compelled to shuttle back and forth between the image, the caption, and the caption's original location. There seems to be no logic governing the selection of narrative detail to be echoed in an image, no clear principle of correlating sentences and phrases with images. The arrangement of the series of photographic reproductions does not always parallel the order of Auster's reminiscences. Moreover, the yoking together of images and narrative snippets seems to be quite capricious: sometimes two consecutive sentences or even phrases are dignified with images, sometimes two, three, or even four images are chained to one phrase, sometimes one and the same image is referenced several times in the narrative, and sometimes the narrative goes on for several pages without being graced with a single image. Thus, although the captions create bridges between the narrative and the images and although they bring the public images into the realm of Auster's personal universe, this bridging of the individual and the public seems – for the most part – to be arbitrary, random, whimsical, tenuous, and quite feeble.

It could be argued, of course, that the seemingly haphazard and erratic selection of phrases and images as well as the often arbitrary coupling of the verbal and the visual is emblematic of the working of memory as Auster defines it. In the opening pages Auster writes that all he remembers are "remnants," "vestiges," and "shards" of his earliest thoughts: "You can remember only some of it, isolated bits and pieces, brief flashes of recognition that surge up unexpectedly at random moments – brought on by the smell of something, or the touch of something, or the way the light falls on something in the here and now of adulthood" (4). This fragmentary nature of memory is underscored by the narrative strategy of offering lists; as in *Winter Journal*, Auster offers long inventories of events, annotated with self-reflexive comments like the one that sums up a catalogue of about thirty items: "Random, unrelated events, connected only by the fact that they all occurred in the year of your birth, 1947" (64). Randomness, Auster insists again and again, is the name of the game in his *Report from the Interior*. However, Auster's visual "charting of the workings of [his] young mind" (45) does reveal some patterns and thematic preoccupations. Most of the images that can be arranged into clusters are impregnated with violence, fear, and disappointment; hardly any of the pictures function as a straightforward 'illustration' that merely reiterates what is said.[9] In the course of the book, he proceeds to cre-

---

[9] The concept of 'illustration' is far from clear; its relation to the written text is sometimes seen

ate recurrent motifs and to devise multiple ways through which he 'troubles' the link between reading and viewing.

4 Marvels and Anguish

For Auster, ontological distinctions between real and fictional objects and creatures (including human beings) become erased by the magic of pictures; all images, irrespective of their provenance, actively configure his sense of his being in the world. The opening line, infused with a biblical idiom, reads: "In the beginning, everything was alive" (3). Auster then mentions a number of everyday inanimate objects which, to his young self, appear to be endowed with *élan vital* and human characteristics; for instance, "scissors could walk," "the face of the clock was a human face," "the grill on the front of [the] car was a grinning mouth with many teeth," "the branches of trees were arms" (3). The narrator employs anthropomorphism to render a sense of magic and wonder. Magical and wondrous, too, appears to be the first image in the Album section. It is a still from *A Trip to the Moon*, a 1902 French black-and-white silent film directed by Georges Méliès. One of the most iconic and frequently referenced images in the history of cinema, it presents the moment of the capsule landing on the moon. The text accompanying it reads: "There was no problem in believing that the man in the moon was an actual man" (3). This movie, we may recall, is loosely based on a number of literary sources, of which Jules Verne's *From Earth to the Moon* (1865) and, in all likelihood, H. G. Wells's *The First Men in the Moon* (1901) are the most important. Méliès's movie tells the story of a group of astronomers who journey to the moon in a rocket-like capsule propelled by a cannon shot. The rocket lands straight in the eyeball of the anthropomorphically presented moon, causing convulsions of pain to contort its face and blood to ooze out of the pierced eye. The pastoral world of wonders and magic that the narrative creates is thus simultaneously confirmed and undercut by the opening image: while this image offers a paean to human technological ingenuity in its doubling of the construction of a space rocket with the invention of the cinema, the film still surreptitiously signals one of the main themes in Auster's memoir, that of violence and suffering.

---

as decorative, sometimes as explanatory or even interpretive. For a review of the existing scholarship on the subject see Marsh and White (2003). My use of single inverted commas is meant to indicate how problematic the term is.

The spasms of agony displayed on the moon's humanoid face resonate with images of anguish in a vast majority of other pictures: of soldiers afflicted with frostbite, of children in danger of contracting polio, of the biblical Isaac about to be sacrificed by his father, of prisoners beaten by guards, of African Americans hurt in race riots, and of students clubbed by police. The science-fictional rocket that hurts the moon is echoed in the pictures of rifles, knives, clubs, tanks, military jets, and the nuclear mushroom cloud. This assembly of images may be seen as a testimonial to the "jolt" that Auster experienced upon seeing the movie *The War of the Worlds* (1953) when he was just six years old: the lesson he learned, he writes, was that "[i]n the face of evil, God was as helpless as the most helpless man" (16). Suffering, the images suggest, is overwhelmingly and inexplicably present in the lives of individuals and societies across time and space.

Figure 1: A series of four images (5, 6, 7, and 8) taken from animated films for children. Source: Auster 2013: n. pag. Images from *Oceantics* (Pat Sullivan Cartoon), *The Window Washers* (Paul Terry Cartoon), and *Felix in Hollywood* (Pat Sullivan) are in the public domain.

That cruelty and misery lurk behind magic is slyly implied by a series of four images taken from animated films for children (figure 1). The images are linked by the line that declares the young child's sentiment that the cartoon characters "are real, that these raggedly drawn black-and-white figures are no less alive than you are" (7). The top image features a silhouette of a black cat in an upright position, pacing, a frown on its face, as if it were lost in angry thoughts. The second image shows three mice on a table, pumping water from a bottle onto the face of a seated farmer who, shocked, is leaning back to avoid the mischief; in the third, the same farmer chases a cat. The final image shows a black cat guffawing, the interjection "HA HA" reinforcing the sense of its amusement (or perhaps derision). The sequential arrangement of the four images invites the reader/viewer to construct a story line: the cat schemes to harass the farmer and manages to make the mice carry out its plans; the farmer realizes that the cat is behind the mice's mischief, so he chases the cat to punish it but fails in his pursuit of the villain who rejoices in the success of the prank.[10] By spinning such a story, the reader/viewer is encouraged to do exactly what Auster's narrative resolutely refuses to provide: to create cohesion and causality. Such narrative cohesion, however, turns out to come at the cost of disregarding the fact that the four cartoon images come from three different movies: the first from *Oceantics* (1930, produced by Pat Sullivan), the second and third from *The Window Washers* (1925, produced by Paul Terry), and the fourth from *Felix in Hollywood* (1923, produced by Pat Sullivan). The images reference different cartoons, different narratives, and different characters: whereas Felix the Cat is a Sullivan character, the cat in Terry's cartoons is named Henry the Cat.[11] The farmer in Terry's cartoons is called Al Falfa (or Alfalfa) and referred to as 'Farmer Gray' by Fred Sayles, the host of a 1950s TV program for children. For the young narrator, such distinctions are immaterial; he believes that all of these characters live in an alternate universe, the magic of which stems from the violation of ontological boundaries: not only can a cat behave like a human being, but it can even look like one (as indicated by the strikingly similar faces of the farmer and the cat he is chasing). The arrangement of the cartoon figures draws the reader/viewer into this world

---

10 Kibédi Varga notes that we are inclined to interpret series of images "whether they are accompanied by words or not [...] as exclusively narrative, because they require us to spend time on them and to follow them" (1989: 36). He reiterates the point by claiming that "[e]ven if nothing seems in reality to link the elements to which the successive images refer, we are tempted to accept the 'post hoc ergo propter hoc' fallacy and establish between them a chronological, hence a narrative, order." Such narrativization of images is central to comics; see McCloud who notes "[a]lchemy at work in the space between panels which can help us find meaning or resonance in even the most jarring of combinations" (1993: 73).

11 The creation of the Felix the Cat figure is often attributed to Pat Sullivan, but in fact it was Otto Messmer who conceived the figure; see Crafton 1982 (esp. 301–346) and Canemaker 1991. In creating Henry the Cat, Crafton remarks, Terry "tried to sap some of Felix's popularity," but the character "never achieved stardom" (1982: 290).

of cross-species metamorphosis. By extension, all the images in the Album section undergo a similar transformation: whether they are fictional pictures (like the ones from film cartoons or the Bible illustrations) or photographs of real people (such as the baseball player Hank Greenberg or the actress Hedy Lamarr), they share the same universe in Auster's book, both expressing and actively shaping the narrator's sense of the world and himself. They are, it could be argued, an integral part of him.

While the caption to the sequence of the four cartoon pictures emphasizes a child's magical world view, the incident that Auster recalls is actually one of a brutal rupture of the belief in a "land of marvels" (7). An avid watcher of a television program called *Junior Frolics*, hosted by 'Uncle Fred' (Fred Sayles), the then five-year-old Auster is taken by his mother to the studio in Newark from where the program is broadcast. No Farmer Gray or Felix the Cat meet the boy; instead, the characters can be seen on the screen of a small television set in a small studio room. Profoundly disappointed, the young Auster feels that "a nasty trick has been played on [him]" (9). Viewed in the context of recalling this bitter childhood experience, the image of the laughing cat acquires a much darker tone: the cat appears to be laughing at the boy's naiveté.

5 Family Matters

As in the studio incident, the images in the Album section are predominantly linked to the narrative moments of bitterness, disappointment, fear, and a sense of failure; no pictures are connected to the (relatively rare) moments of joy and happiness. This is especially extraordinary in the case of pictures that depict family relations, in particular those between fathers and sons. Take the story of Auster, age six, attempting to chop down a little fruit tree with an ancient ax that he has found in the family garage. The ax being far too heavy for the boy, he has to give up his plan, the tree's bark barely pierced in a few places. The boy's physical failure is juxtaposed with the success of young George Washington at felling a cherry tree, the story of which is "the essential American myth" (55) to American readers. But the contrast between the success of one boy in cutting down the tree and the failure of another to do so does not end there: unlike George Washington, who confesses his misdeed to his father, Paul never lets his parents know what he has done. In this, he feels that he has failed to measure up to Washington's honesty and his "commendable virtue and moral strength" (56). This event is echoed in the reproduction of an engraving by John C. McRae (after a painting by George Gorgas White) titled *Father, I Can Not Tell a Lie: I Cut the Tree* (1867: Auster 2013: image 35). In the picture, we see an adult male figure gingerly holding a boy's right hand, his other arm gently touching the boy's shoulder. Benevolently looking down at the boy, the man appears to be protecting and comforting him. The aura of gentility and love is enhanced by the pastoral setting against which the two figures are depicted. The engraving provides what Auster omits in his narrative: the myth has it that after the son's confession Washington's father embraced him and declared that his son's honesty was worth more than a thousand trees. By contrast, young Paul, we can presume, fears that his father will punish rather than forgive him, and thus he never confesses his deed. The interaction between the text and the image suggests a yearning for a father's presence, for his love and forgiveness. Instead, Auster's father is cunningly aligned with the figure of the Old Testament God, "an angry and demented psychopath" (75), while the young Auster, who self-identifies as an outcast, is associated with the innocent victims of such a God's unjust acts of vengeance.

This motif of family dynamics haunted by violence and injustice reappears in a sequence of three images illustrating biblical scenes (figures 2a, 2b, and 2c). All three are brought together by the caption "... studying the principal stories of the Old Testament, most of which horrified you to the core ..." (75). The first image represents Cain's murder of Abel, the second illustrates the biblical story of Isaac tricked by his wife, Rebekah, to mistakenly bless their son Jacob instead of the first-born Esau, and the third picture shows Abraham about to sacrificially kill his son Isaac. Each of the pictures was created by a different artist who used a different medium of expression: the first image is an engraving by the English artist T. O. Barlow (1824–1889), the second a woodcut by the German artist Julius Schnorr von Carolsfeld (1794–1872), and the third an oil painting on copper by the Italian painter Jacopo da Empoli (1551–1640). By gathering images made by artists of different nationalities, working in different historical periods, and with different media, Auster universalizes the theme of latent and explicit violence in dysfunctional families. Although verbally the three images are linked to Auster's reflections on the picture of the Old Testament God, narratively they are aligned with the narrator's meditations on his "broken" family and his feeling of being "exposed to the elements, unprotected, and vulnerable" (46).

As shown, the word–image interactions in *Report from the Interior* appear to be straightforward only when glanced at casually, the way Auster himself first reads the tear in the family portrait he writes about in *The Invention of Solitude*. If the reader/viewer pores over the interactions "with a fascination bordering on mania" (Auster 1982: 14), s/he may discover puzzling games. For instance, the image of a candelabrum is accompanied by the caption "... no Sabbath meals on Friday night, no lighting of candles ..." (67).

Figures 2a/b/c: A sequence of three images (60, 61, and 62) illustrating biblical scenes. Source: Auster 2013: n.pag. The biblical image of Cain killing Abel by T. O. Barlow is reproduced with the permission of © Lebrecht Music & Arts. "Jacob Taking Blessing from Esau" (© Bettmann) and "The Sacrifice of Isaac" (© Corbis Historical) are reproduced with the permission of Getty Images.

182 — Danuta Fjellestad

The phrase is taken from a passage in which Auster muses on his lack of awareness of his ethnic heritage: regarding themselves as "Americans who happened to be Jews" (68), his parents were indifferent to Jewish rituals. Remarkably, the reader does not see a Sabbath candelabrum but a Hanukkah menorah used for the annual eight-day festival of light. The menorah's candles are all lit, in contradistinction to what the caption says. This disjunction between the words and the images, the substitution of a (verbal) Sabbath candle piece with a (visual) Hanukkah menorah, sparks off a number of possible interpretations: the image may be read as resonating with Auster's alleged ignorance of Jewish traditions, as reinforcing the point about his parents' indifference to Jewish rituals, or as Auster's pulling a trick on the readers/viewers, testing their knowledge of Jewish culture. The reader's powers of perception are repeatedly quizzed, the visual archives that Auster draws upon simultaneously evoking and eradicating images' illustrative powers, pointing to ambiguity, fissure, paradox, and deception.

6 The Politics of Contradictions

The intricate intermedial games Auster plays are particularly pronounced when the reader/viewer is faced with seemingly disparate pictures which, upon closer inspection, turn out to be brought together to make more subtle points, or when the trajectory of the narrative and the sequence of images seemingly lack alignment. For instance, thinking back to the 1952 presidential election, the first he ever experienced, the narrator makes a series of comments that serve as captions to four election-related images. He starts with the observation that "[p]olitics was a nasty sport, you now realized, a free-for-all of bitter, unending conflict [...]" (58). A few lines later the following three points occur in one sentence: "The Cold War was in full bloom then [...]"; "[...] the Red Scare had entered its most poisonous phase [...]"; "[...] the only noise from the zeitgeist loud enough for you to hear was the bass drum sounding the alarm that the Communists were out to destroy America" (59). The four images linked to these recollections are a reproduction of the "Vote Stevenson" poster; a reproduction of a newspaper heading "Truman says Russia set off atom blast" from an article published in *The Sun* on September 24, 1949; a snapshot of Joe McCarthy at one of the public hearings; and a picture of a "Crusade for Freedom" propaganda poster asking for donations of "truth dollars" to fund Radio Free Europe. However, this series of pictures related to 1950s politics is disrupted by two images placed after the "Vote Stevenson" poster. One is a reproduction of J. L. G. Ferris's painting *The First Thanksgiving 1621* (1932), the other a still from the TV series *The Lone Ranger* (1949–1957), featuring the masked Lone Ranger and Tonto with the iconic white horse, Silver. Related to a narrative segment in which the narrator recalls the childhood stories about 'Indians' and which comes after the section about the Cold War (59–63), the images do not follow the story's linear development but are embedded in the politics of the 1950s. Auster thus visually aligns the Red Scare – the fear of the rise of communism – with the fear-mongering embodied in the representation of "red men" as "ruthless killers, enemies of civilization, plundering demons who attacked white homesteaders out of pure, sadistic pleasure" (60). The arrangement of pictures suggests that this chronologically earlier fear of and hostility towards the Indians do not only resonate with the Cold War hysteria of the 1950s but that anti-Communist attitudes are also nestled within 'anti-red' prejudices.

However, the implied congruity between the two types of sinister "red men" clashes with the picture of Native Americans marketed to the child-protagonist as kind, generous, and able. Both the painting and the film still depict, after all, moments of compassionate interaction between the indigenous and white populations. This apparent comradeship between two ethnic groups stands in contrast to the verbal–visual rhetoric of discord and divisiveness within white Americans that informs the images of the 1950s politics. In the 1952 campaign poster "Vote Stevenson," antagonism and rivalry are visualized in a remarkably vivid way. With the question "Which will be safer for you?" at the top, the poster contrasts the failures of "the party of Hoover" with the successes of "the party of Roosevelt" in a diptych-like fashion, the photograph of the Democratic Party presidential hopeful Adlai Stevenson, in an oval frame, placed at the center. Three drawings, arranged vertically under the year "1932," surround one side of Stevenson's photograph; "bread lines," "homeless," and "banks closed" are the words used to sum up Hoover's legacy. To the other side of the presidential candidate three images, placed under 1952 and also vertically arranged, are captioned by "higher wages," "better homes," and "social security." Like in the case of 'redness,' the virtues and failures of political parties are arbitrarily assigned; disseminated through a variety of predominantly visual media (such as television, film, posters, and paintings), they shape the young narrator's worldview as inherently incoherent and contradictory. This lack of intrinsic logic is echoed in the assembly of pictures in the Album section, in which the reader/viewer encounters a haphazard multiplicity of others and their representations of the world.

7 Dislodging the Autobiographic 'I'/'Eye' in Word and Image

While the memories of public and private experiences are – however loosely – braided together in the three narrative parts of *Report from the Interior*, the visual material in the Album part is conspicuously void of the personal. However, the reader of the Faber and Faber edition of the book is confronted with two photographs of the author, placed paratextually on the dust jacket. In the lower right-hand corner of the front cover, we see a somewhat fuzzy image of the upper torso of a young boy, *en face*, his eyes but dark slits, due, we may surmise, to the blinding sun (figure 3). Behind the boy there is an even fuzzier image of a parked car (presumably the blue 1950 DeSoto which Auster mentions in *Winter Journal*). This blurry black-and-white snapshot (which comes from the author's private collection) stands in stark contrast to the sharply focused photographic portrait of the adult Auster (taken by the professional Danish photographer Lotte Hansen), reproduced so often that it has become an iconic public image of the writer. Placed on the back cover, the image of Auster's adult face appears to be emerging from the surrounding darkness, his eyes open and unflinchingly staring right at the viewer. The two dust jacket photographs literally enclose the narrative that evolves between the book's covers. Significantly, the clear-eyed adult is not looking at the blurry picture of his younger self; instead, both the child and the adult are looking at the readers/viewers or, to be more correct, at the photographers who are the recipients' avatars. Communicated by the medium of photography, and thus molded by camera lenses, the boy and the adult become indeed "figment[s] of someone else's imagination" (44–45). These paratextual private photographs resonate with the focalizing technique employed in *Report from the Interior*, thus emphasizing Auster's intermedial approach to representing acts of retrospective and contextual self-representation.

At the beginning of "Time Capsule" the narrator expresses his anguish at the lack of photographic documentation of his life: "no more than a few photographs exist of you from your early childhood to your mid-thirties." The dearth of visual evidence of his life strikes him as peculiar: "For a person born in the mid-twentieth century, the era of the inexpensive camera, the postwar boom days when every middle-class American family gripped by shutter-bug fever, your life is the least documented of anyone you have ever known" (177). This lack of photographs, the narrator's comment implies, bespeaks his parents' aloofness if not neglect; after all, as Susan Sontag argues, "[n]ot to take pictures of one's children, particularly when they are small, is a sign of parental indifference" (1977: 8). The narrator's brooding over a lack of photographic traces of

Figure 3: The photograph of the author on the front cover of the dust jacket of the Faber & Faber edition of the book. Source: Auster 2013. The snapshot of Paul Auster as a child is reproduced with his gracious permission.

himself reverberates with an incident in *The Invention of Solitude*: rummaging through his father's bedroom, Auster finds "a very big album, bound in expensive leather with a gold-stamped title on the cover – This is Our Life: The Austers" (1982: 14). The album is left empty; it seems that "no one had ever bothered to fill it" (14). In *Report from the Interior*, Auster assembles an album out of the visual material that is available to him: (reproductions of) book illustrations, film stills, newspaper clippings, public photographs, posters, paintings, etc., all in the public domain. Together, these images have the flavor of a scrapbook rather than a family album; they document a historical exterior in which the writing self is embedded; they are, we could say, a memoir of a historical period re-created from the public archives of images.

That *Report from the Interior* refuses to gratify the reader's/viewer's eye with a display of personal images should not, perhaps, come as a surprise, given the fact that from the very beginning the reader is immersed in a narrative that violates autobiographical conventions of first-person narration. Employing a highly unorthodox mode of second-person narration – rare in both fictional writing and life writing – Auster stages a complex push-and-pull game of intimacy and distance between the writing subject, the subject written about, and the reader.[12]

---

12 Lejeune (1988: 7) acknowledges the possibility of an autobiography written entirely in the second person, but promptly adds that he is not aware of any such text. Listing autobiography in the second person as one among many modes of life narrative, Smith and Watson (2001: 185) provide references to three examples of this genre. In *Patterns of Childhood* (1980), they observe,

The grammatical choice of 'you' underscores a distance in time and perspective as well as tensions in intellectual and emotional attitudes between the established sixty-five-year-old writer and his much younger self, while simultaneously pulling the reader into the position of the addressee. The 'you' narration, as Fludernik notes, invites "active participation and even identification by real readers"; it "always alerts the current listener to pay attention since he or she may be directly called upon to react" (1994: n. pag.; see also Phelan 1994). But Auster 'troubles' any comfortable alignment of the reader with the addressee by disrupting the second-person mode of narration with the third- and the first-person ones. Dominant in the first part of *Report from the Interior*, in the second part, "Two Blows to the Head," the second person is edged out of the center as Auster describes the actions of the male protagonists in *The Incredible Shrinking Man* and *I Am a Fugitive from a Chain Gang*. The shifts between 'he,' 'you,' and 'I' are underscored by explicit comments such as "I am Robert Scott Carey" (107) or "Scott Carey is you" (110). In the "Time Capsule" section, the 'I' is embedded in the 'you': the passages quoted from the letters are all written in the first person, but are addressed as 'you' in the concurrent comments.[13]

In its departure from the generic impositions of autobiographical writing, Auster's *Report from the Interior* seems to be even more radical than the much celebrated *Roland Barthes by Roland Barthes* (1975). In his memoir, Barthes thwarts readerly expectations of a conventional autobiography by resorting to anecdotes and fragments and by shifting between first- and third-person pronouns. Simultaneously, however, he accommodates the expectations of disclo-

---

Christa Wolf "often uses the second person to address both her childhood memories and those of Germans during the Hitler years," while Marya Hornbacher, in *Wasted: A Memoir of Anorexia and Bulimia* (1998), "shifts into 'you' to insist on her reader's identification with her descent into the dark night of anorexic's self-erasure." While the second person does indeed appear in both texts, in neither of them is it the dominant mode of narration: Wolf weaves the 'you' in and out of vignettes and incidents written from a 'neutral' third-person perspective while Hornbacher for the most part follows the convention of first-person narration. Smith's and Watson's third example (2001: 60), *Change Series* (1986), is a series of quilts created by Faith Ringgold to chronicle her struggle to lose weight; it comprises images and narrative comments of which only some are in the second person. Nuruddin Farah's *Maps* (1986) or Jennifer Egan's "Black Box" (2012) are further examples of fiction in which the second-person perspective is extensively used. However, it is the narrative mode employed in Jay McInerney's *Bright Lights, Big City* (1984) that Auster's autobiographical text resembles the most in that both fit into the category that DelConte labels "complete-coincident second-person" (211).

13 Auster's narrative technique could be viewed as a corrective to DelConte's claim that second person "is always also *either* first- *or* third-person" (2003: 204; emphasis added). Auster's narrative technique in *The Winter Journal* and *Report from the Interior* implies that second person is both first and third person.

sures of private moments by reproducing forty-four photographs of himself, his family members, friends, and places related to his life. Even if in the accompanying captions (which at times are quite lengthy) Barthes questions the common assumption of the photographic image's documentary power and its ability to 'speak' the subject, the photographs (most of which are snapshots) do provide the reader with a sense of Barthes's private life.[14] As this essay has made clear, Auster violates both the 'I' and the 'eye' of the autobiographical contract.

The interior of Auster's autobiographic subject is configured by an assembly of print artifacts (newspapers, novels, poems, and posters), films, television programs, book illustrations, paintings, drawings as well as radio, music, sounds of supersonic jets and telephones, and so on. These heterogeneous media enter into complex and complicated relations with each other and with the narrative in which they are lodged. They 'speak' the writing subject's always already intermedial sense of selfhood, making the reader wonder alongside the narrator if selfhood is but "a figment of someone else's imagination" (44).

Works Cited

Adams, Timothy Dow. 1998. "Photography and Ventriloquy in Paul Auster's *The Invention of Solitude*". In: G. Thomas Couser and Joseph Fichtelberg (eds.). *True Relations: Essays on Autobiography and the Postmodern*. Hofstra: Greenwood Press. 11–22.
Adams, Timothy Dow. 2000. *Light Writing and Life Writing: Photography in Autobiography*. Chapel Hill, NC: University of North Carolina Press.
Auster, Paul. 1982. *The Invention of Solitude*. London: Penguin.
Auster, Paul. 2012a. *Winter Journal*. New York: Henry Holt and Company.
Auster, Paul. 2012b. "*Winter Journal:* Paul Auster in Conversation with Paul Holdengräber". New York Public Library, 1 October. <https://www.nypl.org/audiovideo/winter-journal-paul-auster-conversation-paul-holdengräber?nref=90281> [accessed 10 May 2016].
Auster, Paul. 2013. *Report from the Interior*. London: Faber and Faber.
Barrett, Laura. 2009. "Framing the Past: Photography and Memory in *Housekeeping* and *The Invention of Solitude*". *South Atlantic Review* 74 (1): 87–109.
Barthes, Roland. 1981. *Camera Lucida*. Translated by Richard Howard. New York: Hill and Wang.
Barthes, Roland. 2010 [1975]. *Roland Barthes by Roland Barthes*. Translated by Richard Howard. New York: Hill and Wang.
Canemaker, John. 1991. *Felix: The Twisted Tale of the World's Most Famous Cat*. New York: Pantheon.

---

14 For an excellent analysis of photographs in *Roland Barthes by Roland Barthes* see Pedri 2008.

Crafton, Donald. 1982. *Before Mickey: The Animated Film 1898–1928*. Cambridge, MA: MIT Press.

DelConte, Matt. 2003. "Why *You* Can't Speak: Second-Person Narration, Voice, and a New Model for Understanding Narrative". *Style* 37 (2): 204–252.

Eakin, Paul John. 1992. *Touching the World: Reference in Autobiography*. Princeton, NJ: Princeton University Press.

Eakin, Paul John. 2004. "Introduction: Mapping the Ethics of Life Writing". In: Paul John Eakin (ed.). *The Ethics of Life Writing*. Ithaca, NY: Cornell University Press. 1–16.

Edwards, Natalie, Amy L. Hubbell, and Ann Miller. 2011. *Textual and Visual Selves: Photography, Film, and Comic Art in French Autobiography*. Lincoln: University of Nebraska Press.

Egan, Jennifer. 2012. "Black Box". *The New Yorker* June 4 and 11: n. pag. <https://www.newyorker.com/magazine/2012/06/04/black-box-2> [accessed 15 January 2018].

Espejo, Ramón. 2014. "Coping with the Postmodern: Paul Auster's *New York Trilogy*". *Journal of American Studies* 48 (1): 147–171.

Farah, Nuruddin. 1984. *Maps*. Harmondsworth: Penguin.

Fludernik, Monika. 1994. "Second-person Narrative as a Test Case for Narratology: The Limits of Realism". *Style* 28 (3): 445–479.

Gilmore, Leigh. 1994. "The Mark of Autobiography: Postmodernism, Autobiography, and Genre". In: Kathleen Ashley, Leigh Gilmore, and Gerald Peters (eds.). *Autobiography and Postmodernism*. Amherst: University of Massachusetts Press. 3–18.

Hirsch, Marianne. 1997. *Family Frames: Photography, Narrative, and Postmemory*. Cambridge, MA: Harvard University Press.

Hughes, Alex and Andrea Noble. 2003. "Introduction". In: Alex Hughes and Andrea Noble (eds.). *Phototextualities: Intersections of Photography and Narrative*. Albuquerque: University of New Mexico Press. 1–16.

Kibédi Varga, A. 1989. "Criteria for Describing Word-and-Image Relations". *Poetics Today* 10: 31–53.

Lejeune, Philippe. 1975. *Le pacte autobiographique*. Paris: Seuil.

Lejeune, Philippe. 1988. *On Autobiography*. Minneapolis: University of Minnesota Press.

Lennon, J. Robert. 2012. "Review of *Winter Journal*". *The Guardian* August 15: n. pag. <https://www.theguardian.com/books/2012/aug/15/winter-journal-paul-auster-review> [15 January 2018].

McCloud, Scott. 1993. *Understanding Comics: The Invisible Art*. New York: Harper Perennial.

McInerney, Jay. 1984. *Bright Lights, Big City*. New York: Vintage.

Marsh, Emily and Marilyn Domas White. 2003. "A Taxonomy of Relationships between Images and Texts". *Journal of Documentation* 59 (6): 647–672.

Martin, Brendan. 2008. *Paul Auster's Postmodernity*. New York: Routledge.

Nealon, Jeffrey T. 1996. "Work of the Detective, Work of the Writer: Paul Auster's *City of Glass*". *Modern Fiction Studies* 42 (1): 91–110.

Nelson, Deborah. 2014. "Comics and Autobiography: Phoebe Gloeckner, Justin Green, Aline Kominsky-Crumb, Carol Tyler". *Critical Inquiry* 40 (3): 86–103.

Peck, Dale. 2004. *Hatchet Jobs: Writings on Contemporary Fiction*. New York: The New Press.

Pedri, Nancy. 2008. "Documenting the Fictions of Reality". *Poetics Today* 29 (1): 155–173.

Phelan, James. 1994. "Self-Help for Narratee and Narrative Audience: How 'I' – and 'You'? Read 'How'". *Style* 28 (3): 350–365.

Rajewsky, Irina O. 2005. "Intermediality, Intertextuality, and Remediation: A Literary Perspective on Intermediality". *Intermédialités* 6: 43–64.

Rubenstein, Roberta. 1998. "Doubling, Intertextuality, and the Postmodern Uncanny: Paul Auster's *New York Tragedy*". *Lit: Literature Interpretation Theory* 9 (3): 245–262.

Rugg, Linda Haverty. 1997. *Picturing Ourselves: Photography and Autobiography*. Chicago: University of Chicago Press.

Smith, Sidonie and Julie Watson. 2001. *Reading Autobiography: A Guide for Interpreting Life Narratives*. Minneapolis: University of Minnesota Press.

Sontag, Susan. 1977. *On Photography*. New York: Farrar, Straus, and Giroux.

Sorapure, Madeleine. 2002. "Paul Auster". In: Hans Bertens and Joseph Natoli (eds.). *Postmodernism: The Key Figures*. Oxford: Blackwell. 19–24.

Wolf, Werner. 1999. *The Musicalization of Fiction: A Study in the Theory and History of Intermediality*. Amsterdam: Rodopi.

Wolf, Werner. 2011. "(Inter)mediality and the Study of Literature". *CLCWeb: Comparative Literature and Culture* 13 (3): 2–9. <https://docs.lib.purdue.edu/cgi/viewcontent.cgi?article=1789&context=clcweb> [accessed 15 January 2018].

Silvia Schultermandl
Auto-Assembling the Self on Social Networking Sites: Intermediality and Transnational Kinship in Online Academic Life Writing

Abstract

This essay discusses social networking sites (SNSs) as locales of transnational kinship building and intermedial life writing. Through a critical analysis of *Family Line-Ups*, a curated online art project which features family photographs and personal narratives, this essay investigates intermedial representations of family and kinship which throw into relief the constructed nature of transnational families. In particular, the gaps between the visual and the verbal texts featured on *Family Line-Ups* highlight the tension between the verbal and visual representations of family genealogy. In this light, intermedial representation of kinship in social networking sites are read here as rhizomatic storytelling which pushes the boundaries of the auto/biographical genre at the same time as it calls into question notions of identity in a networked world.

1 Social Networking Sites as Intermedial Rhizomes

The World Wide Web is full of digital self-expressions which depict the personal and the mundane as means of creating a cultural archive of the present. On social networking sites (SNSs) such as Twitter, Facebook, Storify, Pinterest, and Instagram, these "everyday" autobiographies (Smith and Watson 1996) rely on verbal and visual materials to express online lives and identities. Because of SNSs, "millions of individuals on a daily basis now produce online selves in interaction with both other people and software applications" (McNeill 2003: 65).[1] In the

---

[1] This phenomenon of the Web 2.0 caused a noticeable collapse of the boundaries between offline and online lives (Fischer 2006). The effects on everyday lives have been noted within many fields of study, and the general consensus is that SNSs are sources of empowerment and vulnerability at the same time: notions of a democratic (easily accessible and affordable) usage coa-

field of literary studies, SNSs have generated new insights into how autobiographical practices affirm everyday life as a productive space for self-life writing. At the same time, the rise of SNSs also highlights anew the importance of intermediality studies to provide frameworks with which to capture the particular communicative nature of online media (Emden and Rippl 2010: 1).

As is perhaps the internet itself, the various practices of online intermedial life writing are best understood through the metaphor of the rhizome which, in Gilles Deleuze and Félix Guattari's terms, implies "lines of articulation or segmentarity, strata and territories; but also lines of flight, movements of deterritorialization and destratification" (2007 [1987]: 3) and thus captures the infinite connectivity as well as the ruptures and discontinuities characteristic of online life writing. To think of these narratives as rhizomatic ones ties in with contemporary assertions in the field of auto/biography studies where the narrating subject is commonly understood to be "fragmented, provisional, multiple, and in progress" (Smith and Watson 2002: 9). The online, interactive, and malleable nature of autobiographical expressions on SNSs epitomizes this fluidity on the levels of content and form. Similarly, Gillian Whitlock and Anna Poletti note that "[t]he materiality of the individual's online presence – layout, uses of images and text, connection to others' sites through networking functions – is in flux" (2008: xviii).

My essay discusses online academic life writing and the intermedial strategies through which the authors represent themselves and their family genealogies. The academic context of the examples of online life writing discussed here is worth emphasizing because the academic disciplines of the contributing authors and the respective academic context of the persons who curated the submissions are important. I will elaborate on this context below, but I want to briefly connect recent developments in the study of online life writing to my project. In particular, my essay investigates the potential of transnational kinship building through SNSs via the intermedial practices of constructing online lives. This potential applies, of course, to online autobiographical practices in general (cf. Zuern 2003; McNeill and Zuern 2015; Poletti and Rak 2014). Still, my discussion of *Family Line-Ups* calls attention to the constructed nature of family genealogy precisely through its intermedial representation in the form of "media combinations" and "intermedial references" (Rajewsky 2005: 52–53). In Rajewsky's terms, media combinations denote the practice of "combining at least two convention-

---

lesce with issues of user security and big data mining on the one hand and new social division along the infamous 'digital divide' (Youngs 2004) between internet-savvy users and those who lack the resources to participate in this form of online communication culture.

ally distinct media or medial forms of articulation" (2005: 52) whereas intermedial references are "meaning-constitutional strategies that contribute to the medial product's overall signification: the media product uses its own media-specific means, either to refer to a specific, individual work produced in another medium [...], or to a specific medial subsystem [...] or to another medium *qua* system" (52–53). As my chapter will show, tension permeates the aesthetic rendering of the individual examples featured on the project website: while the photos foreground the similarity among the family members through a common visual iconography, the verbal narratives exemplify the mechanisms of constructing family lineage through the interpretation of family photography. Because these ekphrastic texts are never only descriptions of the photos but always also interpretations of their overall function within the construction of a sense of familiarity within the authors' family histories, the examples featured on the website throw into relief both the properties of the visual and verbal media of self-representation and the dynamics of claiming a collective past through auto-ethnographic self-positioning.²

In this vein, the examples of online life writing featured on *Family Line-Ups* show that texts and kinship are coherent narratives dynamically constructed out of available multi-medial materials. Auto-assembling is a practice which extends the common definition of life writing to include specifically intermedial forms of representation. It is connected to Whitlock and Poletti's term "autographics," a term which accounts for the ways in which autobiographical practices on SNSs are shaped by "a new mode of autobiographical storytelling, where the telling becomes a kind of shorthanded showing and telling" (2008: xvi). This notion of auto-assembling resonates with the rhizomatic character of postmodern identity narratives and honors ways in which intermedial narratives of selfhood and kinship innovate the autobiographical genre.

2 Reading an Old Genre in a New Light

When Sidonie Smith acknowledges, in her Presidential Address to the Modern Language Association in 2011, a veritable "memoir boom" on the contemporary literary market, she in no small part credits the role of online media in the dissemination of life narratives. Certainly, contemporary life writing appears in

---

2 Sidonie Smith and Julia Watson have pointed out the autoethnographic situation of the text–image relationship where the photos are "described and thematized within the narrative" (2002: 18).

myriad artistic formats, many of which challenge existing assumptions about autobiographical genres (cf. Smith and Watson 1992; 1996; 2002). Online life writing, critics concur, is one of the most recent contributions to the genre of life writing which urges us to reconceptualize what actually constitutes "life" and "writing" (Smith and Watson 2010: 183–190). To what degree online autobiographical practices are still about the life of a 'real' person is an issue explored in two leading academic journals of life writing (*Biography* and *European Journal of Life Writing*) in the form of special issues on the post-human (cf. Zuern 2003; Whitlock and Couser 2012; Heinrich and Soeting 2015; McNeill and Zuern 2015). It is therefore not surprising that scholars acknowledge the innovative features of online autobiographical practices by introducing terms which often eschew the etymological roots of the words 'self' and 'writing' in the commonly used terminology of auto/biography studies. Smith and Watson, for instance, use the term "enacted life narratives" (2002: 9) in order to highlight the performative gestures of documentary film, performance art, online writing, and virtual representations of lives, all of which, they argue, need to be considered as autobiographical practices. What is interesting for this collection on intermedial life writing is a general tendency in these neologisms to highlight the multi-medial agency of the author/curator/performer of online life narratives. For instance, Whitlock and Poletti coin the term "online autographics" to describe the practice of uploading visual content (2008: xv) and employ the term "auto assemblages" to describe the layers of "multimodal texts" generally featured on SNSs (2008: xx). Similarly, Laurie McNeill introduces the term "auto/curating" (qtd. in McNeill and Zuern 2015: xv) to designate the practice of expressing personal information through the compilation and circulation of one's favorite things. All of these examples of how the terminology has changed with the onset of online autobiographical formats and their digital nature emphasize the deeply networked and reciprocal nature of (re)posting, (re)tweeting, blogging, (re)pinning and liking inherent to online life writing practices.

This new terminology also reminds us of the rhizomatic nature of online narratives and enactments which privilege connectivity and interaction over the singular status of the liberal subject common in the autobiographical genre's initial inception. This rhizomatic quality of online practices of auto-assembling or auto/curating stresses that it is no longer categories such as 'authenticity' or 'veracity' that stand at the center of interest in the study of online life writing but the performative strategies through which self-expressions are created and enacted. Personal narratives are rhizomatic in the sense that an individual, insular narrative "is merely an illusion because many other stories can exist alongside this one that don't get illuminated at the moment" (Sermijn et al. 2008: 641). And in their online format, personal narratives are fundamentally relational or refractured through engagement with the lives of their significant others: the lives presented are often interactive; they are co-constructed; they are linked to others – family, friends, employers, causes and affiliations. (Smith and Watson 2013: 70–71)

To think of online identity narratives as rhizomatic connects ongoing discussions in auto/biography studies to the phenomenon of networked communication. If autobiographical writing used to be mainly defined by the stable narrating 'I' which can be held accountable through what Philippe Lejeune has termed the 'autobiographical pact,' then the advent of SNSs has brought about new forms of online expressions of the self which are, paradoxically, not so much about the self. Of course, postmodern, feminist, and transnational autobiographies in general are replete with depictions of bifurcated, fluid, and contingent subjectivities; they are themselves expressions of a rhizomatic selfhood and often "narrate the experience of textual production" through their "highly metaliterary" nature (Davis 2016: 5). Nevertheless, the rhizomatic applies particularly forcefully to SNSs because of the rhizomatic connections the Web affords. While the content is self-selected and designed to represent individual identities, the networked nature of SNSs highlights the collective context rather than the position of the individual.

The notion of accessing the selves of other people through their online autobiographical practices also raises questions about the constituency of the self in the networked constellation with other 'authors' and 'readers' on SNSs (Whitlock 2012). In "There Is No 'I' in Network: Social Networking Sites and Posthuman Auto/Biography" (2012), Laurie McNeill points towards this relational constituency of online selves as well as to the post-human aspects of the virtual lives we are living and composing at the same time. Similarly, McNeill's essay "Teaching an Old Genre New Tricks" (2003) analyzes the genre innovations of online diaries, both on the level of narrative form and as aesthetic experience. For McNeill, these two are interrelated: the global reach of online diaries which can be openly accessed on the Web and the dissemination of sensitive content accessible by an anonymous reader make the confessional tone of diaries especially effective in an online setting. The phenomenon McNeill theorizes is the closeness between the autobiographical subject and the overwhelming number of readers who have potential access to his or her life story. Therefore, in addition to the connection between questions of autobiographical subjectivity and its medial transformation, the concept of the rhizome also captures the complexity of these kinship constellations.[3]

---

[3] Kinship, according to Linda Stone, is "an ideology of human relationships" which brings into

In the following, I will look at online academic life writing and the strategies of articulating family genealogy and kinship building through intermedial auto assemblages. My primary example is *Family Line-Ups*, an online art project which ran as a web log for almost a year (23 August 2012 through 22 July 2013) and continues as a Facebook page and as a secured Twitter account to this day. *Family Line-Ups* was first initiated by American studies scholars Dana Mihailescu, Roxana Oltean, and Mihaela Precup at the University of Bucharest as part of their research project "Cross-Cultural Encounters in American Trauma Narratives: A Comparative Approach to Personal and Collective Memories." At heart, *Family Line-Ups* invites participants to relate their family genealogy by providing portraits of three family members and by reflecting in writing on their personal relationship to these portraits (hence its subtitle "Trans-Generational Encounters in Family Photography"). The narratives mostly revolve around individual connections to family traumata induced by war, poverty, diaspora, loss, and exile. They are personal testimonies of survival and celebrations of cultural heritage. But more than anything, they are examples of the constructed nature of family genealogy, both through oral and written stories as well as through family photography, and the ways in which we make sense of the gaps and fissures in our own past. The intermedial auto assemblages on *Family Line-Ups* illustrate that remembering means "actively creat[ing] the meaning of the past" (Smith and Watson 2002: 9).

At the center of my discussion are four prominent feminist scholars in the US featured on the project webpage: literary studies scholars Nancy K. Miller and Julia Watson; historian Dina Copelman; and sociologist Ethel Brooks. Their examples of multi-medial auto assemblages raise issues about representations of transnational family genealogies. The relationship between the photos and the texts they use to reflect on their family histories, respectively, points toward a tension between the personal artifacts these feminist scholars show and the narratives of the cultural context they tell. All four scholars engage the transnational as a differential between their present lives in the US and their families' lives in Eastern Europe on the one hand and as a concept through which to describe the material realities of their families' diasporic lives on the other. Their transnationalism is one that destabilizes the nation-state as a required representational category of identity and advances an image of the nation-state as "contested, interrupted, and always shot through with contradiction" (Briggs et al. 2008: 627). This idea of a transnational differential connects the constructed nature of the

---

sharper focus the "cultural ideas about how humans are created and the nature and meaning of their biological and moral connections with others" (2000: 6).

nation-state to the constructed nature of family genealogy; in both cases, the auto assemblages that the four authors submitted to *Family Line-Ups* negotiate their transnational relationships to their Eastern European 'origins' via the deconstruction of the family narratives they inherited.

3 Assembling Family Genealogy Online

Family Line-Ups is different from everyday autobiographical expressions on social networking sites: While online life writing is generally open to laymen and professional authors alike, *Family Line-Ups* regulated the flow of submissions by issuing a call for contributions which predetermined the thematic as well as the methodological context for the submissions it received. To this end, the photos and narratives the contributors submitted respond to prompts that the project organizers inserted into the call for contributions. This call specifically situates cultural studies methodologies at the center of the submissions' overall nature: by referring to Roland Barthes's musings on photography in *Camera Lucida* (1981 [1980]) and by citing the analytical work of Nancy K. Miller on the genre of life writing, the organizers put forth a theoretical framework within which the contributors may engage their auto-ethnographic constructions of selfhood and kinship ties. The questions the organizers ask are indicative of critical conversations in the fields of memory studies, visual culture, and auto/biography studies and thus unmistakably link the submissions to academic practices of analysis and critique. Still, despite the editorial interventions of the project organizers, *Family Line-Ups* makes use of the same representational strategies on its Facebook page and Twitter account as millions of other everyday autobiographers do.

This imprint of the discourses of cultural studies and critical theory is also mirrored in the texts the contributors submitted alongside their family photos, in which they narrate their family genealogies and reflect on their family photograph's role in constructing a sense of kinship. Of the 20 profiles[4] accessible through the project website, all participants are artists, scholars, authors, psychoanalysts or professors, either in the humanities (especially in literature) or the social sciences. This creates a certain homogeneity through the style and register of academic discourse, despite the fact that the narratives the contributors tell and the national and cultural histories into which they inscribe themselves

---

[4] Nineteen are intermedial auto assemblages consisting of photos accompanied by a verbal narrative; one consists of a film and a written narrative.

are very diverse. They all define family genealogy as a socially constructed narrative, but some do so in particular through the intermedial representation of the mechanisms of constructing kinship. In the examples I have selected for my discussion, the ways in which the verbal narratives engage the photos show that tension between the verbal and the visual captures the complex dynamics of narrativizing family memory.

The photos are arranged in chronological sequence, tracing family histories over three generations and ending with a photo of the contributor, either a recent one or one that is several decades old. This means that, for some submissions, the genealogical narrative told by the photo sequence ends in the present; for others it ends in the author's childhood and is connected to the present only through the hand-written letters accompanying the photos. For instance, while Brooks, Watson, and Miller present themselves as adult women looking back at female ancestors from a contemporary point of view, Copelman offers an image of her childhood and thus visually inscribes herself into her family's collective past. In both cases, however, the sequence of photographs suggests a close connection between the individual members through a visual presentation which foregrounds similarity through the angles, frames, and iconography on which it relies. For instance, the three photos that Brooks submitted are portraits of herself, her mother, and her grandmother, and the physical resemblance the photos display (the heart-shaped face, the texture of the hair, the piercing eyes, and a confident body posture) establish a strong matrilineal connection among the three generations of women (figure 1). A reading of the photos suggests that Brooks chose these three photos precisely because of the genealogy they document. This reading is confirmed by her verbal narrative.

Figure 1: Triptych of Ethel Brooks's visual narrative of family genealogy. Source: Brooks. "Ethel, Charlotte, Ethel." *Family Line-Ups*.

In addition to the sense of kinship the contributors may communicate through their choice of photos, there are editorial interventions on the part of the project organizers which highlight this impression of closeness. For instance, the art project uses the same black frame to arrange the three photos in a symmetrical triptych, creating a sense of uniformity among the nineteen examples. Moreover, all auto assemblages operate in the same format: the photos are arranged chronologically, from the oldest to the most recent. This emphasis on a seemingly teleological development is not atypical of academic autobiographies (even postmodern ones) which may present class mobility at the same time as they claim a sustained relationship to the past. In both cases, the black passepartout around the photos functions as a framing device which underscores connectivity and manifests the idea of a strong sense of genealogy, much in the way that triptychs have been employed throughout Western culture.[5]

In addition to the photos, the auto assemblages comprise short personal narratives, some dated and signed in epistolary fashion, others written as personal testimonies. These written texts offer interpretations of the visual archive of the authors' families; they project personal stories onto the photos in order to create connections between individual and collective histories (figure 2). They are narratives of progress and upward social mobility, connected to the linear development of the medium of photography from black-and-white to color, and from analog formats to the digital archive of the Web. However, in most auto assemblages featured on *Family Line-Ups*, contributors realize at some point in their narratives that the family stories they have heard all their lives foreground some genealogical connections and conceal others, a fact which emphasizes the constructed nature of family as both a lived experience and as an institution.[6] Expressions like 'discovered,' 'learned,' 'found out,' and 'realized' abound. In this light, the verbal narratives serve as means to de-construct prevalent family stories the authors 'inherited' from their parents and grandparents and to re-construct more inclusive ones which are less driven by societal norms of the patriarchal family and its instrumentalization as the nucleus of society. In terms of their assemblage on the interface, the written texts are also set off against a black frame, but clearly disconnected from the triptych of photos.

The gaps between the visual and the verbal texts in each of the auto assemblages featured on *Family Line-Ups* call attention to the tension between the ver-

---

[5] I am indebted to the editors of this fine collection for pointing out the cultural capital of the triptych as a prominent art form within and beyond the context of religious paintings.

[6] My distinction between experience and institution goes back to Adrienne Rich's groundbreaking study on motherhood, *Of Woman Born: Motherhood as Experience and Institution* (1995 [1976]).

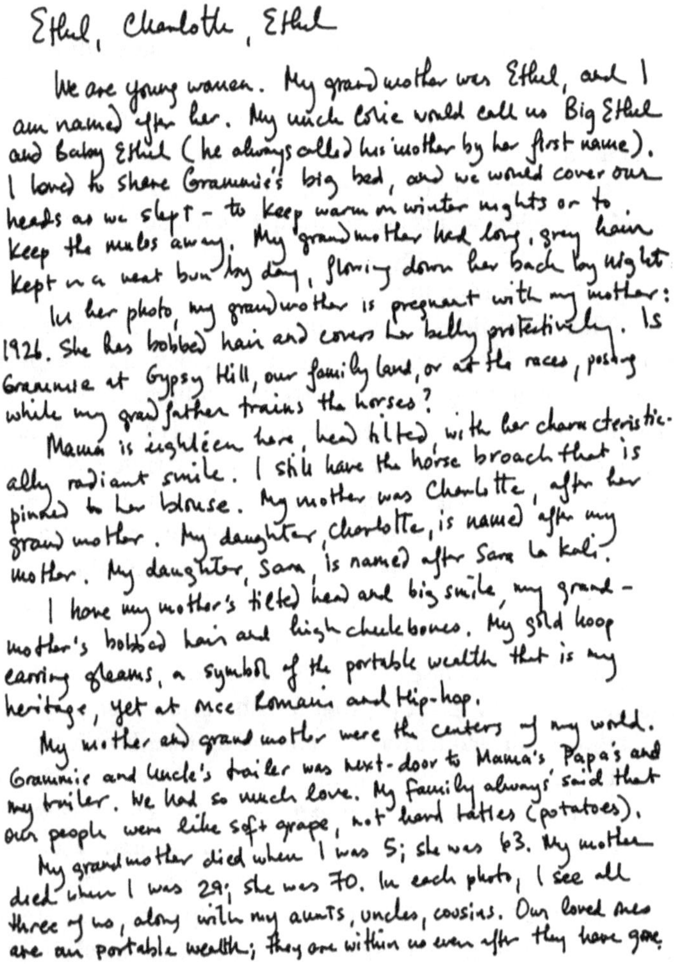

> **Ethel, Charlotte, Ethel**
>
> We are young women. My grandmother was Ethel, and I am named after her. My uncle Louie would call us Big Ethel and Baby Ethel (he always called his mother by her first name). I loved to share Grammie's big bed, and we would cover our heads as we slept – to keep warm on winter nights or to keep the mulos away. My grandmother had long, grey hair kept in a neat bun by day, flowing down her back by night.
>
> In her photo, my grandmother is pregnant with my mother: 1926. She has bobbed hair and covers her belly protectively. Is Grammie at Gypsy Hill, our family land, or at the races, posing while my grandfather trains the horses?
>
> Mama is eighteen here, head tilted, with her characteristically radiant smile. I still have the horse broach that is pinned to her blouse. My mother was Charlotte, after her grandmother. My daughter, Charlotte, is named after my mother. My daughter, Sara, is named after Sara la kali.
>
> I have my mother's tilted head and big smile, my grandmother's bobbed hair and high cheekbones. My gold hoop earrings gleam, a symbol of the portable wealth that is my heritage, yet at once Romani and Hip-hop.
>
> My mother and grandmother were the centers of my world. Grammie and Uncle's trailer was next-door to Mama's, Papa's and my trailer. We had so much love. My family always said that our people were like soft grapes, not hard tatties (potatoes).
>
> My grandmother died when I was 5; she was 63. My mother died when I was 29; she was 70. In each photo, I see all three of us, along with my aunts, uncles, cousins. Our loved ones are our portable wealth; they are within us even after they have gone.

Figure 2: Ethel Brooks's hand-written narrative accompanying her family photos. Source: Brooks. "Ethel, Charlotte, Ethel." *Family Line-Ups*.

bal and visual representations of family genealogy. The verbal narratives offer explanations for the choice of photos. In some cases, they imply that the authors grapple with a family secret which is contained in the photos. A photo documenting the existence of a relative who never appears in family stories of the past, for instance, is a common theme, as is the fact that the authors question the ways in which family stories have been passed down to them. This critical engagement with the visual archive of their collective past can best be understood via Marianne Hirsch's concept of postmemory which describes

> the experience of those who grew up dominated by narratives that preceded their birth, whose own belated stories are evacuated by the stories of the previous generation shaped by traumatic events that can be neither understood nor recreated. (1997: 22)

In line with the feminist and poststructuralist approaches they bring to their academic work, Miller, Watson, Brooks, and Copelman deconstruct the linear and coherent narratives they grew up hearing and thereby uncover the many fissures within kinship discourses that have been glossed over for the sake of a unified and normative sense of genealogy. Miller, for instance, starts her letter by asserting that her family "tree had been neatly pruned," a metaphor which captures her parents' attempt to assimilate and to disconnect from their Eastern European Jewish heritage upon immigration to the United States.

What is true for Miller's example of the exclusion of cultural difference is also true for cases of illness, death, and social stigmatization. For instance, Watson rewrites the story of her grandmother Julia, a story that focuses on her grandmother's psychological illness without accounting for the circumstances of immigration and poverty that shaped her life early on. Watson's story, entitled "Looking for Julia," displays considerable awareness as to how her family constructed her grandmother's illness as a matter of her grandmother's idiosyncrasy without acknowledging how the other family members' lives were affected by the same cultural discourses that pronounced grandmother Julia 'crazy.' When Watson discovers that her grandmother's admission to a mental hospital coincided with her family's financial struggles during the years of the Great Depression, she speculates how class, gender, and health were interconnected factors in her grandmother's diagnosis of 'insanity.' With this in mind, Watson's re-writing of her grandmother's story bears the imprint of her own desire for a strong feminist genealogy, her search for a female ancestor whose defiance and persistence, not whose victimization and submission, connect her to her granddaughter: "Now, when I look at her photo, her gaze locks mine – I see the determination and defiance of a young woman pleased with her fine appearance and hungry for adventure and a better life." Watson's reconstruction of her grandmother ascribes a great deal of agency to a woman who figures in the collective memory of Watson's family only as a victim and as an invalid.

The emphasis on continuity of features which distinguish their families from others is also central to the auto assemblages submitted by Brooks and Copelman. In Brooks's case, this is a central theme of the personal narrative in which she explains the commonalities between herself, her mother, and her grandmother, in part by meditating on the inheritance of female first names: "My grandmother was Ethel, and I am named after her. My uncle [...] would call us Big Ethel and Baby Ethel (he always called his mother by her first name)." For Copelman, the motif of reading addresses the quest for belonging after many months of unsettlement and unrest, both in the sense of the coerced mobility of diasporans and the feeling of cultural uprootedness away from the family's Romanian origins:

> One evening, my father walked into my room and told the sulking eight[-]year[-]old that hard as it might be to believe, once I settled into a language (English, presumably, but I wasn't betting on it) and could read comfortably, life would improve: worlds to explore, words to craft my own worlds. (Or was it a curse? – here I am, still reading, writing).

The tone of these hermeneutic forays into deconstructing existing and inherited narratives of familial identity and of a sense of kinship is suffused with suspicion. The contributors communicate a sense of confusion amidst their attempts to de-essentialize existing versions of the family history and to appropriate them in a meaningful way so that they may bear a connection to their current lives. While the verbal narratives differ in their rhetorical appeal, they all display the underlying parameters in the concept of the family, which implies that genealogy is not something inherited or retrieved from memory, but constructed and re-mediated.

4 Doing Family History on SNSs

Family Line-Ups exemplifies that family history is not so much a static relic of the past but an ongoing practice with its own potential and limitation. This has been acknowledged readily in postmodern literary studies of narrative fiction and life writing as well as in the study of visual culture (cf. Balestrini 2013, 2015; Hirsch 1994, 1997; Rose 2010). In Hirsch's sense of postmemory, "the past is thus actually mediated not by recall but by imaginative investment, projection, and creation" (2012: 5). *Family Line-Ups* stages these interpretative acts of family photos in a quasi-familial context, naturalized through the familiar practice of engaging with family history by looking at family albums and offering verbal narratives of the stories that the photos 'contain.' The art project thus simulates a practice very familiar to the authors and readers of these auto assemblages, a practice which Gillian Rose terms "*doing* family photographs" (Rose 2010: 17) in order to emphasize the interpretative practices of engaging with what family photos offer and conceal at the same time. In Rose's understanding of the term, family photographs are not only to be understood as images but also as a practice, consisting of taking, collecting, storing, remediating, and narrating family snap shots (Rose 2010: 16–21). In this light, Copelman's suggestion that the three photos she assembled "contain all those thousands of words" refers to the polysemic quality of images and the rhizomatic narrative of selfhood.

By bringing together verbal and visual narratives of family history, *Family Line-Ups* allows us to interrogate the media-specific properties of the auto assemblages in relation to their representations of family and kinship. The verbal narratives function as attempts to decode the pictures, and the mixed-media installation lays bare the dynamics of assembling a family genealogy out of the rhizomatic relationships between the authors and their kin and, as I will show in the final part of this essay, also with the intention of subsuming the reader into the web of kinship constellations online life-writing practices generate. As meta-photographic texts "which place family photography into narrative contexts, either by reproducing them or by describing them" (Hirsch 1997: 8), these auto assemblages have the potential to disrupt the familial gaze that reproduces the feeling of kinship the authors might exhibit in relation to family photos (Hirsch 1997: 53–54) and present family genealogy not only as a multiplicity of constructed narratives but as a process which is full of ruptures and fissures. Because the auto assemblages on *Family Line-Ups* evoke both Deleuze and Guattari's philosophical concept of assemblage and the artistic practice of mixed-media collages, the relationship between the verbal and the visual materials calls attention to the multi-faceted, fluid, and contingent selfhood of online lives.

While the auto assemblages on *Family Line-Ups* consist of media combinations of visual and verbal media, "each one present in their own materiality" (Rajewsky 2005: 52), the written texts themselves feature ekphrastic passages which illustrate both the complexity of narrativizing photos and of narrating family genealogies. Most of the verbal narratives contain direct references to the photos and highlight the narrator's subjective point of view. In phrases like "*I think* of the photos here" (Copelman; emphasis added), the practice of looking at photos and engaging with them in an attempt to reconnect with family history becomes evident. When Copelman connects the photo of her three-year-old self to the present with the statement "and *here* I am, three years old, in front of a bookcase in the home of my father's brother" (emphasis added), she offers a description of the photo at hand by evoking its deictic reference signifying both the present moment of looking at the photo and the past moment of the event during which it was taken. This is also true for Brooks's description of her mother's photo: "Mama is eighteen *here*, head tilted, with her characteristically radiant smile" (emphasis added).

At the same time, however, these ekphrastic moments in the written texts show that the memory work that goes into the descriptions of family members relies heavily on the subjective interpretations by the authors of the auto assemblages. Gabriele Rippl asserts that the "highly self-reflexive quality of contemporary ekphrastic texts [...] demonstrates the inadequacy of verbally representing visual data" (2010: 49). Like Rippl, James A. W. Heffernan highlights that in ekphrasis description is always also interpretation and imagination: viewers "gaze on a still silent image to which they impute an independent life and from which they seek to solicit a voice, to hear a confession. But no matter how attentively they listen, the voice is inevitably their own, a product of their own reflections" (2015: 40). Copelman's phrase "I think of the photos here as a narrative of 'people of the book' (assign as many meanings as possible to that phrase)" emphasizes this interpretative procedure as typical of the "intergenerational acts of transfer" (Hirsch 2012: 2) in the ongoing engagement with postmemory, the kind of memory we have only because we have heard stories about events in which we did not participate ourselves.[7] This includes subjective readings of the photos as well as potential misreadings, as Brooks's question indicates: "Is Granny at Gypsy Hill, our family land, or at the races, posing while my grandfather trains the horses?"

The interpretation of the family photos in the ekphrastic moments of the written verbal narratives characterizes ekphrasis as a rhizomatic practice which foregrounds possible readings of the photo out of a myriad of stories the photo 'contains.'[8] Ekphrasis is rhizomatic in the sense that it is not merely a verbal rendering of a visual text but an interpretation along the "lines of articulation" and "lines of flight" (Deleuze and Guattari 2007 [1987]: 3) which co-exist in postmodern narratives. By throwing into relief the mechanisms of kinship building through the intermedial relationship between image and text, *Family Line-Ups* links internet connectivity to intermedial life-writing practices. This enables kinship building on two distinct levels: on its Facebook page and Twitter account, *Family Line-Ups* depicts the dynamic practices of online life writing; at the same time, the connectivity these SNSs enable also establishes a network of users whose virtual community expresses kinship ties through a shared sense of interest, history, and identity.

---

[7] The phrase 'people of the book' alludes to literacy and literature at the same time as it alludes to Jewish identity; the subsequent parenthetical commentary highlights Copelman's emphasis on interpretation and deconstruction.

[8] Compare also Rippl's essay on intermedial life writing and autofiction in this collection.

5 Kinship-Building Online

The politics of representation of family genealogy I have discussed above are not particular to *Family Line-Ups*; in fact, they may describe any project in family photography and storytelling. What is particularly noteworthy about *Family Line-Ups*, however, is its online format and the discussion of family and kinship, online reading, and transnationalism it initiates. If we consider the web format of *Family Line-Ups* not a default (because it was more easily manageable to collect, display, and build an archive of the 20 submissions than any form of non-virtual presentation, e. g., a museum installation) but a deliberate inscription into ongoing trends to negotiate transnational family ties online, we might want to move the conversation away from the politics of representation of the individual submissions and the project as a whole, and direct the discussion towards the level of reception. Precisely because online media create a sense of immediacy and interactivity, the weblog, Twitter, and Facebook can enable a sense of kinship between the subject/object of narration and the reader, who may like, retweet, or engage in other forms with the submissions. This allows readers to respond to or even concern themselves intensively with the family history of another person, known or unknown, albeit not with the person her/himself in most cases. Watson and Smith concur that "[o]nline lives are never only about the self" (2014: 70–71). Similarly, Andrew Hoskins insists that in the age of digital archives and other practices of mediating information online, memory is not collective or re-collective but connective "through the flux of contacts between people and digital technologies and media" (qtd. in Hirsch 2012: 22). In other words, the interactive nature of online media itself creates a potential ground for kinship to emerge between the reader and the text.

Online writing can thus serve as a means of kinship building in which connections among readers and authors can occur spontaneously. Viviane Serfaty, for instance, argues that this emerging community of readers and authors depends on the anonymity and distance as well as the connectivity and interactivity online writing enables. At its root, so Serfaty claims, is the "urge to be recognized and connected with others" (2004: 37) and to "merge public and private spaces" (2004: 46). In the particular case of Mommy blogs, for instance, online connections sometimes even replace embodied relationships, and *ersatz* kinship structures emerge out of shared values, struggles, and desires (Friedman 2013). These *ersatz* kinship constellations effortlessly cross national borders via the Web and can thus establish and maintain transnational communities. In this light, online media have shaped the ways in which we maintain family ties across time and space, enabling a form of transnational connection that is more easily sustained than are embodied practices of kinship. It is true, as Sherry Turkle argues, that online technology "redraws the boundaries between intimacy and solitude" (2013: 30); at the same time, the category of family itself "is undefined and redefined in the combination of mass mobility and cheap and accessible international interaction" (Friedman and Schultermandl 2016: 11).

The connectivity described above operates on the level of affect, where it allows for the emergence of a feeling of kinship among individuals and groups who are otherwise not related. These kinship connections are rhizomatic: among the seemingly endless connections the Web might facilitate, a Facebook page foregrounds some connections over others in the sense of the rhizome. In the specific case discussed here, the accompanying Facebook page and Twitter account interlace *Family Line-Ups* with a dynamic environment whose thematic focus lies on feminist, queer, and transnational revisions of normative family models. And while verbal interaction with the Facebook posts are rudimentary, consisting mostly of expressions of agreement in the form of minimal verbal comments or emoticons and in the number of 'likes,' it is embedded in a substantial network of posts which pursue similar projects of broadening the concepts of family and kinship. For example, the Facebook page is linked to a variety of other texts, including other projects in family photography which pursue topics such as father–daughter relationships (Radcliff), queer families (Rosenberg), and family life in socialist Eastern Europe (Totnoi). While the verbal and iconic replies offer clues about the affective work of online auto assemblages of family genealogy, the links to other projects of similar focus create a strong intertextual digital archive of online lives performed by individual users and curated via the Facebook page. Kinship is therefore not only represented in intermedial form; it is also enacted through the connectivity inherent to SNSs.

This enacted practice links the Facebook page to other fast-paced participatory media technologies and redirects the emphasis away from personal representation and toward kinship building in the form of liking, retweeting, and linking. This creates a plethora of connections and makes available a new archive of similar cases of postmemory work in other national, socio-cultural, geographical, and temporal contexts. In line with Michael Rothberg's concept of "multidirectional memory" (2009: 3), these enacted practices of kinship building connect *Family Line-Ups* to related efforts to unearth family genealogies that counter normative family models, theorize the legacies of transnational family bonds, and engage with the material realities of diaspora since the final decades of the twentieth century. In this sense, *Family Line-Ups* is a portrait of an historical era, marked geographically by the experience of dissent in Eastern Europe and subsequent immigration to the United States. At the same time, the historically and geographically specific nodes of identity construction that the auto assemblages on *Family Line-Ups* perform can also be linked to historical recovery work elsewhere which shares family genealogy as a conceptual frame for its exploration of postmemory and (trans)nationalism.

6 Kinship as Imaginative Reconstruction

In *Living Autobiographically: How We Create Identity in* Narratives (2008), Paul John Eakin proposes that our lives eventually become stories and that these stories counter the assumption of a coherent self (8–17). Eakin highlights the constructed nature of autobiographical stories by labeling them performances of "imaginative reconstruction" (21). These imaginative reconstructions may follow prevalent tropes in the establishment of – if not coherent selves, then at least – coherent narratives. In *Family Line-Ups*, these tropes also resonate with a literary tradition of narrating immigration and multiculturalism on the one hand, and feminist and cultural materialist recovery work on the other – a tradition which the four authors I examine in this chapter have shaped with their own work as teachers and scholars. In both instances, a subtle subtext defines the US-American context from which the four contributors submitted their auto assemblages as the cultural ground on which their personal development was possible.

As is generally the case with academic autobiographies, an element of the success story can also be seen in the cases I discuss here. In the field of American studies, immigrant success stories are often met with a critical eye towards their depictions of the socio-political circumstances in the US, which have some immigrant groups prosper and others struggle. By zooming in on the narratives of a family rather than on the socio-cultural context of their ancestors' respective generations, the authors featured in *Family Line-Ups* emphasize the practices of establishing a sense of kinship among family members as though kinship and belonging resulted primarily from the family members' efforts. For instance, the auto assemblages by Miller, Watson, Copelman, and Brooks foreground their own agency within the construction of family genealogy, but they do not spend much time addressing the question of how their agency stands in relation to the agentic potential of the family members they describe. This leaves many questions about kinship building – both embodied and digitalized – unanswered.

One question that must be asked is how a sense of kinship and relationality manifests itself linguistically and how the family narratives Miller, Watson, Copelman, and Brooks tell are encoded by their own levels of literary and academic writing skills. While their auto assemblages meditate on the interpretation of the visual archive of their family members through verbal genealogical narratives (with all expected gaps and fissures), they do not address the modes used to translate informal family stories into an elevated register. The verbal narratives, for instance, are written in a personalized but still professional register not unrelated to the academic diction the authors have mastered. But questions of language such as immigrant dialects and class sociolects are issues their families surely experienced. These issues would provide an occasion for the authors to reflect on the differences in power and privilege between the three generations they describe, to investigate their own roles in narrating a family history, and to scrutinize the heterogeneity within their own families.

Still, questions about linguistic translation within the representation of family memory are implicitly addressed through the use of ekphrasis in the auto assemblages on *Family Line-Ups*. Ekphrasis functions here as a rhetorical mode of addressing a variety of ethical issues of online life narratives. As Rippl has suggested, ekphrasis allows us to raise questions through which "to reconstruct the concepts of representation and mimesis which predominate in specific historical periods and cultures" (2010: 49). The ekphrastic moments in *Family Line-Ups* highlight how representation and mimesis interact in intermedial life-writing practices. On top of that, through their online nature, they not only entertain questions about representation and mimesis but also about specific forms of medialization. To think of ekphrasis through the concept of the rhizome – where interpretations of family photos foreground certain stories and conceal others – expands our understanding of the creative possibilities which the autobiographical genre in its conjunction with digital practices of representing and creating kinship yields.

Works Cited

Balestrini, Nassim Winnie. 2015. "Life Writing in the Internet Age: Miranda July and the Limits of Art as Social Practice". *Arbeiten aus Anglistik/Amerikanistik* 40 (1–2): 127–150.

Balestrini, Nassim Winnie. 2013. "Photography as Online Life Writing: Miranda July's and Harrell Fletcher's *Learning to Love You More* (2002–2009)". In: Alfred Hornung (ed.). *American Lives*. Heidelberg: Winter. 341–353.

Barthes, Roland. 1981 [1980]. *Camera Lucida: Reflections on Photography*. Translated by Richard Howard. London: Vintage Books.

Briggs, Laura, Gladys McCormick, and J.T. Way. 2008. "Transnationalism: A Category of Analysis". *American Quarterly* 60 (3): 625–648.

Brooks, Ethel. "Ethel, Charlotte, Ethel". *Family Line-Ups*. <http://www.familylineups.com/ethel-brook/> [accessed 15 January 2018].

Davis, Rocío G. 2016. "Foreword: Empathy and Life Writing". *Concentric: Literary and Cultural Studies* 42 (2): 3–8.

Deleuze, Gilles and Félix Guattari. 2007 [1987]. *A Thousand Plateaus: Capitalism and Schizophrenia*. Translated by Brian Massumi. Minneapolis: University of Minnesota Press.

Eakin, Paul John. 2008. *Living Autobiographically: How We Create Identity in Narrative.* Ithaca, NY: Cornell University Press.

Emden, Christian J. and Gabriele Rippl. 2010. "Introduction". In: Christian J. Emden and Gabriele Rippl (eds.). *ImageScapes: Studies in Intermediality*. Oxford: Peter Lang. 1–18.

Family Line-Ups. <http://www.familylineups.com/> [accessed 30 November 2016].

Fischer, Hervé. 2006. *Digital Shock: Confronting the New Reality*. Montreal: McGill.

Friedman, May. 2013. *Mommyblogs and the Changing Face of Motherhood*. Toronto: University of Toronto Press.

Friedman, May and Silvia Schultermandl (eds.). 2016. *Click and Kin: Transnational Identity and Quick Media*. Toronto: Toronto University Press.

Heffernan, James A.W. 2015. "Ekphrasis: Theory". In: Gabriele Rippl (ed.). *Handbook of Intermediality: Literature – Image – Sound – Music*. Berlin: De Gruyter. 35–49.

Heinrich, Tobias and Monica Soeting (eds.). 2015. *Beyond the Subject*. Special Issue of *European Journal of Life Writing* 4.

Hirsch, Marianne. 2012. *The Generation of Postmemory: Visual Culture after the Holocaust*. New York: Columbia University Press.

Hirsch, Marianne. 1997. *Family Frames: Photography, Narrative, and Postmemory*. Cambridge, MA: Harvard University Press.

Hirsch, Marianne. 1994. *The Mother/Daughter Plot: Narrative, Psychoanalysis, Feminism*. Indianapolis: Indiana University Press.

Lejeune, Philippe. 1988. *On Autobiography*. Translated by Katherine Leary. Minneapolis: University of Minnesota Press.

McNeill, Laurie. 2003. "Teaching an Old Genre New Tricks: The Diary on the Internet". *Online Lives* 26 (1): 24–47.

McNeill, Laurie. 2012. "There Is No 'I' in Network: Social Networking Sites and Posthuman Auto/Biography". *Biography* 35 (1): 65–82.

McNeill, Laurie and John David Zuern (eds.). 2015. *Online Lives 2.0*. Special issue of *Biography* 38 (2).

Miller, Nancy K. (2002). *But Enough About Me: Why We Read Other People's Lives*. New York: Columbia University Press.

Poletti, Anna and Julia Rak (eds.). 2014. *Identity Technologies: Constructing the Self Online*. Madison: University of Wisconsin Press.

Radcliff, Jack. 2014. <http://www.jackradcliffe.org/alison-c37w> [accessed 30 November 2016].

Rajewsky, Irina O. 2005. "Intermediality, Intertextuality, and Remediation: A Literary Perspective on Intermediality". *Intermédialités* 6: 43–64.

Rich, Adrienne. 1995 [1976]. *Of Woman Born: Motherhood as Experience and Institution*. New York: Norton.

Rippl, Gabriele. 2010. "English Literature and Its Other: Towards a Poetics of Intermediality". In: Christian J. Emden and Gabriele Rippl (eds.). *ImageScapes: Studies in Intermediality*. Oxford: Peter Lang. 39–65.

Rose, Gillian. 2010. *Doing Family Photography: The Domestic, the Public and the Politics of Sentiment.* Surrey: Ashgate.

Rosenberg, David. 2013. "Traditional Families – Who Also Happen to be Gay". *Slate.* <http://www.slate.com/blogs/behold/2013/02/04/alix_smith_states_of_union_aims_to_portray_gay_families_in_traditional_settings.html> [accessed 30 November 2016].

Rothberg, Michael. 2009. *Multidirectional Memory: Remembering the Holocaust in the Age of Decolonization.* Stanford, CA: Stanford University Press.

Serfaty, Viviane. 2004. *The Mirror and the Veil: An Overview of American Online Diaries and Blogs.* Amsterdam: Rodopi.

Sermijn, Jasmina, Patrick Devlieger, and Gerrit Loots. 2008. "The Narrative Construction of the Self: Selfhood as Rhizomatic Story". *Qualitative Inquiry* 14 (4): 632–650.

Smith, Sidonie. 2011. "Presidential Address 2011 – Narrating Lives and Contemporary Imaginaries". *PMLA* 126 (3): 564–574.

Smith, Sidonie and Julia Watson. 2014. "Virtually Me: A Toolbox About Online Self-Presentation". In: Anna Poletti and Julie Rak (eds.). *Identity Technology.* Madison: University of Wisconsin Press. 70–95.

Smith, Sidonie and Julia Watson. 2010 [2001]. *Reading Autobiography: A Guide for Interpreting Life Narratives.* Minneapolis: University of Minnesota Press.

Smith, Sidonie and Julia Watson (eds.). 2002. *Interfaces: Women, Autobiography, Images, Performance.* Ann Arbor: University of Michigan Press.

Smith, Sidonie and Julia Watson (eds.). 1996. *Getting a Life: Everyday Use of Autobiography.* Minneapolis: University of Minnesota Press.

Stone, Linda. 2000. *Gender and Kinship: An Introduction.* 2nd ed. Boulder, CO: Westview Press.

Totnoi. 2016. <https://www.flickr.com/groups/totnoi/pool/> [accessed 30 November 2016].

Turkle, Sherry. 2011. "The Tethered Self: Technology Reinvents Intimacy and Solitude". *Continuing Higher Education Review* 75: 28–31.

Whitlock, Gillian and G. Thomas Couser (eds.). 2012. *(Post)Human Lives.* Special issue of *Biography* 35 (1).

Whitlock, Gillian and Anna Poletti. 2008. "Self-Regarding Art". In: Gillian Whitlock and Anna Poletti (eds.). *Autographics.* Special issue of *Biography* 31 (1): v–xxiii.

Youngs, Gillian. 2004. "Cyberspace: The New Feminist Frontier?". In: Karen Ross and Carolyn M. Byerly (eds.). *Women and Media: International Perspectives.* Malden, MA: Blackwell Publishing. 185–209.

Zuern, John David (ed.). 2003. *Online Lives.* Special Issue of *Biography* 26 (1).

Nassim Winnie Balestrini
Intermedial On/Offstage Auto/Biography: Lin-Manuel Miranda's *Hamilton*, Hip Hop, and Historiography

Abstract

Lin-Manuel Miranda wrote the libretto and the music for *Hamilton: An American Musical*, created the lead role both in the Off-Broadway (Public Theater) and the Broadway productions (Richard Rodgers Theater), and co-authored the book *Hamilton: The Revolution*, which provides the lyrics of the musical as well as the history of its production. Both the stage show and its companion volume rely on intermedial discourse that intersects autobiographical and biographical narratives. By doing so, *Hamilton* emphasizes metahistorical reflections concerning Alexander Hamilton's legacy/ies, agency, and power in writing history/ies as well as the role of democratic participation in understanding American history and in relating this history to an encouraging sense of selfhood. Performance theorist Diana Taylor's inquiry into the consequences of the repertoire-vs.-archive dichotomy in historical studies as well as social psychological research on heroism serve as frameworks for explaining how the transmedial *Hamilton* narrative adapts a Founding Father's biography into a call for social cohesion in what Miranda perceives as a nation of immigrants.

1 Historiographic Processes and Practices

Lin-Manuel Miranda, the lyricist and composer of the 2015 smash hit *Hamilton: An American Musical*, seems well-aware of the potential impact of autobiography and biography. As historiographic genres, they can affect individuals' sense of self and sense of (particularly national) belonging. The musical presents an array of historical personages from the era of the American Revolution and the Early Republic. Yet, the Broadway show makes use of a twentieth- and twenty-first-century sonic landscape that ranges from Broadway stock songs via R&B ballads and Beatles-style Brit pop to concept rap. Visually, *Hamilton* yokes past and present together through period costumes "from the neck down" combined with coiffures of the 2010s (Miranda and McCarter 2016: 113). The sung-through musical zeroes in on processes, products, and repercussions of historiography –

i. e., of the methods and trajectories of written histories – rather than on the American Revolution itself. *Hamilton* conjures up scenarios of misrepresented or forgotten individuals, and contrasts these with the transformation of the collective memory of Alexander Hamilton as a Federalist with aristocratic leanings into Alexander Hamilton as an allegorical stand-in for unappreciated, hardworking, relentlessly knowledge-hungry, and verbally virtuosic immigrants.[1]

Miranda's meta-historiographical outlook extends beyond performances of the musical into printed matter – a realm which is significantly more affordable and accessible than outrageously priced theater tickets. In April 2016, during the first year of the Broadway run, Miranda and his co-author, Jeremy McCarter, published *Hamilton: The Revolution: Being the Complete Libretto of the Broadway Musical, with a True Account of Its Creation, and Concise Remarks on Hip-Hop, the Power of Stories, and the New America*. Analogous to the visual language that strives to bridge the temporal chasm between Alexander Hamilton's world and the everyday lives of current theater audiences, this hefty volume cleverly merges eighteenth-century book aesthetics – as the somewhat pompous and verbose title already indicates – with intermedial features of bestselling hip-hop life writing.

The musical and the companion volume constitute an overall artistic and sociopolitical project which interlaces autobiography and biography in relational life writing (Smith and Watson 2010: 256). The auto/biographical trajectory links Hamilton's era with the contemporary world of the artists involved in the musical. This multi-faceted life narrative relies, to a large extent, on being mediated by words; at the same time, the stage performance and the companion volume combine multiple media that collaborate in conveying the central theme of how history is written. Contemplating both of these artifacts together – and doing so in light of Diana Taylor's reflections on 'repertoire' and 'archive' – reveals that Miranda combats the ephemerality and limited accessibility of stage performances by publishing a tangible mass market book. This comparatively durable format implicitly elevates the collected materials about the musical's genesis, its contributors, and its early performance history to the status of ostensibly stable historical documents to be archived and appreciated by future generations.

Miranda's version of Hamilton's biography has developed a multifaceted transmedial presence, meaning that it is narrated within and according to the

---

[1] For a thoughtful discussion of the historiographic focus, see Nereson 2016: 1046, 1047, 1054, and 1055. Regarding the myriad prizes and other acknowledgments that *Hamilton* and its creators received in 2016, see Nereson 1046–1047.

medium-specific affordances of several media (Rajewsky 2005): an onstage musical, a book, a cast album on CD, and a proliferation of spin-off materials online and onstage, among them an extensive parody entitled *Spamilton: An American Parody* (premiere: July 19, 2016 at the Triad Theater in New York City). This transmedial phenomenon inextricably interlaces autobiographical and biographical narratives as well as writing/performing practices of the involved artists and reading/viewing/listening practices of audiences.

By addressing his verbal prowess, this transmedial project represents Hamilton as a social hero according to social psychology definitions. Like a hip-hop artist, he uses words to promote his views on American democratic social structures. This innovative link between a Founding Father's legacy and hip hop reinforces the internal auto/biographical and century-transcending connections as well as the meta-historiographical discourse on what counts as momentary or long-lived, as negligible or significant. These elements support the central argument regarding the impact of competing historiographies on individuals' sense of self in the United States today and in years to come. The printed history of adapting Hamilton's biography into a viable Broadway musical proposes that the longevity of art resides in those who witness a performance and then adapt it. Thus, artistic adaptations of historical narratives become points of departure for democratically oriented participation in re-thinking auto/biographies across time, space, and political ideologies.

2 Transforming the Repertoire into an Archive

My chapter title adopts hemispheric American studies and performance studies scholar Diana Taylor's terminology. Her terms, which capture competing concepts of knowledge production and distribution, can be applied to the relation between historiography and musical theater as reciprocal adaptive processes. Taylor defines "'[a]rchival' memory" as residing in seemingly stable materials such as "documents, maps, literary texts, letters, archaeological remains, bones, videos, films, cds" whereas the "repertoire [...] enacts embodied memory – performances, gestures, orality, movement, dance, singing – in short, all those acts usually thought of as ephemeral, non-reproducible knowledge" (Taylor 2003: 19–20). She also asks whether ephemerality denies performance the ability to inquire into the past in a manner that meets the "archival stability" requirement associated with written history (2006: 68). According to Taylor, our understanding both of performance and of historical studies needs to be revised so as not to preclude the idea that only one of the epistemologies associated with archive-based historical writing offers "socially legitimate ways of understanding the past" as well as "predictive power" (2006: 68).

Miranda and McCarter's co-authored *Hamilton: The Revolution* deliberately taps into a widely accepted sense of archival stability and legitimacy associated with history books, especially if they contain what are considered historical documents. Accordingly, the book provides images, facsimiles, and transcripts of written texts related both to Hamilton's era and to the life and times of Miranda and his fellow artists. More specifically, several design-related and structural features of *Hamilton: The Revolution* take up an aesthetic of hip-hop life writing that has been evolving since the early twenty-first century. These features bridge gaps between oral performance and written discourse, between performative personae and socially defined roles, as well as between artistic representation and politicized commentary.

Publishing a historiographic book about a Broadway show during its first-year run is not simply a gimmick, although it certainly constitutes merchandize connected with a wildly successful production. More importantly, the diligently composed and designed book ensures that the makers of the musical get to write their own history and thus adapt a repertoire into an archive rather than leaving this task to others. What we have here is historiography adapted into musical theater, and musical theater – with all its trimmings, paratexts, contexts, links to the past, and projections into the future – adapted into historiography. In tune with Taylor, the musical and the monograph argue in favor of dissolving the archive–repertoire dichotomy for the sake of perceiving agency and coincidence as major contenders in creating collective memory.

As expressed in the book's subtitle, Miranda and McCarter argue that the musical's innovative impetus is as revolutionary as the historical events depicted in the musical. Within their respective contexts, some goals and impacts of the political upheaval and the artistic intervention are indeed comparable. Beyond artistic innovation, the musical's book and lyrics also contemplate who Alexander Hamilton, the other Founding Fathers, and several contemporary women were, how they have not yet been remembered, how they may be remembered one day, and what the United States could be like in the future (Miranda and McCarter 2016: 10). The story of "two revolutions" (2016: 10), as Miranda and McCarter put it, is not a mere analogy between two clearly delineated phenomena frozen in time. Rather, these phenomena possess amorphous edges that must constantly be adjusted to ongoing processes. Thus, the musical "continues" (2016: 11) the revolution by pointing towards the future realization of its ideals. Just as Taylor questions the neat juxtaposition of the "repertoire" which, as indicated, "enacts embodied memory – performances, gestures, orality, movement, dance, singing" and which supposedly consists of "ephemeral, non-reproducible knowledge" (2003: 19–20), with the ostensibly stable "archive," Miranda implies that innumerable performances of previously archived history connect past, present, and future. Specific elements of the historiographically themed performances develop a life of their own when taken over by viewers and listeners, so that the representation of history is continuously changed and adapted. And – somewhat ironically – the printed, materially rather stable monograph creates a Tayloresque archive, but not without questioning the implications of producing a stable or uninterested historiographic record. Representing history remains an ongoing process of adaptation which, in the case of Miranda's *Hamilton*, combines and crosses media boundaries.

The design of the book demonstrates adaptive processes through various visual and verbal features, and through merging features of eighteenth-century print culture and of hip-hop life writing. The large dimensions of the 228-page volume (22 cm wide, 26.5 cm tall, and 4 cm thick) make it a substantial tome. Irregular paper edges imitate the now obsolete practice of separating pages with a knife. The spine, which reads *Hamilton The Revolution* (without an intervening colon) and which features the Broadway show's emblematic five-pointed star, plays with Hamilton as subject and object, as author and part of the revolution. The top point of the star is the silhouette of a man in eighteenth-century garb, raising his left arm and pointing his index finger straight upwards. Thus, the musical is visibly present through the stylized star used on the program booklet, the cast recording's CD booklet, the YouTube channel, the piano-vocal score, and so on. Like the overall title, the headings of the acts and numbered subsections emulate long, descriptive chapter titles of eighteenth-century novels like Henry Fielding's *Tom Jones* (1749). These headings frequently straddle the eighteenth- and twenty-first-century revolutions. Their stilted, slightly ironical, and pun-oriented style evokes both revolutionary era discourse and rap lyrics. The book features black-and-white and color photographs, contemporary photographs made to look like daguerreotypes, typeset and handwritten words, yellowed parchment-like pages with black script, and pages with white text printed onto color photographs of Broadway performances. Some of these elements fit conventional notions of archival material, whereas readers will recognize other features from current contexts.

The most significant contemporary context relevant to life-writing studies is an evolving trend to package hip-hop life into carefully designed coffee table–sized publications that combine verbal narrative, images, and visual design with music as a central theme. Prime examples are Eminem's *The Way I Am* (2008) and Jay Z's *Decoded* (2011). Like *Hamilton: The Revolution*, these *New York Times* bestsellers contain a relational autobiographical narrative that also includes the life stories of other individuals, an artistic manifesto in defense of hip hop, lyrics from various albums, photographs, and facsimiles of the artists' creative work (Balestrini 2015, 2016, and 2018).

Some of these intermedial publications feature images of hip-hop artists' handwritten lyrics. In light of Taylor's call to rethink the archive-versus-repertoire dichotomy, these visual reproductions serve as comments on the standing of hip hop and of ethnic or socioeconomic groups that, for the longest time, have not been considered part of the artistic mainstream. In Jay Z's monograph, a verse written onto a brown paper bag symbolizes his claim on his home turf through his artistic work (2011: 6). In Eminem's book, the heading "Ghost Trapped in a Beat: Original Handwritten Lyrics from the Personal Collection of Marshall B. Mathers III" (2008: 153) introduces a section of photographs of the rapper's notebook sheets covered in longhand. The phrase "Original Handwritten Lyrics" calls up the culturally highbrow imaginary of artistic value rooted in original, unique, and painstakingly created art that deserves conservation. Turning such material evidence of creative work in progress into 'sacraliz[ed]' documents (Levine 1988: 86) counteracts negative attitudes towards rap as being a spontaneous, thoughtless, and ephemeral repertoire rather than an art form with its own historical archive.

Accordingly, *Hamilton: The Revolution*, whose graphic design was produced by the company that created Eminem's volume, includes two sections entitled "The Pen & The Pad" (Miranda and McCarter 2016: embedded in ch. III and ch. XXII, 36–37, 202–203). Annotations added to photographs of Lin-Manuel Miranda's notebooks explain the creative process. Detailed side notes also abound in the representation of song lyrics – a feature shared with Jay Z's volume. These annotations contain autobiographical accounts about when, where, and why Miranda developed certain artistic ideas; they explain the poetics of his versatile style; they pay homage to Broadway and hip hop through pointing out allusions and adaptations of elements from revered works; and they comment on patterns within audience responses and on revisions in the course of developing and performing the show. Like the photographs of the notebook pages, the annotations thus make the lyrics look like an annotated Shakespeare edition or a modernist poem that requires erudition or scholarly explanation – an impression that situates Miranda's lyrics within the ostensibly stable realm of canonized, socially appreciated art. Furthermore, the annotations emphasize that art and life are in constant flux, and that adaptive processes contribute to producing knowledge and to working towards social change. The back and forth between the historical Hamilton's world and the world of the musical may avert experiencing the book solely as a high-quality scrap book. Instead, Miranda and McCarter offer an inquiry into how inside and outside perspectives on two historical eras and on ostensibly real and fictional worlds inform each other.

The intersecting eras and auto/biographies dominate the book's text right from the beginning by immediately linking the future of an individual with that of a nation, and by foreshadowing analogies between the sensibilities of twenty-first-century artists involved in the musical and of the historical personages they represent on the stage. The book is dedicated to the authors' sons "who will come of age with our young nation" (Miranda and McCarter 2016: 5). The "young nation" may hint at the musical cast which metaphorically resembles the newly founded nation of the revolutionary era. The multiethnic group of artists then embodies the work's interpretation of the United States as a nation of immigrants. Miranda and McCarter's reference to their children echoes the depiction of Hamilton and Burr as fathers in the early 1780s. In the song "Dear Theodosia" (2016: 128–129), they voice their insecurities when facing their offspring that "will come of age with our young nation" (128). Having both grown up without a father, which is yet another nod to a recurrent hip-hop theme, Hamilton and Burr pledge to be different (129), thus taking on the double roles of Founding Father and biological father. This tender ballad addressed to posterity also prefigures one of the final numbers in the musical, in which Hamilton's adversaries ruefully acknowledge that "The World Was Wide Enough" (272–275) – which is another plea to overcome partisan divisions.

Secondly, the song "Helpless" (Miranda and McCarter 2016: 71–77) depicts the courtship and marriage of Elizabeth Schuyler and Alexander Hamilton. It is written in the style of an R&B rap duet, somewhat like Jay Z and Beyoncé's "Crazy in Love" (2003). The love plot as a stock element makes the characters seem more approachable, but McCarter identifies a more serious purpose. He argues that the contemporary song style facilitates understanding a historically remote era: "Lin uses the conventions of a pop song to help a 21st-century audience understand 18th-century social distinctions" (Miranda and McCarter 2016: 69). The visual images of the performed scene plus the lyrics are preceded by a transcription of a love poem Hamilton wrote for Eliza, which is visually 'authenticated' through a facsimile of his signature (69). Archive and repertoire, thus, become mutually reinforcing and even indistinguishable. At the same time, Miranda adapts Hamilton's biography to the argumentative bent of the libretto and thus, as numerous annotations describe, re-writes some historical facts for the sake of a workable show. Such biographical myth-making finds its autobiographical analogue in pointed interpretations of Miranda and his co-workers as artists. For instance, McCarter claims: "Here is another *Hamilton* paradox: Half a century after verse storytelling – the technique that worked so well in *Medea*, *Tartuffe*, and *Othello* – was declared dead on the American stage, it has been revived by someone who learned it not in a textbook or in a drama school but from listening endlessly to 'Friend or Foe,' 'Everything Is Fair,' and the first album by The Pharcyde" (103). This juxtaposition of supposedly natural, folk-based genius versus painstakingly learned craft sounds defiant and functions as part of the overall you-can-make-it-if-you-work-hard trajectory. As a literary and cultural historian, I see a potential danger in perpetuating a binary opposition between popular and elite cultures while simultaneously celebrating that the former intruded into the marketplace of the latter. Furthermore, one might ask why popular culture should not teach an aspiring artist lyrical techniques. Buying into the natural-genius-of-the-common-man myth, even though Miranda attended a prep school and graduated from Wesleyan University, seems counterproductive to confirming the innovative power of his work. It does, however, reflect the ongoing intra-cultural conflict as to how the social and ethnic background of an artist may impact the reception of his/her work.

Hamilton: An American Musical adapts historiography, and *Hamilton: The Revolution* provides a history of the musical. In both cases, staking a claim as to who writes history in which ways and for whom goes along with evaluating and selectively presenting the respective archive. The musical undermines the notion that historiography must remain a white, mainstream domain. It shows that ostensibly well-known historical personages and events can be seen quite differently and that previously unheard perspectives serve to re-construct the implications of events – and texts – for the future. In order to avoid coming across as monolithic and one-sided, the monograph is polyvocal, presents archival material as part of fluid meaning-making processes, and ties together past, present, and future. The adaptation of the adaptation asserts that historiography is a never-ending series of adaptive projects, i. e., that it is a repeatedly realized, dynamic repertoire rather than a static archive.

3 The Future-Oriented Auto/biographic Heroization of Verbal Power

In addition to stressing the long-term effect of whether and how a person is remembered in official histories, the musical and the companion volume construct the authors' desired and perceived impact of Alexander Hamilton and of hip-hop culture as being rooted in wielding words. When Miranda performed his first Hamilton rap at a White House event in 2009, he proposed that "Treasury Secretary Alexander Hamilton" was the Founding Father "who embodies hip-hop" (qtd. in Miranda and McCarter 2016: 15; see also "Lin-Manuel Miranda Performs"). One of the markers of this analogy is Hamilton's immense output of persuasive political rhetoric and the central role that his verbal prowess played in his social rise from a poor West Indian half-orphan to a powerful figure during the Revolution and the Early Republic. Both the musical and the companion volume point out that verbal power can be abused to misrepresent just as it can be used to empower, and that verbal representations exert a strong impact on understanding oneself in relation to larger social contexts.

Relational life writing serves to interlink depictions of the past, the present, and of future prospects. *Hamilton: The Revolution* transcends the biographical focus on Alexander Hamilton in two ways: first, through autobiographical reflections by onstage characters as well as offstage creators and recipients; and second, by the proposition that everyone who is exposed to the musical will potentially propel its sociopolitical significance into the future. To highlight this vision of the Hippocratic aphorism *vita brevis, ars longa*, Miranda and McCarter juxtapose it to the limits imposed on presidential terms. Ironically, official written histories may emanate from federal authorities like a presidential office. Miranda's approach to characterizing the potential multiplication effects of artistic renderings of history resembles a twenty-first-century variant of Percy Bysshe Shelley's claim that "poets are the unacknowledged legislators of the world" (1993: 765). Significantly, in the case of *Hamilton*, the largely anonymous audience members and fans become multiplying factors for a specific perspective on United States history.

A central element in triggering the desire to become such a multiplier is the depiction of the central character as a heroic figure. This raises the question as to which notions of heroism currently prevail in the United States. Cultural anthropologists have been describing notions of heroism through locally rooted field work. Empirical researchers in social psychology have taken up such culturally perpetuated concepts and have, for instance, studied how lay ideas of the heroic correlate with attitudes towards democracy. These insights are of interest when contemplating Miranda's work as a hip-hop-inspired social justice project because his intermedial auto/biographical representations are meant to foster a higher sense of self-worth among previously and currently disadvantaged people. These individuals are to translate the affective impact of Miranda's version of Founding Father heroism into a specific understanding of the United States and of their own positionality within the nation. In order to achieve that, Miranda blends his brand of Hamiltonian heroism with twenty-first-century hip-hop empowerment.

The obvious lack of reliable and comprehensive data on audience responses again raises the specter of theater as ephemeral repertoire – a specter which adulatory responses mentioned in *Hamilton: The Revolution* are to disperse because they confirm the timeliness of reading the Revolution and the Early Republic through the lens of the United States as an immigrant nation. As historian Jacquelyn Dowd Hall suggests, life writing that engages with controversial historical legacies may serve as a vehicle of "social critique" that can only be satisfactorily interpreted by readers who "leaven [...] politics with poetics" (1998: 441). According to Hall, "[p]olitics demand that we choose a side, take a stand. Poetics demand that we hold seemingly contradictory beliefs at the same time, that we embrace multiple levels of meaning, that we think metaphorically" (1998: 441). Literary scholar Suzanne Keen – who works with sociological data on reading practices – develops her typology of affective responses to literature along similar lines. Among other things, she distinguishes between empathy-focused structures that target "the maker's in-group" and those that go beyond this group, which she calls "ambassadorial" because they "go [...] out into the world to recruit readers/viewers/audiences by means of emotional fusion with current causes" (Keen 2016: 20). The historiographic and auto/biographical components in both instantiations of Miranda's Hamilton are geared towards critiquing national shortcomings and encouraging recipients to bridge gaps between contending factions.

3.1 Hamilton as a Hero in Chernow's Biography

Social psychologists Franco, Blau, and Zimbardo differentiate between those who are considered born heroes and those who are seen as having exerted themselves to achieve heroic status. This distinction juxtaposes predetermined heroic traits with acquired ones, which presuppose a "growth mindset" (Franco, Blau, and Zimbardo 2011: 100). An eighteenth-century hero elect evokes class-based chivalry, whereas the more modern growth mindset allows a broader social distribution of heroism. Such concepts remain in flux and "the question of what the term 'hero' will mean for this generation is yet to be answered" (Franco, Blau, and Zimbardo 2011: 112). Lay concepts of heroism cluster around "risk-taking" (which implies danger to one's own well-being for the sake of someone else or for a higher cause) and "empathy/service" (Becker and Eagly 2004: 164), i. e., altruistic acts triggered by morally laudable rather than selfish motivations. Furthermore, three situations prevail in the test subjects' minds: "martial (military) heroism, civil heroism, and social heroism" (Franco, Blau, and Zimbardo 2011: 100). Social psychologists agree that heroes have perceived psychological and social uses (Kinsella, Ritchie, and Igou 2015a: 1 and 2015b: 114) and that these are part of each individual's "heroic imagination" (Zimbardo qtd. in Franco, Blau, and Zimbardo 2011: 111). The give-and-take between positive and negative traits of a real or imagined hero triggers an inner struggle, a "dissonance" (Franco, Blau, and Zimbardo 2011: 102, 103, 111), particularly when assessing heroism that may serve someone as a coping mechanism in difficult sociopolitical predicaments (Kinsella, Ritchie, and Igou 2015: 8–9). Analogous to heroism as either an inherent or an acquired personal quality, recent studies argue that those who prefer prominent heroic leaders regard democracy in the United States today as celebrating specific individuals' "exclusive" status; by contrast, those who favor grassroots everyday heroism of widely unknown, even anonymous non-celebrities share an "inclusive" view of American democratic society (Zimbardo, Breckenridge, and Moghadam 2013: 222 and 2015: 507, 512).

Which of these lay conceptions of heroism, then, apply to Alexander Hamilton in the musical, the companion volume, and in Ron Chernow's biography *Hamilton* (2004), which inspired Miranda in the first place? And which reading practices do these representations encourage? Ultimately, both Chernow and Miranda direct recipients' sympathies via their respective depiction of Elizabeth Schuyler Hamilton. Through the musical's performances and outreach activities as well as through the co-authored book publication, Miranda's transmedial engaging with Hamilton's legacy reaches the offstage world and encourages responses by lay perceivers of heroism.

Chernow's biography – a *New York Times* bestseller that participates in the ongoing boom of Founding Father publications for the mass market – shuttles between the entity view and the growth mindset, but the author then closes his text with an emphatic effort on dissolving dissonance within the implied reader's mind. Chernow introduces his Hamilton as an archetypal immigrant who "re-creates himself" (2004: 4) and who undergoes "a rapid metamorphosis into a full-blooded American" (92), which would imply that such metaphorical full-bloodedness is not inherited but merit-based. On the other hand, the narrative also contains references to Hamilton's "Mozart-like" (250) giftedness and to his superhuman capacities, descriptions of which blur the boundary between born genius and hard-working ambition (30, 33, 61, 232, 250, 353, 426, 444). The ostensible hero's central achievement is his verbal prowess as an author and orator, with which he supposedly penned "his way out of poverty" (37) and became the "foremost political pamphleteer in American history" (493).

Chernow's Hamilton is a military hero aware of risks and perfectly willing to sacrifice his life (72). More than that, he is "a fearless, swashbuckling intellectual warrior who excelled in bare-knuckled controversy" (59). Such argumentative heroism firmly plants him in the civil and social realms, particularly whenever Hamilton embraced controversial stances and stood up for a higher law (see, for instance, 196). Strikingly, Chernow's characterization of Hamilton creates a strong sense of dissonance, which is not only based on the author's hyperbolic style when describing Hamilton's strengths and weaknesses. Chernow criticizes Hamilton's support of the anti-immigrant Alien and Sedition Acts (572) and repeatedly diagnoses Hamilton's "egotism, outsize pride, and quick temper" (153; also see 232, 237, 406, 418, 453, 492, 514, 534, 619). In contrast, he partially downplays Hamilton's best-known extramarital affair by citing the extreme stress of professional and political labor (363). Chernow even offers a pseudo-psychoanalytical explanation according to which Hamilton was supposedly "ensnared by a sexual obsession" which forced him to regress to "the sensual, dissolute world of his childhood" (368).

The biography thus heroizes Hamilton as a rhetorical and political genius as well as military leader; it partially de-heroizes him through his character flaws; and it finally re-heroizes him through the depiction of Hamilton's fatal duel with Aaron Burr and of Elizabeth Schuyler Hamilton. Supposedly, the loving husband and father was both "incapable of turning the other cheek" (683) and ethically laudable because he threw away his fire during the duel (689). Aiming at readers' heartstrings, Chernow juxtaposes the misunderstood Hamilton with his hitherto invisible wife (130, 528), whose achievements the biographer sufficiently appreciates. She exemplifies the implied reader who remembers Hamilton's achievements while forgiving his shortcomings and who dedicates the rest of her life to helping the downtrodden, particularly orphans. She thus serves to dispel the substratum of dissonance in Hamilton's heroism and becomes a model for emulation.

3.2 *Hamilton: The Revolution* on the Stage and on the Page

Chernow wrote a 900-page book to convey his perspective on Hamilton. Most musicals comprise far fewer spoken and sung words, and they present music, dance, stage sets, and a set of scenes whose plot more often than not leads towards a sense of closure. Obviously, a successful Broadway show must attract large audiences over an extended time period. How could one make the American Revolution and the Founding Fathers exciting enough to achieve this? American musical theater is certainly studded with heroic protagonists, some of whom have impressed specific versions of American history on the minds of generations. Among these, musicals about the American Revolution are not prominent (Nereson 2016: 1055). The 1969 musical *1776* (Stone and Edwards 2014), for instance, depicts the Continental Congress debates about declaring independence. The dialogue and songs are highly jocular in tone, and the Founding Fathers come across as rather dusty and selfish buffoons. *Hamilton* takes a markedly different approach.

Miranda's construction of his protagonist's heroic status rests on three pillars: words as the driving force in Hamilton's life story, his afterlife in historical memory, and his appeal to specific twenty-first-century audiences. The musical suggests that it was first and foremost Hamilton's linguistic and rhetorical (rather than physical or military) prowess that allowed him to escape the poverty of his Caribbean home. Accordingly, the musical brings a Hamilton to life whose thirst for knowledge and relentless drive toward openly debating his political vision render him an ideal truth-seeking and fearless fighter for freedom and equality. The musical's finale, then, adeptly redirects the work's focus away from the historical personage per se towards the viewers' own world by shifting attention to Hamilton's wife and companions as they contemplate how he will be historicized. Hamilton's heroism as a supposed underdog who evolved into a remarkable identification model is thus placed within a metahistoriographical reflection on the ideological subtexts of who is remembered in which way. By implication, viewers who take up the musical's conceptualization of heroism may perpetuate it within their views on the history of the American Revolution and on the United States today.

Heroism and revolution occur on multiple levels in the musical and the companion volume. The American Revolution and the Early Republic provide the subject matter, and the characters are portrayed according to their respective roles during these turbulent times. Musically, *Hamilton*'s hybrid approach pushes the boundaries of the Broadway musical genre by combining a broad range of styles including R&B, Beatles-era Brit Pop, Broadway ballads, and rap. The intermedial forms of representation transform specific artistic styles into figurative renderings of specific social relations – as in the superimposition of the rap battle as a musical and dramatic form onto political debates in the post-revolutionary era. Furthermore, both the libretto and the other texts in the companion volume intersect the historiography of revolutionary era heroes with historical narratives of hip-hop artists whose achievements Miranda acknowledges through a dense web of verbal and sonic allusions and through detailed annotations.

The musical certainly includes war-related scenes of martial heroism. But the shift to the battle of ideas poses the main challenge to making *Hamilton* a viable musical that expounds on the conundrums of founding a new nation (see Nereson 2016: 1052). For instance, instead of ending the first act on the spectacular note of the American victory at Yorktown, it closes with the question "What Next?" (Miranda and McCarter 2016: 127) and raises the specter of the new nation's failure. This question is verbalized in a stage-effective manner first by – of all people – King George III and reiterated by George Washington in act two (2016: 163).

The musical's sung-through libretto comprises more words than most Shakespeare plays (Miranda and McCarter 2016: 250). It foregrounds the notion that many questions remain inconclusive and subject to coincidences and power relations among those who get to create historical narratives that interpret the past and affect the future. Oskar Eustis, the artistic director of the Public Theater, i. e., the theater in which Hamilton ran off-Broadway, perceives Miranda as a modern-day Shakespeare in the sense that he "takes the language of the people, and heightens it by making it verse" and that he "tells foundational myths of his country" which result in "mak[ing] the country the possession of everybody" (Eustis qtd. in Miranda and McCarter 2016: 103). Eustis's perspective as a theater practitioner is complemented by Questlove's as a hip-hop great who served as executive producer of the *Hamilton* cast album. Rather than seeing Miranda as a certain type of artist, Questlove stresses that "[j]ust from the way the story is told, I feel like hip-hop is now a legitimate filter – though it's always been legitimate to me. It's as vital and important as dancing or poetry or singing" (Questlove qtd. in Miranda and McCarter 2016: 197). These perspectives demonstrate some of the chasms *Hamilton* has been trying to straddle through its artistic means and its self-representation. Rather than reading Miranda's hip-hop-infused Broadway show as selling out to shallow presentism or to a 'usable past' rhetoric for merely commercial reasons, the trajectory of superimposing two eras is to encourage dedication to improving the contemporary United States by reinvigorating a specific take on revolutionary ideology. In the companion volume, the lyrics of the musical are thus printed alongside images of the performers in action so that hip-hop poetry and eighteenth-century scenarios share numerous pages. Also, the book contains offstage photos of the performers in 'regular' clothing which visualize their own back-and-forth between being an individual artist and citizen and embodying a role. Chapters that narrate their social backgrounds, their artistic careers, and their readings of the *Hamilton* experience complete the intermedial intricacies of auto/biography and historiography as well as the depiction of what can be classified as their heroic contribution to the current revolution that parallels the earlier one.

A triangle of heroism, knowledge, and freedom as the American Revolution's goal is established early on in the musical. In the first musical number, Aaron Burr calls Hamilton "a hero and a scholar" (Miranda and McCarter 2016: 11), and Hamilton says: "I will lay down my life if it sets us free" (26). At the same time, the libretto verbally intersects rap as a verbal war and the American Revolutionary War. For instance, Lafayette's military contributions go along with rapid-fire rapping skills, which Miranda annotates by calling Lafayette a "speed demon," "rap god," and "military superhero" (Miranda and McCarter

2016: 118n2).² Outside the musical, Miranda and the actor-singer Chris Jackson, who embodied George Washington in the first Broadway production, also performed in the improvisation rap group called Freestyle Love Supreme – a cooperation which Miranda describes with a military metaphor: it "was a little like being in a band together and a little like sharing a fox hole" (Miranda and McCarter 2016: 58).

Continuing the war/rap analogy, the musical numbers entitled "Cabinet Battle #1" and "Cabinet Battle #2" (Miranda and McCarter 2016: 161–163) pit Hamilton and his political opponents against one another in rhetorical combat. The first cabinet battle establishes Hamilton's morally higher ground by depicting him as an abolitionist concerned with a stable Early Republic as opposed to Thomas Jefferson who, as a slave owner, is interested in regional and personal advantages. The second one depicts him as taking up a controversial issue that may have cost him his long-term reputation, that is, his critical stance toward the French Revolution (Miranda and McCarter 2016: 192). Cautioning against military participation "in every revolution in the world" because they will "never stop" (Miranda and McCarter 2016: 193), Hamilton implicitly foreshadows current foreign policy debates (193n4). A third cabinet battle, focused on slavery (212–213), was unfortunately cut – ostensibly because it interrupted the dramatic coherence of the musical. Not unexpectedly, one of the main criticisms of the musical has been that the slavery debate should have been more prominent, that African American historical characters do not have major roles, and that Native Americans are absent (see McMaster 2016; Monteiro 2016; Nereson 2016: 1047). Slavery and abolitionism are certainly mentioned in the libretto and the companion volume (for references in the lyrics, see Miranda and McCarter 2016: 16, 27, 97, 122, 152, 161–162; for further references, see 27, 97, 122n7, 131, 152n4, 208, 212–213). Retaining the third cabinet battle would, however, have highlighted these references and would have complemented the casting strategy, particularly the selection of black performers to embody three U.S. presidents (Washington, Jefferson, and Madison). Reproducing these lyrics in the 'memoirs' of the musical, if I may call the book such, crucially contributes to the heroic status of the show's creators who pushed the envelope in multiple contexts but who were not successful on all accounts.

The focus on the difficulty of governing the new nation in the second act facilitates seeing Alexander Hamilton and other characters who are struggling with positioning themselves within an evolving sociopolitical matrix as engaging in

---

2 Miranda's notes are placed in the margins of the main text. References to his notes will be indicated by page number, lower-case "n," and note number.

acts of "social heroism." Such heroism does not require "immediate physical peril" but involves "considerable risk and personal sacrifice in other dimensions of life" because individuals are "trying to [...] push [...] toward a new ideal that has not yet found wide acceptance" (Franco, Blau, and Zimbardo 2011: 100). Dramatizing the characters' attempts to formulate sociopolitical ideals coheres with Chernow's and Miranda's argument regarding the potentially constructive or destructive power of words. This, in turn, prepares audience members as well as readers of the companion volume for the closing section of the show and for the outlook promoted by the book. For instance, Hamilton hurt his own reputation when he published the so-called Reynolds pamphlet that, on the one hand, disproves accusations of corruption during his tenure as Treasury Secretary but that, on the other hand, describes his extramarital affair with Maria Reynolds who – with her husband – blackmailed him for several years. Also, the conflict that leads to the fatal duel between Burr and Hamilton develops through an exchange of angry letters. Instead of ending the musical with Hamilton's dramatic death, the libretto returns to Miranda's central concern: historiography as mediating – and thus adapting – relational auto/biographies in order to define one's sense of belonging.

4 Towards Future Archives

The musical walks a thin line between broad appeal and innovation. According to Miranda and McCarter, the collage of musical genres is to serve as an entry point for a variety of audience members with different preferences (2016: 94) and as "another way of saying that American history can be told and retold, claimed and reclaimed, even by people who don't look like George Washington and Betsy Ross" (95). As Daveed Diggs, who embodied Jefferson, argues, "seeing a black man play Jefferson or Madison or Washington when he was a kid in Oakland might have changed his life" (149). Audiences also reacted strongly to seeing non-white actors dressed in Continental Army uniforms, "young men and women from communities that have seen their freedom infringed for hundreds of years, win freedom for us all" (113). In addition to the visually perceivable multi-ethnic casting, the show heroizes – in Miranda's words – Hamilton as both "the prototype of an immigrant striver (hard-working, ambitious, desperate to prove himself)" and "the model New Yorker: opinionated, hyperverbal, always on the make" (38). Thus, the show anchors its version of Hamilton in the history of the U.S. as a nation of immigrants and in a locally rooted self-image, in both cases casting its net back into the past and out into the audience and their heroic imaginaries of the future. The intermedial combination of words, music, and visual signs in both the musical and the companion volume "continues," according to Miranda and McCarter, the core of Hamilton's revolution as described by Henry Cabot Lodge: "the creation of a national sentiment" (11). Whereas such an emerging national consciousness has traditionally not been depicted as multiethnic, Miranda and McCarter emphasize that this shared feeling is to celebrate and to emerge from a diverse population (88).

Rather than ending the musical with the protagonist's death in a duel, the coda to his demise proffers what Miranda designates as "the key to the whole musical" (Miranda and McCarter 2016: 120n2): "Who lives, who dies, who tells your story" (280–281). The musical provides an explicit answer by adapting Chernow's use of Hamilton's wife as a framing device. In the course of the musical, she proceeds from pleading to become part of her husband's narrative in the song "That Would Be Enough" (110) to refusing to be part of her husband's life story after she learns of his affair with Maria Reynolds in "Burn" (238) and to finally spending the last five decades of her life as the guardian and promoter of her deceased husband's legacy. Significantly, the instability of archival material in Taylor's sense becomes clear when, in the second song, she sings "I'm erasing myself from the narrative. / Let future historians wonder / How Eliza reacted when you broke her heart" (238). She emphasizes the power to deny access to documents by "[b]urning the letters that might have redeemed" (238) her husband. The third song, "Who Lives, Who Dies, Who Tells Your Story?" (280), contrasts the fact that Hamilton has been less prominent in official histories of the revolution with Eliza's efforts to the contrary – efforts that were primarily based on publishing Hamilton's papers and an extensive biography, that is, on creating an archive of ostensibly stable documents which, in the musical, are presented as adaptable and malleable materials with which to reflect on the present. The volatility of preserving and then interpreting so-called documents contributes to the relative lack of closure in the musical, which the book publication ironically amends by including facsimiles of eighteenth-century and twenty-first-century materials related to the historical Hamilton and to *Hamilton: The Musical*. Significantly, audience members are among those who step into Elizabeth Schuyler Hamilton's shoes in continuing the legacy of the American Revolution. Just as she took up social causes, primarily through caring for orphans, audience members are to support disadvantaged or otherwise suffering people.[3] Miranda and McCarter make this obvious both verbally and visually, for instance by comple-

---

[3] In this context, more research needs to be done regarding the depiction of risk-taking heroes and altruistic characters, and of a possible division along gender lines (see Becker and Eagly 2004).

menting facsimiles of Hamilton's writings (see, for instance, 48, 165, 227) with a facsimile of high-school student Esteisy Seijas's rap on gay marriage (158).

Nevertheless, one needs to address that wealth amassed by success in commercial hip hop or on Broadway tends to raise eyebrows regarding the effectiveness of a sociopolitical message aimed at individuals who are economically and otherwise disadvantaged. With hip-hop braggadocio, the musical's Lafayette and Hamilton link their backgrounds with their contribution to the successful revolution, as expressed in the line "Immigrants: We get the job done" (Miranda and McCarter 2016: 121). Miranda and McCarter's published history of the musical's off-Broadway and Broadway runs stresses the importance of involving audiences that cannot afford regular Broadway tickets, in particular high-school students. Students have been working creatively with the musical (156–159), and the musical will be licensed for amateur productions in the early 2020s (160) which – Miranda hopes – may feature actors of all races playing the Founding Fathers as well as female actors embodying male characters (160). The book *Hamilton: The Revolution* ends with an appeal to the belief in *vita brevis, ars longa* or: presidential terms are short whereas art lives on in the body politic. This is a hopeful promise that, beyond the ending of President Obama's second term, the musical will offer a site for participatory and inclusive democracy based on a growth mindset that encourages everyone to become a social hero.

The archive that Miranda and McCarter's companion volume creates is designed to function as an instrument of wielding historiographic power by verbalizing and visualizing the agency of groups that are, in common usage, not regarded as historians at all. The intermedial intersections between onstage and offstage identities and realities belie the dichotomy between repertoire and archive. More than that, they promote the concept of empowering what has commonly been regarded as an ephemeral repertoire to become an archive created by geographically wide-spread multitudes of participants involved in developing "socially legitimate ways of understanding the past" which have "predictive power" (Taylor 2006: 68). For instance, the title of chapter VII "On the Character of George Washington and the Character of Chris Jackson [i. e., of the singer-actor embodying the first U.S. president in the musical]" (Miranda and McCarter 2016: 58) playfully puns with the double meaning of individual traits of a historical personage and a contemporary man as well as a *dramatis persona*. Similarly, the image of President Obama (285) speaking from a lectern and thus being visually coded as an officially accepted orator is followed by the penultimate page of the entire book, which combines an image of Miranda as Hamilton on the stage, half-bent over a desk strewn with papers, followed by bio blurbs of Miranda and McCarter plus a list of people to whom the authors extend their thanks.

Outside the musical performances and the book publication, the transmedial life narrative also extends to online formats. The more broadly accessible YouTube channel *Hamilton: An American Musical*, to some extent, compensates for the limited accessibility of Broadway shows in New York City and on tour. The rap video entitled "Wrote My Way Out," which is placed prominently on the channel's opening page, confirms the centrality of words and of transgenerational concerns. This song from the 'Hamilton Mixtape,' from which the musical emerged, features Nas, Dave East, Lin-Manuel Miranda, and Aloe Blacc. The lyrics depict words as possible sources of hope and of improving one's bleak situation. The New York cityscape (which is reminiscent of countless other rap music videos) and the foregrounding of young children and adolescents who mouth the words vocalized by the adult performers places the central theme of the glamorous Broadway musical into the more commonly recognizable context of hip hop as a socially engaged art form which not only references multiple modes and media of expression but also transforms them artistically. That words have an impact particularly in the contexts of immigration and the image of the United States of America as a nation must be crystal clear to anyone who observes how language carries ideological baggage and bears practical consequences. On February 23, 2018, the U.S. Citizenship and Immigration Services deleted the phrase "nation of immigrants" from its mission statement. The new version reads: "U.S. Citizenship and Immigration Services administers the nation's lawful immigration system, safeguarding its integrity and promise by efficiently and fairly adjudicating requests for immigration benefits while protecting Americans, securing the homeland, and honoring our values" ("About Us"). Rather than stipulating possible benefits of immigration or expressing pride in a long history of immigration, this statement centers on in-group self-protection. The transmedial auto/biographical narrative of *Hamilton*, by contrast, fosters a perspective on the United States that verbalizes, visualizes, and sonically portrays diversity as a wellspring of a democratic future.

Works Cited

"About Us". U.S. Citizenship and Immigration Services. <https://www.uscis.gov/aboutus> [accessed 1 March 2018].

Balestrini, Nassim Winnie. [forthcoming 2018]. "Intermedial Hip-Hop Life Writing". In: Justin D. Burton and Jason Lee Oakes (eds.). *Oxford Handbook of Hip-Hop Music Studies*. Oxford: Oxford University Press.

Balestrini, Nassim Winnie. 2016. "Hip-Hop Life Writing and African American Urban Ecology". In: Catrin Gersdorf and Juliane Braun (eds.). *America after Nature: Democracy, Culture, Environment*. Heidelberg: Winter. 287–307.

Balestrini, Nassim Winnie. 2015. "Strategic Visuals in Hip-Hop Life Writing". *Popular Music and Society* 38 (2): 224–242.
Becker, Selwyn W. and Alice H. Eagly. 2004. "The Heroism of Women and Men". *American Psychologist* 59 (3): 163–178.
Chernow, Ron. 2004. *Alexander Hamilton*. New York: Penguin.
Eminem, with Sacha Jenkins. 2008. *The Way I Am*. Designed by Headcase Design. New York: Dutton/Penguin.
Franco, Zeno E., Kathy Blau, and Philip G. Zimbardo. 2011. "Heroism: A Conceptual Analysis and Differentiation Between Heroic Action and Altruism". *Review of General Psychology* 15(2): 99–113.
Hall, Jacquelyn Dowd. 1998. "'You Must Remember This': Autobiography as Social Critique". *The Journal of American History* 85(2): 439–465. <http://www.jstor.org/stable/2567747> [accessed 1 February 2018].
Jay-Z [Shawn Carter]. 2011. *Decoded*. Expanded Edition. New York: Virgin Books/Spiegel & Grau/Random House.
Keen, Suzanne. 2016. "Life Writing and the Empathetic Circle". *Concentric: Literary and Cultural Studies* September: 9–26.
Kinsella, Elaine L., Timothy D. Ritchie, and Eric R. Igou. 2015a. "Lay Perspectives on the Social and Psychological Functions of Heroes". *Frontiers in Psychology* 6, article 130: 1–12.
Kinsella, Elaine L., Timothy D. Ritchie, and Eric R. Igou. 2015b. "Zeroing in on Heroes: A Prototype Analysis of Hero Features". *Journal of Personality and Social Psychology* 108 (1): 114–127.
Levine, Lawrence. 1988. *Highbrow/Lowbrow: The Emergence of Cultural Hierarchy in America*. Cambridge, MA: Harvard University Press.
"Lin-Manuel Miranda Performs at the White House Poetry Jam". The Obama White House, 2 November 2009. <https://www.youtube.com/watch?v=WNFf7nMIGnE> [accessed 5 March 2018].
McMaster, James. "Why *Hamilton* Is not the Revolution You Think It Is". *HowlRound*, 23 February 2016. <Howlround.com/why-hamilton-is-not-the-revolution-you-think-it-is> [accessed 15 December 2017]
Miranda, Lin-Manuel and Jeremy McCarter. 2016. *Hamilton: The Revolution: Being the Complete Libretto of the Broadway Musical, with a True Account of Its Creation, and Concise Remarks on Hip-Hop, the Power of Stories, and the New America*. New York: Grand Central Publishing.
Monteiro, Lyra D. 2016. "Race-Conscious Casting and the Erasure of the Black Past in Lin-Manuel Miranda's *Hamilton*". *Public Historian* 38(1): 89–98.
Nereson, Ariel. 2016. "Hamilton's America: An Unfinished Symphony with a Stutter (Beat)". *American Quarterly* 68(4): 1045–1059.
Rajewsky, Irina. 2005. "Intermediality, Intertextuality, and Remediation: A Literary Perspective on Intermediality". *Intermédialités* 6: 43–64.
Shelley, Percy Bysshe. 1993. "From A Defence of Poetry". In: M. H. Abrams (ed.). *The Norton Anthology of English Literature*. 6th ed., vol. 2. New York: Norton. 753–765.
Smith, Sidonie and Julia Watson. 2010. *Reading Autobiography: A Guide for Interpreting Life Narratives*. Minneapolis: University of Minnesota Press.

Stone, Peter and Sherman Edwards. 2014. "1776". In: Laurence Mason (ed.). *American Musicals 1950–1969: The Complete Books and Lyrics of Eight Broadway Classics*. New York: Library of America. 553–644.
Taylor, Diana. 2006. "Performance and/as History". *TDR/The Drama Review (1988–)* 50(1): 67–86.
Taylor, Diana. 2003. *The Archive and the Repertoire: Performing Cultural Memory in the Americas*. Durham, NC: Duke University Press.
"Wrote My Way Out". <https://www.youtube.com/channel/UCKhSqWRvBtjlivrs_xeT5aQ> [accessed 1 March 2018].
Zimbardo, Philip G., James N. Breckenridge, and Fathali M. Moghadam. 2015. "Culture, Militarism, and America's Heroic Future". *Culture & Psychology* 21(4): 505–514.
Zimbardo, Philip G., James N. Breckenridge, and Fathali M. Moghaddam. 2013. "'Exclusive' and 'Inclusive' Visions of Heroism and Democracy". *Current Psychology* 32: 221–233.

Ina Bergmann
Emily Dickinson, Intermediality, and Life Writing: An Interview with Susan Snively

Susan Snively is guide, discussion leader, and film scriptwriter for the Emily Dickinson Museum. She is the founder and was the first director of the Writing Center at Amherst College, where she worked from 1981 until 2008. In the course of her career, she taught courses in writing and autobiographies of women, and she continues to lecture and give readings. Furthermore, she has published four collections of poems – *From This Distance* (1981), *Voices in the House* (1988), *The Undertow* (1998), and *Skeptic Traveler* (2005) – and has received numerous prizes and awards for her writing. Besides her poetry, Snively has published essays both personal and critical, and, most recently, a novel, *The Heart Has Many Doors* (2015), about the relationship between Emily Dickinson and Judge Otis Phillips Lord. She is also the screenwriter and narrator of two documentary films in the three-volume series *Angles of a Landscape* on Emily Dickinson: *Seeing New Englandly* (2010) and *My Business Is to Sing* (2012).

Ina Bergmann: You have been a practitioner in various practices of life writing for decades. For example, you published *Composing Yourself: A Guide to Writing Personal Statements* (1983), and you have taught courses on writing and women's autobiographies. What is your view of life writing as a personal or even private genre? What are its goals and benefits, especially for women?

Susan Snively: You speak of life writing as encompassing many genres, including film, memoir, and just about everything else. Of course, among its many forms are the autobiographical essay, film, memoir, and poem. It may begin as a private act – a diary entry, or an intimate letter, or even a fantasy inscribed as a story, or part of the draft of a work not meant to be seen right away. This 'private' act may be left to be discovered later, hidden in a strongbox, or attached to a will. But writers are sneaky, and love to hide and yet be discovered at the same time. "Good to hide, and hear 'em hunt!" a Dickinson poem (# 842) begins. Life writing is dramatic, evasive, and full of coded messages – that is part of its power. For women, it can be a subversive act. Subversive acts are fun and full of mischief. Women need to make mischief, in order to defy power or propriety, but also to give life to their words.

IB: You are also a prolific and prize-winning poet. Often, your poetry takes its incentive from the lives of famous women, as in your ventriloquist poem "Mary, Queen of Scots" from your collection *Voices in the House*. And, of course, your poetry is inspired by the life and work of Emily Dickinson, for example in "The View from Dickinson's" from the same collection or "Elegy for Sarah" from the earlier *From This Distance*. In the latter poems, biographical and autobiographical materials seem to blur. What is your specific interest in exploring women's lives in your poetry?

SS: I like exploring other lives in whatever form I choose. Right now it's prose more than poetry. Over the past eight years, since I retired from Amherst College, I've given talks for the Dickinson Museum Poetry Discussion Group, which meets once a month. I've talked about Dickinson's winter poems, her letters to Judge Otis Phillips Lord, her poems about balloons, imprisonment, secrecy, and lately, the art of hiding. The discussions are always lively, and it's a pleasure to hear what other Dickinson readers think. So this is a mutual exploration, assisted by tea, coffee, and cookies.

I don't write to engage in rescue or missionary work, but to put words on paper. Women's lives – the ones I've written about, and certainly the ones I've read about – are infinitely interesting because they often challenge convention. But they're interesting in other ways as well: because of their connections to other people, their daring escapades (whether real or imaginary), their talent for disguise, and their attempts to change their own and others' lives. Men also write about women, and vice versa. Everybody, whatever their gender, is a potential subject, full of threat, promise, and adventure.

IB: Poetry can be considered a genre that is prone to the use of ekphrasis, which is an intermedial device. Emily Dickinson made frequent use of it, despite her declaration "I would not paint – a picture –" in one of her poems (# 505). Which specific opportunities does ekphrasis offer to a poet? Are there any particular ekphrastic poems by Emily Dickinson and/or from your own oeuvre which you would like to discuss here?

SS: Two visual artists whose work Dickinson knew were Thomas Cole, described as the founder of the Hudson River School of landscape artists, and Frederic Church. Cole's series "The Voyage of Life" (1842) was copied many times, and Dickinson probably saw it when she attended Mount Holyoke Female Seminary in 1847–1848. Cole, a devout Christian, depicted the voyage as a spiritual quest. He infused the landscape with divine meaning and remarked in his "Essay on American Scenery" (1836): "We are still in Eden" (12). Dickinson was not conventionally pious, but she admired Cole and even signed a letter to Sue Gilbert, her sister-in-law, "Cole" (# 214). She would no doubt have been moved by the images of glowing, angelic guides who help the voyager through the stages of his life.

Frederic Church, a pupil of Cole, ranged wide for subjects like the Chimborazo, the Arctic, the Connecticut River Oxbow, and dramatic landscape events. Dickinson probably knew Church's stunning depiction of the Aurora Borealis, because of a dramatic sighting of the phenomenon in New England, in September 1851. She wrote a letter to her brother, Austin, about the "excitement in the village. The sky was a beautiful red, bordering on crimson, and rays of a gold pink color were constantly shooting off from a kind of sun in the centre [...] Father happened to see it [...] and rang the bell *himself* to call attention to it" (# 53).

Later, she wrote this poem (# 290). Its bold language combines "vaster attitudes" with the humility induced by awe.

> Of Bronze – and Blaze –
> The North – tonight –
> So adequate – it forms –
> So preconcerted with itself –
> So distant – to alarms –
> An Unconcern so sovereign
> To Universe, or me –
> Infects my simple spirit
> With Taints of Majesty –
> Till I take vaster attitudes –
> And strut opon [sic] my stem –
> Disdaining Men, and Oxygen,
> For Arrogance of them –
>
> My Splendors, are Menagerie –
> But their Competeless Show
> Will entertain the Centuries
> When I, am long ago,
> An Island in dishonored Grass –
> Whom none but Daisies, know –

The fiery colors, the celestial display, the drama of the cosmos doing whatever it likes – all of these elements keep human beings in their earthly place. Dickinson is a genius at many things, and here she both brags and marvels, in one of her memorable performances. Confined to the reality of mortal flesh and grass, she also plays with daisies. (The alternative word in the last line was "Beetles.") Daisy was one of her nicknames. The image of her "strutting upon her stem" conveys a radical charm. (She spelled "upon" "opon.") Whenever I read or recite the poem, I feel gleeful, like a child who has successfully tricked the grown-ups into believing a wild story.

Emily Dickinson read widely and deeply about dramatic events of all kinds. She had a particular fascination with volcanoes, although she never witnessed a volcanic eruption. Articles in newspapers and scientific journals, engravings in publications, illustrations, and reproductions of volcanic events – Vesuvius erupted seven times during her lifetime – inspired her interest in seeking metaphoric connections between these events and the "fire, and smoke, and gun" (# 165) of her own powerful passions. In another, undated poem (# 1705), she combines lessons from her geography book with revelations of her own wild heart:

> Volcanoes be in Sicily
> And South America
> I judge from my Geography
> Volcano nearer here
> A Lava step at any time
> Am I inclined to climb
> A Crater I may contemplate
> Vesuvius at Home

IB: Life writing encompasses biographical work in a multitude of media. It also blurs the ostensible divide between fact and fiction, just consider the highly popular genres of biofiction and biopics. For you, what are the differences between the biographical work on Emily Dickinson you have done, on the one hand, as a guide at the Amherst Homestead and as a scriptwriter for the *Angles of a Landscape* series, and, on the other hand, as a novelist in *The Heart Has Many Doors*?

SS: Learning to be a guide under the tutelage of Cindy Dickinson – the former director of programs and interpretation at the Dickinson Museum, who is not related to the poet – gave me a chance to re-read everything I had read before, but this time with the purpose of bringing Emily Dickinson alive in new ways, refreshed by reading criticism and biography, by talking with colleagues, and by re-reading her poems and letters. The biographical work merged with the film script when my friend Terry Y. Allen, who had written the script of the first film in the *Angles of a Landscape* series, *The Poet in Her Bedroom* (2009), asked me to help write the second script, *Seeing New Englandly*, produced by filmmaker Ernest Urvater. I also wrote and narrated the third film in the series, *My Business Is to Sing*, based on Carolyn Lindley Cooley's book, *The Music of Emily Dickinson's Poems and Letters* (2003). The titles, of course, come from Dickinson's poems. We never considered any other source as useful as these.

At every point in this project, we were excited to discover images familiar to Dickinson; to visit museums and other sources in our valley full of smart, talented people; and to rediscover the poet's poems and letters. Each project took 18 months – interrupted by my writing a novel about the romance between the poet and Judge Otis Phillips Lord, published as *The Heart Has Many Doors*. Ernest Urvater is a filmmaker, a physicist, a musician, and a joy to work with. His wife Terry Y. Allen, journalist, writer, and Dickinson guide, helped us shape these films in her capacity as an expert editor.

I began the novel in 2010 after re-reading Millicent Todd Bingham's powerful little book, *Emily Dickinson: A Revelation* (1954). In it, Bingham brought to light the letters Dickinson had written to Judge Otis Phillips Lord, her father's best friend, described by Bingham as the poet's "last great love" (3). The letters had been discovered after Emily Dickinson's death and kept by Austin Dickinson, who gave them to his lover, Mabel Loomis Todd. She in turn gave them to her daughter after forty years.

Re-reading them, I was again struck by how passionate, mischievous, and surprising they are. Judge Lord was a mighty figure on the Massachusetts Supreme Court. He could be a tiger in the courtroom, but he had a warm, funny, affectionate nature, and he had known Emily Dickinson all her life. After his wife died in 1877, it is assumed that their long friendship blossomed into love.

I take many liberties in the novel, such as giving the dignified judge a tattoo in an interesting place, taking the pair on a romantic picnic in a Sunderland meadow, and allowing Dickinson to take a secret trip to Salem (his home). Although the novel rests on verifiable historical facts and contains characters who actually existed, it is a love story, and I allow its events to create some mayhem in the Dickinson family.

It's odd to think that I was writing film scripts and the novel at the same time. They all required research and much exploring in libraries, museums, and the occasional graveyard. I loved doing that. The novel took me a long time, and I received good advice from my writer friends. Bingham's book truly was a revelation, and I think she helped bring to light an Emily Dickinson who deserved to shine forth in a new way, together with her wise, brilliant, tempestuous Judge Lord.

IB: The two films in the *Angles of a Landscape* series for which you wrote the scripts are entitled *Seeing New Englandly* and *My Business Is to Sing*. They imply a connection between biography and intermediality. You mentioned that these titles are taken directly from Dickinson's writings. Would you mind elaborating a bit more on what made you choose these titles, and, of course, how they relate to the respective agendas of the films?

SS: *Seeing New Englandly* comes from a poem that begins "The Robin's my Criterion for Tune – / Because I grow – where Robins do – " (# 256). The poet is at one with her native landscape, inseparable from its creatures and seasons. The film is filled with images that evoke the New England that Dickinson took as her subject, and where she 'grew' as a poet.

IB: In *My Business Is to Sing*, Emily Dickinson's poetry becomes associated with music. Why is this specific intermedial approach to Dickinson's life and work so productive?

SS: The subtitle of Cooley's excellent book is "A Study of Imagery and Form." She writes in her Preface: "Recognizing the importance of music to Dickinson's verse can intensify a reader's awareness of the aesthetic richness of the Dickinson canon [...]" (1). As Carolyn points out, the poems contain a whole orchestra of instruments: drum, trumpet, bugle, flute, pipe organ, violin, mandolin, bells, banjos, and guitars. The human voice sings, warbles, trills, booms, and makes what Mabel Loomis Todd called "startling little poetic bombs" (qtd. in Cooley 66). Singing, of course, brings together music and poetry. Bird-song, which the poet knew well and could probably imitate, makes "A Music numerous as space – / But neighboring as Noon" (# 783).

We learn from Cooley – as well as from re-reading the poems and letters – that Dickinson was quite musical from an early age, picking out little tunes – "moosic" (10) – on her Aunt Lavinia's piano, taking lessons, playing hymns, ballads, classical pieces, opera choruses, and sentimental songs. She played for her family and friends, and in her 20s composed "weird & beautiful melodies" (Kate Scott Anthon qtd. in Cooley 18) later remembered by friends – although, alas, she simply improvised these marvels and never wrote down the notes! In Amherst, Springfield, Boston, Cambridge, Washington, D.C, Philadelphia, and elsewhere she would have heard concerts and recitals. Jenny Lind sang in Northampton in 1851, and when the family heard the 'Swedish nightingale,' Emily Dickinson's father disliked all the bird-trills and warblings, and sat "looking *mad* and *silly*." Her description of her father's reaction appears in a letter she wrote to Austin on July 6, 1851 (# 46). Reading it always makes me laugh.

Music is inseparable from Dickinson's poems. It is frequently remarked that one could sing all of Dickinson's poems to "The Yellow Rose of Texas," which isn't true, but I wouldn't stop anyone from amusing a crowd by trying. Many are written in Common Hymn Meter, but her rhythms and images are so supple and original that we see how her particular music transformed a conventional meter to suit her own uses. *My Business Is to Sing* uses lots of music: Irish songs, Schubert, traditional hymns by Isaac Watts, brass bands, and opera. It also features a musical setting written by composer Alice Parker, who said of the poem, "The sweet joy mixed with her own anguish stood in stark contrast – as night and day, as human despair and natural rebirth" (qtd. in Cooley 140). I can't read this poem (# 1420) without thinking of Parker's music:

> One Joy of so much anguish
> Sweet nature has for me
> I shun it as I do Despair
> Or dear iniquity –
> Why Birds, a Summer morning
> Before the Quick of Day
> Should stab my ravished spirit
> With Dirks of Melody
> Is part of an inquiry
> That will receive reply
> When Flesh and Spirit sunder
> In Death's Immediately –

Dickinson's poems mention twenty-two species of birds, whose songs reveal their own "intimate delight" (# 1265). We also include the sounds of crickets, cats, dogs, horses, frogs, and flies. "Musicians wrestle everywhere" (# 157), the poet wrote, and some of them never took lessons or played in any orchestra but nature itself.

IB: The topics that *Seeing New Englandly* discusses with regard to Emily Dickinson's life and work oscillate between the private and the public. Education and health are issues that concern the poet's private life, while historical events such as the Civil War and polar expeditions are more general concerns of her time. Why did you choose exactly these topics for this biographical film?

SS: Some of our topics emerged from questions we are asked when we guide visitors at the Museum. New England, especially Massachusetts, has always been a center of education. Dickinson's grandfather Samuel Fowler Dickinson helped to found Amherst College in 1821; her father and brother both served as its treasurer. The poet's attendance at Mount Holyoke Female Seminary was important to her, although she stayed only one year – not unusual. The family library was a treasure trove, with fine editions of Shakespeare, Emerson, and classical works, and a remarkable work about Arctic exploration written by explorer Elisha Kent Kane. Kane was one of many explorers who tried to find British explorer Sir John Franklin who had disappeared while trying to locate the Northwest Passage. This tragedy – never completely resolved – was the subject of many newspaper stories, even dramas, poems, and novels. Dickinson alludes to it in several poems and letters.

As for the Civil War, we now know that Dickinson wrote the majority of her nearly 1,800 poems during the years of the Civil War: 1861–1865. Her poems are not topical, but the War is an underlying presence in her poems about death, violence, and conflict. Amherst lost several dozen citizens, black and white, during the War. "It feels a shame to be Alive – / When Men so brave – are dead –," she writes in poem # 444, written in 1863.

We also include a section called "The Eyes of the Poet" about Dickinson's eye trouble – *anterior uveitis*, which affected her irises and threatened her vision. Staying in Cambridge with her cousins so that she could be treated by an eminent ophthalmologist, she felt exiled to a sort of prison. In 1864 and 1865 she had to be away from home for months at a time. Luckily for her – and for the rest of the world! – her eyes improved and she was reunited with her family and her big dog, Carlo.

IB: *Seeing New Englandly* also combines visual elements such as landscape shots, paintings (portraits and landscapes), and photographs as well as shots of books (illustrations and text), poems, and hand-written letters with audio elements such as narration, poetry recitals, and music. In what way does this intermediality enhance the biographical work of the film? And how does intermediality figure within the aesthetic experience of viewers?

SS: Ernest Urvater, the film-maker, had done other films, including one on *Berthe Morisot* (1989), and *The Poet in Her Bedroom*, the first film of the series, as well as other documentaries. He knew that the film had to include, and emphasize, the passing of the seasons as a theme in Dickinson's poetry, the physical evidence of writing and reading that Dickinson fans enjoy, and the "Titanic Opera[s]" (# 593) the poet heard and saw in her own neighborhood. With wonderful museums in Springfield, Mount Holyoke and Smith Colleges, Amherst College, and a trove of fine libraries – not to mention the Dickinson Museum itself – we had a lot to choose from. My husband contrived a plain bird-feeder so that we could capture birds having lunch; Ernie hurried out into the snow to capture an image of Dickinson's cousin Sophia Holland's grave; I did a lot of research on the Luminist painters known to the poet; furthermore, her manuscripts were made available to us for filming. I have done a lot of narrating, and we had wonderful sound-people to work with. Ernie selected much of the music, except for Mendelssohn's "Elegie" (1845), which ends the film – I chose that one because I love it and believe that Dickinson herself played it. I am unable to prove that, but she played a lot of Schubert, some Beethoven, and the usual classical composers music teachers assign to their pupils. There is also a scene in my novel, *The Heart Has Many Doors*, where she plays the piece for Judge Otis Lord, and a chapter depicting her attendance at a concert in Boston. She may have done so, because she refers to Anton Rubinstein in one of her letters (# 390), and he often played in Boston's Music Hall. It's sometimes hard for me not to believe that what I imagined and turned into a novel might not have happened at all.

IB: Is there an advantage of the filmic biography over more conventional forms of biography, such as the book? And if so, is this plus (for the recipient) directly connected to the film's (greater) intermediality?

SS: I don't believe I ever heard or knew the word 'intermediality' until this interview project. I suppose that if the films work for people, it's because they reveal how Dickinson exists in many realms of art and brings together art, music, poetry, and all of its myriad subjects. I doubt if Dickinson would have used the word, but she would have known what it alludes to – not just known it, but acted out its multiple meanings. And of course, she was ahead of her time as a poet, a thinker, a nonconformist, as a writer of wise and hilarious letters. There are moments in her poems that seem like little films. You could make a tiny film of her poem "A Bird came down the Walk" (# 328), or "Two Butterflies went out at Noon" (# 533), or "Because I could not stop for Death" (# 712), or even "Alone and in a Circumstance / Reluctant to be told / A spider on my reticence / Assiduously crawled" (# 1167), which takes place in the Dickinson privy. She had a dramatic, performative imagination that saw movement and life in everything, including a fly on the windowpane in a room where someone is dying.

"Biography," she once wrote in a letter, "Convinces us of the fleeting of the Biographied" (# 972). In everything I've written about Emily Dickinson, especially *The Heart Has Many Doors*, I often sensed her fleeing around a corner, leading me on a merry chase, accompanied by Judge Lord, her sister Vinnie and brother Austin – he of the long legs – , Lord's nasty niece Abbie tripping over her fancy skirts, her little nephew Ned saying 'Wait for me!,' and big old Carlo, the dog. How wrong it would have felt to capture Emily Dickinson and present her as a kind of biographical trophy. So I don't have an answer to the question of the "advantage of the filmic biography over more conventional forms." This seems like a contest without a winner, and I hope it stays that way.

IB: Thank you very much for sharing your thoughts on Emily Dickinson, intermediality, and life writing with us. We very much appreciate your willingness to participate in this interview and offer your highly-valued perspective on the topic as an experienced life writer in numerous media.

SS: The chance to do this interview allowed me to revisit Dickinson's poems and letters, and experience again their humor, power, and mystery. Responding to the questions helped me clarify my thoughts about the poet and her many sources of inspiration. Other works of art, literature, and music took Dickinson – and now her many readers – to what she called "Enchanted Ground" (# 1118).

Works Cited

Berthe Morisot: The Forgotten Impressionist. 1989. Produced by Ernest Urvater, script written and narrated by Teri J. Edelstein. Sawmill River Productions. DVD.

Bingham, Millicent Todd. 1954. *Emily Dickinson: A Revelation.* New York: Harper and Brothers.

Cole, Thomas. 1836. "Essay on American Scenery". *American Monthly Magazine*: 1–12. <https://www.csun.edu/~ta3584/Cole.htm> [accessed 22 January 2018].

Cooley, Carolyn Lindley. 2003. *The Music of Emily Dickinson's Poems and Letters: A Study of Imagery and Form.* Jefferson, NC: McFarland.

Johnson, Thomas H. (ed.). 2016 [1970]. *The Complete Poems of Emily Dickinson.* London: Faber and Faber.

Johnson, Thomas H. and Theodora Ward (eds.). 1958. *The Letters of Emily Dickinson.* Cambridge, MA: Belknap Press of Harvard University Press.

My Business Is to Sing. Angles of a Landscape: Emily Dickinson. 2012. Produced by Ernest Urvater, script written, narrated, and associate-produced by Susan Snively. Amherst, Massachusetts, Sawmill River Productions. Emily Dickinson Museum. DVD.

Seeing New Englandly. Angles of a Landscape: Emily Dickinson. 2010. Produced by Ernest Urvater, script written, narrated, and associate-produced by Susan Snively. Sawmill River Productions. Emily Dickinson Museum. DVD.

Snively, Susan. 1981. *From This Distance.* Cambridge, MA: Alice James Books.

Snively, Susan. 1983. *Composing Yourself: A Guide to Writing Personal Statements.* Amherst: Amherst College.

Snively, Susan. 1988. *Voices in the House.* Alabama Poetry Series. Tuscaloosa: University of Alabama Press.

Snively, Susan. 1998. *The Undertow.* Contemporary Poetry Series. Gainesville: University of Central Florida.

Snively, Susan. 2005. *Skeptic Traveler.* Cincinnati, OH: David Robert Books/WordTech Press.

Snively, Susan. 2015. *The Heart Has Many Doors.* Amherst, MA: White River Press.

The Poet in Her Bedroom. Angles of a Landscape: Emily Dickinson. 2009. Produced by Ernest Urvater, script written by Terry Y. Allen, narrated by Joni Denn. Sawmill River Productions. Emily Dickinson Museum. DVD.

Wilmerding, John. 1989. *American Light: The Luminist Movement 1850–1875.* Princeton, NJ: Princeton University Press.

Further Reading

"Susan Snively: Author & Speaker". Susan Snively, 2015. <http://susansnively.com> [accessed 23 February 2017].

Nassim Winnie Balestrini
The Respectful Biographer's Empathetic Imagination: An Interview about Intermediality and Life Writing with Brenda Wineapple

Literature scholar, essayist, and nonfiction author Brenda Wineapple has been a prominent voice in American biography since the 1980s. She is the recipient of numerous prestigious prizes and fellowships, such as the Academy Award in Literature from the American Arts and Letters, a Guggenheim fellowship, and a Pushcart Prize. She received the Ambassador Award for Best Biography for *Hawthorne: A Life* (2003), and her *White Heat: The Friendship of Emily Dickinson and Thomas Wentworth Higginson* (2008) was a finalist for a National Critics Circle Award in Biography. Recently named a Public Scholar by the National Endowment for the Humanities (2017), Wineapple is also an elected Fellow of the American Academy of Arts and Sciences and the Society of American Historians. She has taught at leading academic institutions like Columbia University and was director of the Leon Levy Center for Biography at The Graduate School, CUNY. Her first book, *Genêt: A Biography of Janet Flanner* (1989), is the first biography of the journalist. In *Sister Brother: Gertrude and Leo Stein* (1996), Wineapple ventured into relational life writing by presenting a dual biography of the prominent pair of siblings – a feat that she repeated with *White Heat*. Her *Hawthorne* also tackles a canonized author whose inner life has been as much of a mystery as Dickinson's. Her approach of embedding the Dickinson–Higginson correspondence within the sociopolitical context of the time then prepared the broader sweep of her most recent book, *Ecstatic Nation: Confidence, Crisis, and Compromise, 1848–1877* (2013), which offers itself as a magisterial companion piece to the biographies of nineteenth-century literary figures.

Nassim Winnie Balestrini: Ms. Wineapple – throughout your career, you have been bridging the ostensible gaps between fiction and non-fiction, the worlds of literary aesthetics and historiography. What initially drove your interest in writing biographies?

Brenda Wineapple: Prior to writing a biography of Janet Flanner, I'd never been much interested in biography, but when I visited the Flanner/Solano archives at the Library of Congress in Washington, D.C. (I had been thinking about Flanner and her career as a writer/stylist/journalist), I discovered there the riveting correspondence of a community of women who had sustained one another for a lifetime. Since I wanted to do them justice, it seemed to me that biography would be the means for accomplishing just that: for talking about their lives, their commitments, and at the same time preserving their voices as I sought to explore and preserve Janet Flanner's.

NWB: You have several decades of experience in researching and writing biographies, and in teaching the phenomenon of biography in academic contexts. Your work has been highly valued by the most prestigious cultural institutions in the United States and by innumerable readers. Have there been major changes in your approach to biography? If so, which events or thoughts may have triggered these changes of direction or adjustments?

BW: My approach to biography has not changed substantially. What has changed is my interest in biography both as a belletristic genre and as narrative, though I have actually stopped writing biography, partly because I think biographical narrative need not be confined within the conventional brick-like house of biography. Interestingly (at least to me), my book *White Heat* is considered a biography and was a finalist for the National Book Critics Circle in Biography, which was a great honor; yet in the very first chapter to that book, I do say that *White Heat* is not a biography of Emily Dickinson, of whom biography gets us nowhere; nor is it a biography of Thomas Higginson. Of course, that does not mean I did not avail myself of a biographical narrative when it suited me, which it often did. But I saw the book as a book about poetry, about commitments (literary and political), and about the work of two unusual, incompatible friends. Among other things.

NWB: In your career as a professor, what do you find particularly crucial in teaching prospective writers of biographies?

BW: Prospective writers or biographers need in the very first place to be able to write; to eschew jargon (a function of writing well); and as fully as possible to be able to enter the lives of others, to try to see what they saw, feel what they felt; to inhabit what they inhabited in the time, culture, place, skin where they lived. That is, they must be able to exercise a sympathetic imagination while they remember, all the while, to respect the integrity of the other person or persons as separate from the writer. As Richard Holmes once suggested, we try to cross a bridge into the past, but we must recognize too that the bridge is always "broken" (27).

NWB: Which changes, if any, have you observed in how your students approach biography as a genre? And how do you explain certain changes or the lack thereof?

BW: In the academy, insofar as I have a connection to it, I find that students by and large approach biography as they have for a very long time: that is, as the poor relation of literary criticism, to be tolerated if not actively shunned. Of course, I am talking about students of literature, not historians (which is too bad). However, when I teach in MFA programs, which I now mainly do, I find that the students in these programs approach biography as a belletristic adventure in nonfiction, or so I hope, with a distinctive and distinguished classical past.

NWB: Which role did the material form(s) and media, such as verbal narrative, visual images, and sound recordings, which are used to convey biography, play in the process of reconstructing lives? Which ones do you consider particularly central or influential?

BW: When writing/researching biography in sources beyond the written word, I'd say that I use anything and everything, from paintings to photographs, from passports to birth certificates, from recorded broadcasts to brocaded articles of clothing to pressed flowers, from census reports to probated wills, from filmed documentaries (if available) to gravestones. Each and all of these play their prominent part, but as for their influence, that depends on the subject at hand – and those items, objects, documents that have been lost or destroyed and that therefore tell their own story. I cast a wide net, or I try to do that, in order to comprehend and imagine another world and the psyche of a unique person, who is not me.

NWB: What is your advice to authors who are currently trying to emerge as biographers? Should they regard the printed book as the dominant medium for biography, or do they need to take a different approach?

BW: It seems to me that there are wonderful opportunities for other media, such as biographical films – not biopics but actual documentaries. We live in an increasingly visual culture, after all. Me, I'm committed to the written word/printed book, because I consider reading (and writing) one of the great achievements and pleasures of humankind. But other forms of biographical investigation, or narrative, are available, and can be made available. Even an oil painting is a biography of sorts, as is a collage.

NWB: How would you evaluate the role played by filmic biography in shaping the way the depiction of another person's life is perceived at the current moment?

BW: Depends on how many people watch these films, whether about Amy Winehouse or James Baldwin, and how these films are made: conventionally, experimentally, for commercial viewing, for small screens or large. I think film is a marvelous medium, and for those people writing biography, it provides visual information not to be gainsaid: gestures, body language, dress, to name only three. In the hands of those behind the camera not interested in the inner life of a subject, it can evade or avoid much, which is an obstacle to be overcome since a complex exploration of internal as well as the external life of the subject is always the goal of good biography. Then again, because we live in an increasingly visual culture, the influence of a biographical film can be problematic when, in fact, that film reflects the bias or ideological assumptions of the film-maker. Of course, this is the larger problem of biography generally.

NWB: What has been the impact of the internet on biography writing and reading? What are the most significant developments, and where do you see continuities?

BW: The vast number of digitized documents, particularly newspapers and correspondence, currently available to the researcher/writer/biographer is amazing and amazingly helpful. For one thing, in some cases, it assists the biographer in tracking down and using the primary sources needed for her/his work, and this can be extremely helpful because at times such pursuit is just too expensive. (The dirty little secret of biography is its great cost.) Naturally, though, nothing compares with the handling of primary documents – a real, tattered copy of *The Liberator*, say, or a dog-eared old leather-bound diary, the ink turned brown and faded. I have touched a check written by Picasso, the signature so valuable to the receiver that she never cashed the check. What can top that? I have shuddered at a lock of hair from the head of Hawthorne's daughter. On and on. I think the handling of documents, by the way, keeps the biographer humble in the face of a real, other life.

NWB: The technological possibilities of Web 2.0 have shifted parts of internet use toward strongly participatory forms of self-depiction. Do you think that this kind of participatory approach has impacted attitudes toward biography? If so, how?

BW: Probably has had more of an impact on memoir and autobiography, no? In any case, the biographer is a bit of a sleuth, and biography, insofar as it involves detective work, involves discriminating between the false and the true, between the deceiving and the genuine, between desire and reality. We can't always do this carefully, but, for instance, we deploy skepticism as a methodological tool and explore everything while trusting nothing. Perhaps, then, we now need more skepticism, more 'fact-finding,' more source-checking than ever. But that was always the biographer's task.

NWB: In a 2013 interview with *Publishers Weekly*, you argued that with your latest two books, *White Heat* and *Ecstatic Nation*, you demonstrate that the ostensible boundary between an individual's biography and large-scale history was "porous." What is your main strategy as a writer to convince your readers of this porousness? Which aesthetic experience(s) do you want your readers to have in the process?

BW: How do we, how can we, separate ourselves from history? "History is now and England," (38) wrote T. S. Eliot in "Little Gidding," a very personal, historical, spiritual poem while London was being bombed during the Second World War. We live in time; there's no escaping time. And whether we heard bombs dropping near St. Paul's, or smelled the sad, poisoned air of New York City after 9/11, or witnessed the Berlin Wall coming down, or even heard or witnessed or read from afar, we are part of that world. A strategy, I suppose, is to make your reader imagine that world as your subject saw or felt it, and to do this, I suppose one must employ an empathetic imagination to make a reader feel the meaning, consequences, and sound of history. So, again, we're back to knowing as much about the streets, the quality of air, the means of postal delivery, and the cost of a pineapple in the subject's world.

NWB: In a 2010 piece (Keizer, Shapiro, and Wineapple), you write that "[b]iography [...] recovers, or tries impossibly to recover, the conflicts of existence that render the person *behind* the idea both human and unique." Then you go on to say: "We invent the form in which we house those lives, which is the shape of the biography." Thus, I would like to learn more about your process of developing biographical forms that allow you to explore your subject matter. On which media formats do you rely when researching the materials for a biography? How have available archives developed with respect to the available materials? And how has your approach changed over time?

BW: My approach over time has changed insofar as the technology for discovery, which I've already mentioned, has changed. As I said, a good deal of material has been digitized, which is enormously helpful. But your question is really two questions, because you're asking me about developing biographical forms. And that's a separate issue. The form must always fit the subject, so I think each book and, to an extent, one's style changes with the subject. For my Steins book, I had a nineteenth-century novel in mind, even though Gertrude Stein was a vaunted modernist. But they lived overstuffed lives, crammed with pictures and books and people and more people, so I wrote an overstuffed book. And because Hawthorne was consumed with the sins of one's ancestors, I began with his children, on whom he had such a profound influence, as if in their lives we could begin to limn the outlines of his. (I was not, however, looking for causal connections.) Those are two examples of tinkering with the form. And as I said, I never considered or conceived of *White Heat* as a biography, which would straitjacket my elusive subjects and deny me an exploration of the complex relation between reclusiveness and activism in America. So that form involved the central letter that Dickinson wrote to Higginson as introduction and pivot.

NWB: Your works primarily rely on the printed word rather than on a combination of verbal narrative and photographic images or other illustrations. Where do you see the particular potential of written words in bringing to life a person's biography for the reader? Where do you see connections to other visual, auditive (or even olfactory or haptic) media?

BW: Well, I'm a writer so I inevitably rely on (and love) language, which is to say the printed word. How not, and why not? But since it's not polite to answer a question with a question, I would say that I have used photographs as punctuation. Punctuation is an essential vehicle but not always a determinative one. Or, put another way, the Steins' collection is best seen in a series of photographs that help document the change in paintings they collected, and since other people saw that collection, we can too. But it has to be fluid. The problem with photographs is that they stop time, they reproduce an instant of time, and one of the great problems of biography is showing how character changes over time. Regarding the act of translating one thing into another, that is of translating people, places, that which is literally seen into language, I would stress that biography strives to overcome the spaces in-between. Think of dreams: they are intensely visual and colorful. Describe them, and we realize how wide the gap between our experience and our language really is. But poetry closes that gap, and biography, in its typically lumbering way, also tries to do that by creating a poetry that narrates, if the biographer is successful.

NWB: Your husband, Michael Dellaira, is a composer. Sensory historians have been concerned with reconstructing history through understanding sonic environments and their sociohistorical significance. How important is it for you to create a soundscape in your biographical and historical writing? Do you pursue specific trajectories and paths in this endeavor?

BW: Absolutely important. Rhythm – the rhythm of a sentence – is all. (But one medium is not another.) Read the introduction, for instance, to Robert A. Caro's *Power Broker*: it's all rhythm, marvelously so.

NWB: In closing, is there any advice you'd like to give current students and scholars of biography?

BW: I think I have answered this question before but I could say, after Henry James, be someone "on whom nothing is lost" (13). Or, following Melville, I could say, with Ishmael: "Oh, Time, Strength, Cash, and Patience!" (157).

NWB: Thank you so much for your highly-appreciated contribution to this essay collection on intermedial life writing. It is crucial for our project to spark conversation between life writers and scholars, and we hope that this dialogue will continue to foster our understanding of the complexities of life writing.

BW: My pleasure; thank you for inviting me to contribute to your collection.

Works Cited

Caro, Robert A. 1974. *The Power Broker: Robert Moses and the Fall of New York*. New York: Alfred A. Knopf.
Eliot, T.S. 1943. "Little Gidding". *Four Quartets*. New York: Harcourt, Brace. 29–39.
Holmes, Richard. 1985. *Footsteps: Adventures of a Romantic Biographer*. London: Penguin.
Igaz, Paul. "Eccentric Nation: PW Talks with Brenda Wineapple". publishersweekly.com, 14 June 2013. <https://www.publishersweekly.com/pw/by-topic/authors/interviews/article/57825-eccentric-nation-pw-talks-with-brenda-wineapple.html> [accessed 10 February 2017].
James, Henry. 1956 [1888]. "The Art of Fiction". In: Leon Edel (ed.). *The Future of the Novel*. New York: Vintage. 3–27.

Keizer, Bert, Harriet Shapiro, and Brenda Wineapple. (2010). "Table Talk". *The Threepenny Review* 123: 3–5. <http://www.jstor.org/stable/20787844> [accessed 23 December 2016].
Melville, Herman. 2003 [1851]. *Moby-Dick; or, The Whale*. London: Penguin Classics.
Wineapple, Brenda. 1989. *Genêt: A Biography of Janet Flanner*. New York: Ticknor & Fields.
Wineapple, Brenda. 1996. *Sister Brother: Gertrude and Leo Stein*. New York: Putnam.
Wineapple, Brenda. 2003. *Hawthorne: A Life*. New York: Knopf.
Wineapple, Brenda. 2008. *White Heat: The Friendship of Emily Dickinson and Thomas Wentworth Higginson*. New York: Knopf.
Wineapple, Brenda. 2013. *Ecstatic Nation: Confidence, Crisis, and Compromise, 1848–1877*. New York: Harper Perennial.

Note on the Contributors

Nassim Winnie Balestrini is Professor of American Studies and Intermediality and Director of the Centre for Intermediality Studies in Graz (CIMIG) at the University of Graz, Austria.

Ina Bergmann is Associate Professor of American Studies at the University of Würzburg, Germany.

Dennis Bingham is Professor of English and Director of Film Studies at Indiana University-Purdue University Indianapolis (IUPUI), USA.

Danuta Fjellestad is Chair Professor of American Literature at Uppsala University, Sweden.

Christopher J. Lukasik is Associate Professor of English and American Studies at Purdue University, West Lafayette, USA.

Margit Peterfy is Senior Lecturer in American Studies at the University of Heidelberg, Germany.

Hélène Quanquin is Professor of American Studies at Université de Lille, France.

Gabriele Rippl is Professor and Chair of American Literature at the University of Berne, Switzerland.

Silvia Schultermandl is Assistant Professor of American Studies at the University of Graz, Austria.

Susan Snively is a prize-winning poet and novelist. She is also a guide, discussion leader, and film scriptwriter for the Emily Dickinson Museum, and she is the founder and was the first director of the Writing Center at Amherst College, USA.

Daniel Stein is Professor of North American Literary and Cultural Studies at the University of Siegen, Germany.

Brenda Wineapple is the author of prize-winning biographies of Nathaniel Hawthorne, of Gertrude and Leo Stein, and of Janet Flanner. She is also the author of a cultural and political history of mid-nineteenth-century America.

Index

1776   60, 222

abolition   4, 35 f., 38–40, 43–47, 225
Adams, J.A.   16
Adams, Timothy   150
adaptation   3, 12, 52 f., 119 f., 127, 129–131, 213, 215 f., 218
Allen, Terry Y.   52, 54, 236 f.
American Dream   113 f.
American Revolution   60, 211 f., 222–224, 227
American studies   1, 3, 5 f., 196, 207, 213
American Vitagraph Company   65
Americanness   62
An Angel at my Table   95
Anatomy of a Murder   89
Anderson, Alexander   16–21, 24, 32, 102 f.
Angles of a Landscape   5, 233, 236 f.
– *My Business Is to Sing*   233, 236–238
– *Seeing New Englandly*   233, 236–240
– *The Poet in Her Bedroom*   236, 240
archive   36, 100, 120, 133, 172, 182, 185, 191, 199, 201, 205 f., 208, 211–218, 226–228, 245, 249
Armstrong, Louis   4, 119, 129–139, 143
– *Satchmo: My Life in New Orleans*   130
Ashby, Hal   79
– *Bound for Glory*   79, 88
Auster, Paul   4, 167–172, 174–176, 178 f., 181–187
– *Report from the Interior*   4, 167–169, 172, 174, 179, 184–186
– *The Invention of Solitude*   168, 170 f., 179, 185
– *Winter Journal*   168 f., 174, 184, 186
authenticity   5, 104, 157, 194
auto assemblage   193 f., 196 f., 199, 201–204, 206–208
auto/bio/graphics   168
auto/curating   194
auto-geography   153
autobiographical pact   169, 195
autobiographics   130, 139, 143

autobiography   1–4, 9, 11–16, 25–27, 34, 36, 63, 81, 99, 119 f., 123, 130–132, 134, 136, 138 f., 147–150, 152–154, 157–159, 162, 167–170, 185–187, 192–195, 197, 207 f., 211–213, 215–217, 219, 233 f., 249
– Enlightenment autobiography   1
– everyday autobiographies   5
– fictional autobiography   153
– graphic autobiography   120
– graphic musical autobiography   119 f.
– pseudo-autobiography   168
autobiography studies   4, 147 f.
autofiction   147–151, 154, 159–162, 204
autophotographic pact   4, 167, 171

Baldwin, James   248
Balestrini, Nassim   1 f., 5, 44, 52, 63, 100, 147 f., 202, 211, 216, 245
bande dessinée   129, 136
Barker, James Nelson   61
Barlow, T.O.   179, 181
Barnes, Clive   62, 79
Barry, Julian   79, 81 f., 90–93
Barry, Linda   169
– *One Hundred Demons*   169
Barrymore, Drew   111
Barthes, Roland   159, 170, 186 f., 197
– *Camera Lucida*   170, 197
– *Roland Barthes by Roland Barthes*   186
Bartlett, John   104
Bartram, Kent   103
– *Staunch Character*   103
Beale, Edith Bouvier   4, 99, 101–103, 105, 107 f., 110, 114
Beale, Edith Ewing Bouvier   101
Beale, Phelan   101
Bealemaniacs   104
Beat Generation   78
Ben Hur   62
Berger, Daniel   13
Bergman, Ingmar   77
Bergmann, Ina   1 f., 4, 99, 147, 233

Bewick, Thomas   43
Big Edie   101f.
Bigelow, John   24, 26, 34
– *The Autobiography of Benjamin Franklin*   26
Billy the Kid   62
Bingham, Dennis   4, 75, 111
Bingham, Millicent Todd   237
– *Emily Dickinson: A Revelation*   237
biofiction   99, 236
biographical studies   3
biography   1–3, 5f., 11, 13, 18, 22, 35, 37f., 41, 51f., 54–57, 59, 61, 65f, 75f., 99f., 105, 111, 113, 120f., 125, 129–131, 136, 139, 143, 168, 191, 194f, 211–213, 217, 219f., 229, 234, 236, 240f., 246f., 249–251
– biographical drama   4
– biographical film   5, 65f., 239, 247f.
– biographical novel   5
– biographies on television   99
– graphic biography   120f., 125, 138, 140
– graphic musical biography   4, 119–121, 124, 126–129, 139
– new biography   4, 99
Biography   194
biopic   4, 67, 75–77, 79–82, 85, 88, 91–93, 95f., 99, 103f., 111–114, 236, 247
– documentary biopic   2
– Hollywood Renaissance biopic   4, 75
– postfeminist biopic   111f.
Blacc, Aloe   229
black-and-white   75f., 81, 88f., 96, 121, 140, 152, 157f., 160, 170, 175, 177, 184, 199, 215
Blau, Kathy   220, 226
blog   2, 52, 103, 148, 157, 168, 205
Bogdanovich, Peter   90
– *Paper Moon*   90
– *The Last Picture Show*   90
Boker, George Henry   64f.
– *Francesca da Rimini*   64–66
Bolden, Buddy   134f.
Bolter, Jay David   1, 100f., 113, 121
Božović, Velibor   160
Bradlee, Ben   103
Brooks, Ethel   196, 198, 200f, 203f., 207

Brooks, Mel   90
– *Young Frankenstein*   90
Brown, John   44, 52, 124
Bruce, Honey   76, 83
Bruce, Lenny   4, 75f, 78f., 81-96
Buckley, Peter   59
Buddy Holly Show, The   76
Burr, Aaron   217, 222, 224, 226

Caldwell, George S.   58, 103
– *Gristmill*   103
Carmontelle, Louis   13
Caro, Robert A.   251
– *Power Broker*   251
Carolsfeld, Julius Schnorr von   179
Cash, Johnny   119, 125-127, 251
– "Folsom Prison Blues"   125
Cash, June Carter   127
Casper, Scott E.   12, 37, 40, 52, 56–58
Chandler, Elizabeth   46
Chapman, Maria Weston   40f., 44, 46
Chapple, Freda   52
Chernow, Ron   220–222, 226f.
Cheshire, Ellen   111
Church, Frederic   85, 142, 234f.
cinema   4, 51, 55f., 65, 67, 75–80, 88, 92, 104, 175
Citizen Kane   83, 95f.
citizenship   5, 229
civil rights movement   141, 143
Civil War   35f., 239f.
Cole, Teju   147f., 150-152, 156-159, 161f, 234f
– *Every Day Is for the Thief*   156–158
– *Open City*   156
Cole, Thomas   234
– "Essay on American Scenery"   234
– "The Voyage of Life"   234
Collins, Addie Mae   30, 78, 81, 84f., 91–93, 130, 142
Coltrane, John   119, 129, 139–143
– *A Love Supreme*   139–143
– "Alabama"   142f.
– *Blue Train*   140
Columbus, Christopher   62

comics 4, 83, 87, 90, 92, 119f., 124f., 127–130, 141, 143, 151, 177
– comic books 1
– comics as/like music 119, 124, 128f.
communication 6, 53, 169, 192, 195
confession 168, 179, 204
Confessions of St. Augustine, The 168
Conrad, Robert Taylor 63
– *Jack Cade* 63
Cooley, Carolyn Lindley 236, 238f.
Copelman, Dina 196, 198, 201–204, 207
Crandall, Prudence 46
Crockett, Davy 62
Croome, William 22-25
cultural history 3
cultural narratology 3
cultural studies 3
culture 1, 3–6, 9, 11, 13, 27, 51, 54, 56, 58f., 65–67, 75, 78f., 81, 92, 95, 99–101, 103–107, 111, 114, 124, 127–129, 131, 134, 139, 143, 147–149, 151f., 154, 157, 162, 170, 182, 191f., 196f., 199, 201f., 206–208, 218f., 246
Custen, George F. 80f., 85
Custis, George Washington P. 59

daguerreotype 38, 43, 215
dance 52, 75, 77–80, 95, 102, 106, 213f., 222
Dante 64f.
– *Divina Commedia* 64
Davis, Miles 129, 140, 173, 195
Day, Mahlon 13, 16–21, 24, 29, 61, 161, 239
– *Brief Memoir of the Life of Dr. Benjamin Franklin* 13, 16, 18, 29
Deleuze, Gilles 192, 203f.
Dellaira, Michael 251
democracy 5, 12, 63, 219, 221, 228
diary 168, 233, 248
Dickinson, Austin 237
Dickinson, Cindy 236
Dickinson, Emily 5, 233–242, 245f., 250
Dickinson, Samuel Fowler 239
Diderot, Denis 54
Diggs, Daveed 226

digitality 2, 52, 53, 149f, 191, 194, 199, 205-208
– digital age 2, 150
– digital image 52
– digital media 52f.
diptych 183
diversity 5, 168, 229
documentary 1, 3f., 12, 51, 76, 81, 95, 99, 102–107, 109–112, 114, 158, 160f., 187, 194, 233
Dolphy, Eric 140
Döring, Tobias 148, 151–153
drama 51f., 55, 61, 89, 151, 217, 235, 240
– historical drama 52
Dunlap, William 62
– *André* 62
– *Glory of Columbia* 62

Eakin, Paul John 148, 168f., 207
Early Republic 57, 62, 211, 219, 223, 225
East, Dave 101f., 106, 109–111, 139, 229
Ebersole, Christine 104, 109–111
Eisenstein, Sergei 77f., 82
ekphrasis 147, 149–151, 154–156, 159, 161f., 204, 208, 234
Eley, Mike 113
Eliot, T.S. 249
– "Little Gidding" 249
Emerson, Ralph Waldo 114, 239
– *Representative Men* 114
Emily Dickinson Museum 233
Eminem 215f.
– *The Way I Am* 215
Empoli, Jacopo da 179
engraving 3, 10f., 16–26, 31, 37f., 41–44, 178f., 236
Erll, Astrid 100f., 113
Esslin, Martin 52
European Journal of Life Writing 194
Eustis, Oskar 224

Facebook 191, 196f., 204–206
Family Line-Ups 191–193, 196–200, 202–208
Fate Marable Band 132–134
Felix in Hollywood 176f.
Female Literary Association 47

Ferris, J. L. G.   182
– *The First Thanksgiving 1621*   182
Field, Kate   52, 64, 104
Fielding, Henry   215
– *Tom Jones*   215
film   1, 3f., 52, 55, 62, 65f., 75–96, 99, 102–106, 110–113, 130, 151, 153, 167, 169, 172f., 175f., 178, 183, 185, 187, 194, 197, 213, 233, 236–238, 240f., 248
– *film noir*   75f., 80, 96
– silent film   3f., 175
Fischer-Lichte, Erika   52
Fjellestad, Danuta   4, 161, 167
Flanner, Janet   245f.
Fludernik, Monika   186
Forrest, Edwin   63f.
Fosse, Bob   4, 75–96
– *All that Jazz*   77, 81, 93
– *Cabaret*   75, 77, 81f., 85, 89
– *Lenny*   4, 75–78, 80–96
– *Liza with a Z*   77
– *Pippin*   77
Foster, Abby Kelley   44, 46
Foster, Stephen S.   44
Founding Father   5, 211, 213f., 217–219, 221f., 228
Franco, Zeno E.   77, 220, 226
Frank, Robert   129, 158, 170
– *The Americans*   158
Franklin, Benjamin   3, 9, 11–27, 29–34, 52, 239
– *The Autobiography of Benjamin Franklin*   169
Frietchie, Barbara   62
Froemke, Susan   105
Frost, John   22–26, 31
– *Pictorial Life of Benjamin Franklin*   22–25, 31
Fuller-Seeley, Kathryn   66

Garrison, Francis Jackson   35, 37–42, 47
Garrison, Helen Benson   44–47
Garrison, Wendell Phillips   35–37, 39, 42–48
Garrison, William Lloyd   3, 35–48
– *The Liberator*   39, 46-48, 248
Gauguin, Paul   154f.

Georgi, Claudia   52f., 67
Getty, J. Paul   93, 101, 181
Giesa, Felix   124f., 128
Gihon, William   22, 31
Gilbert, R. S.   22, 31
Gilbert, Sue   235
Gilmore, Leigh   130, 148, 154, 168
Gitler, Ira   140
Goffman, Erving   57
Goldman, Albert   78f., 83, 85, 91–93, 95f.
– *Ladies and Gentleman, Lenny Bruce*   83
Goodrich, Samuel G.   13, 18–24, 26, 30
– American School Biography Series   18
– *The Life of Benjamin Franklin*   13, 18f., 26, 30, 32
graphic narrative   1, 4, 139
graphic novel   3, 151
Grey Gardens   102–103
Grey Gardens (musical)   99, 101–107, 109, 111f., 114
Griffith, D.W.   78
Grimké, Angelina E.   44, 46
Grimké, Sarah M.   44, 46
Grusin, Richard   1, 100f., 113, 121
Guattari, Félix   192, 203f.
Guthrie, Woody   79
Guzman, Leonor de   52, 62

Hall, Jacquelyn Dowd   2, 79, 108, 134f., 220, 241
Halttunen, Karen   56
Hamilton, Alexander   5, 211-229
Hamilton, Elizabeth Schuyler   221f., 227
Hansen, Lotte   184
Haskell, Molly   81
Hawthorne, Nathaniel   5, 245, 248, 250
Heffernan, James A.W.   37, 150f., 204
Heim, Alan   81f., 85
Hemon, Aleksandar   147f., 150–152, 158–162
– *The Lazarus Project*   158–161
heroism   55, 62f., 79–81, 126, 211, 213, 219–224, 226–228
Higginson, Thomas Wentworth   5, 245f., 250
Hip Hop   5, 211
Hirsch, Marianne   170, 201–205

historicity 5
historiography 5, 211, 213 f., 218, 223 f., 226, 245
history 3, 23, 26 f., 36, 40, 57, 59, 119, 125, 148, 171, 175, 202–205, 208, 211–215, 218 f., 221–223, 226, 228 f., 249, 251
Hoffman, Dustin 78 f., 84, 86 f., 90, 93 f.
Holiday, Billie 81, 119-122, 129
Holley, O.L. 25, 32
– *The Life of Benjamin Franklin* 25, 32
Holmes, Richard 246
Hovde, Ellen 105
Hornung, Alfred 2, 147 f.
Hoskins, Andrew 205
Howells, William Dean 54
Hughes, Howard 101, 170
hybridity 10, 53, 56, 105, 125, 130, 148, 223
hypermediacy 100 f., 112
hyphenation 4, 148, 151 f.

I am a Fugitive from a Chain Gang 173, 186
I Want to Live 89
icon 4, 13, 99, 103 f., 113 f., 141
– cultural icon 3 f., 93, 99, 113–115
iconography 93, 127, 193, 198
illness 148, 201
illustration 3, 9–14, 16–27, 33, 35–38, 40–42, 63, 130, 138, 149, 158 f., 162, 167, 172, 174, 178, 185, 187, 236, 240, 250
I'm Not There 95
immigration 5, 148, 151, 159–162, 201, 206–208, 211 f., 217, 219, 221, 226, 228 f.
Incredible Shrinking Man, The 173, 186
Indian plays 61
Instagram 191
interdisciplinary 1, 3, 6
intermediality 1–6, 9–11, 18, 25 f., 35, 37 f., 48, 51–54, 56, 59, 61, 63, 67, 75–77, 89, 93, 95 f., 99 f., 106 f., 110, 119 f., 124 f., 127–130, 133, 136, 139, 141, 143, 147–152, 154, 156 f., 159, 161 f., 167–169, 172, 182, 184, 187, 191–194, 196–198, 204, 206, 208, 211 f., 216, 219, 223 f., 226, 228, 233 f., 237 f., 240 f., 245, 251
– diachronic intermediality 101
– intermedia artist 138
– intermedia theory 4
– intermedial turn 53, 147
intermediality studies 1, 2, 192
internet 149 f., 192, 204, 248
interview 5, 76, 79, 81–83, 85, 88–90, 92, 95 f., 100, 120, 168 f., 233, 241 f., 245, 249

Jackson, Chris 36, 42–44, 48, 63, 225, 228
Jacobs, Marc 47, 104, 129
Jay Z 215–217
– *Decoded* 215
jazz 4, 87, 106, 121, 129, 131–136, 138–140, 142 f.
Jefferson, Thomas 64, 225 f.
Jefferson III, Joseph 63
Jocelyn, Nathaniel 41
Jones, Elvin 47, 142
juxtaposition 4, 75–77, 81, 86, 95, 139, 159, 214, 218

Kael, Pauline 78, 86
Kane, Elisha Kent 83, 92, 95 f., 239
Kattenbelt, Chiel 52
Kazan, Elia 77, 85
– *Baby Doll* 85
Keen, Suzanne 220
Kennedy Jr., Joe 101
Kincaid, Jamaica 147 f., 151, 153–156, 161 f.
– *Annie John* 154
– *Lucy* 153–156, 161 f.
– *See Now Then* 154
– *The Autobiography of My Mother* 154
Klein, Calvin 104
Kleist, Reinhard 121, 125–128
– *Cash: I See a Darkness* 125
Knapp, Isaac 44
Kruell, Gustav 35, 37 f., 42, 44 f.
– *The Portfolio of National Portraits* 42
Kübler-Ross, Elisabeth 93
– *On Death and Dying* 93

La Môme 76
Lady Gaga 104
Lady Sings the Blues 81, 91
Lafayette 224, 228
Lazarus, Emma 160f.
– "The New Colossus" 160
Leja, Michael 10
Lejeune, Philippe 169, 185, 195
Lentricchia, Frank 170
– *The Edge of Night* 170
Leypoldt, Günter 113f.
libretto 211f., 217, 223–226
life story 12–14, 17, 75, 99, 101, 103, 119f., 129–131, 136f., 171, 195, 222, 227
life writing 1–6, 9, 51, 55–57, 59, 61, 63, 67, 99, 119f., 130, 141, 143, 147–149, 151f., 157, 159, 161f., 168, 170f., 185, 191–194, 197, 202, 204, 212, 214f., 220, 233, 236, 241, 245, 251
– cinematic life writing 75
– dramatic life writing 56
– musico-comical life writing 4, 119
– online academic life writing 5, 192, 196
– online life writing 192–194, 197, 204
– performative life writing 2, 5
– relational life writing 2, 212, 219, 245
– self-life writing 4, 99, 192
life writing studies 1, 5
Lincoln, Abraham 42–44, 160
Lind, Jenny 238
literary studies 3
Little Edie 4, 99, 101–104, 106f., 110–114
Ljungberg, Christina 53
Lodge, Henry Cabot 227
Lone Ranger, The 182
Longfellow, Henry Wadsworth 57
– "A Psalm of Life" 57
Lord, Otis Phillips 233f., 237, 241
Louis XI 62
Louvel, Liliane 149
Lukasik, Christopher J. 1, 3, 9, 15
Lundy, Benjamin 44

master narratives 2
Mawil 120, 123f.
– *Die Band* 120, 123f.
May, Samuel J. 44, 79

Maysles, Albert and David 99, 102–107, 109–112
– *Gimme Shelter* 102
– *Grey Gardens* 102, 104-106
– *The Beales of Grey Gardens* 103
McCarter, Jeremy 211f., 214, 216–219, 223–228
McConachie, Bruce A. 63
McNair, Denise 142
McNeill, Laurie 191f., 194f.
McRae, John C. 178
– *Father, I Can Not Tell a Lie: I Cut the Tree* 178, 235
media 1–5, 10, 14, 16, 22f., 26f., 35, 37f., 40f., 51–54, 67, 76f., 79, 85, 92, 96, 99–101, 103, 109f., 112, 114, 119f., 124f., 129f., 134, 139–141, 148–151, 153f., 156, 158, 161, 167–169, 179, 183f., 187, 193–196, 199, 203, 205f., 212f., 215, 229, 236, 241, 247–251
– media combination 2f., 10f., 19–21, 169, 192, 203
– medial phenotypes 5
– medial transposition 169
– mixed media 3, 10, 35, 37f., 48, 125, 168
– online media 192f., 205
– optical media 9, 25–27
– social media 2f., 148
media history 25f.
media studies 1, 3, 100
Méliès, George 175
– *A Trip to the Moon* 175
memoir 3f., 12–15, 17f., 22, 36, 99, 103, 148, 157, 168–170, 175, 185f., 193, 225, 233, 249
Mendes, Sam 77, 85
meta-picture 14
Metacom 61
Metz, Christian 88
Meyer, Muffie 105
mezzotint 38
Middle East 151f., 162
migration 147–149, 151, 161f.
Mihailescu, Dana 196

Miller, Nancy K.   129, 170, 196–198, 201, 207
– *But Enough about Me*   170
Miranda, Lin-Manuel   5, 211f., 214–229
– *Hamilton: An American Musical*   211, 218, 229
 – *Hamilton: The Revolution*   211f., 214–216, 218f., 222, 228
Misek, Richard   88
Mitchell, W.J.T.   3, 9–11, 14, 151
Mizrahi, Isaac   104
Monk, Thelonious   129, 140f.
Monkography   141
montage   75–78, 81f., 86, 94, 96
Mount Holyoke Female Seminary   234, 239
movie   3, 65, 67, 75, 77, 79, 81, 88, 104, 112f., 169, 173, 175–177
Muñoz, José and Carlos Sampayo   120–122
– *Billie Holiday*   120, 122,
music   52, 78, 80, 104, 106, 119, 123–125, 127–129, 131–136, 138–141, 143, 169, 172, 181, 187, 211, 215, 222, 226, 229, 236, 238–242
musicals   2f., 106f., 110, 222
myth   2, 111, 136, 178f., 217f., 224

narratology   1
Nas   229
nation   4–6, 42, 48, 85, 196f., 211, 217, 219, 223, 225f., 229
Nation, The   42, 48
Née, François Denis   13
newspaper   51, 54–56, 59, 61, 63, 65, 67, 76, 95, 110, 121, 138, 182, 185, 187, 236, 239, 248
newsreel   76, 95
Nicolson, Harold   56
Nixon   95, 108
Norman, John   13
Nussbaumer, Rolf   172

Obama, Barack   228
Oceantics   176f.
Oldham, Todd   104
Oliver, King   80, 131f.
Oltean, Roxana   196
Onassis, Jackie Kennedy   99, 101f.

Ondaatje, Michael   157
– *Running in the Family*   157
open access   3
Oxford Centre for Life Writing   99

painting   3, 14, 38, 41, 59, 77, 103, 139, 149, 154f., 167, 169f., 172, 178f., 182f., 185, 187, 199, 240, 247, 250
Paquet, Philip   4, 120, 130–135, 137–139
– *Louis Armstrong*   120, 129f., 132f., 135
paragone   151f., 158
paratheatrical   3f., 51, 56, 59, 61, 67
Parisi, Paolo   120, 139–143
– *Coltrane*   120, 139–143
Parker, Alice   104, 129, 239
parlor theatrical   60
Patton   76
Pearson, Roberta A.   65f.
Pease, Elizabeth   46
performance   3, 12, 15, 51–53, 55–57, 59–64, 67, 79, 90, 100, 102, 104, 106, 109–111, 113, 121, 124, 126, 130, 133, 136, 139–141, 207, 211–215, 221, 229, 235
– performance art   53, 194
performance studies   3
performativity   2, 13, 52f., 56f., 129, 140, 151, 194, 214, 241
Perrine, Valerie   82, 90f.
Peterfy, Margit   4, 51, 64
Phillips, Wendel   37f., 40–42, 44
photography   2–4, 10, 38, 41, 76, 93, 102, 127, 131f., 136, 138, 140, 147, 149–162, 167, 169–173, 178, 183–185, 187, 191, 193, 196–206, 208, 215f., 224, 240, 247, 250
picture   9f., 13f., 17–20, 23–26, 35, 37f., 40–42, 44f., 48, 52, 55, 66, 77, 79, 93, 103, 111, 113, 125, 137, 147, 149f., 152f., 155, 158–160, 162, 167f., 170–176, 178f., 182–184, 203, 234, 250
– pictorial histories   10, 18
– pictorial representations   9, 11
– picture personality   65f.
Pillai, Nicolas   129
Pillsbury, Parker   44
Pinterest   191
Pethö, Ágnes   100

plurimediality 52f., 67
Pocahontas 61
Polaschek, Bronwyn 111f.
Poletti, Anna 2, 192–194
Polo, Marco 62
Pontiac 61
popular culture 61, 218
portrait 9, 11, 13f., 17, 23, 35–47, 80, 92, 127, 137f., 142, 152, 155, 168, 171, 179, 184, 196, 198, 206, 240
positionality 2, 5, 219
postcolonialism 154, 157
postmemory 201f., 204, 206f.
postmodernism 168, 193, 195, 199, 202, 204
Precup, Mihaela 196
Priego, Ernesto 129
print culture 3, 9–11, 13, 22f., 26, 215

Quanquin, Hélène 3f., 35, 44, 46
Questlove 224
Quinn, Sally 103
– *Finding Magic* 103

radio 1, 95, 130, 172, 182, 187
Radziwill, Lee 102
Rajewsky, Irina O. 1, 38, 100, 129, 140, 150, 192, 203, 213
Rancière, Jacques 3, 9–11, 14
Read, Deborah 14–22, 25, 158, 251
records 36, 76, 79, 150
relationality 2, 4f., 157, 195, 207, 215, 226
remediation 4, 9, 11f., 16–18, 20, 22–26, 29, 99–101, 104, 106f., 109, 111–115, 121, 126, 129–131, 133, 139f.
repertoire 65, 211–214, 216–219, 228
representation 2, 20, 37, 41, 53, 55, 62–64, 67, 99–101, 104f., 113, 115, 121, 125, 127, 129, 137, 141, 148–152, 162, 168, 170, 183f., 191–194, 196, 198, 200, 203, 205f., 208, 214–216, 219, 221, 223f.
republican motherhood 60
Reynolds, Maria 226f.
rhizome 191f., 195, 206, 208
Rieser, Klaus 113f.
Rigney, Ann 100f., 113

Rimini, Francesca da 52, 62, 64–66
Rippl, Gabriele 1, 4, 119, 129, 147, 150f., 192, 204, 208
Ristori, Adelaide 64f.
Robertson, Carole 142
Rogers, Robert 61, 87, 103
Rose, Gillian 76, 202f., 238
Rothberg, Michael 206
Röttger, Kati 54
Rowe, John Carlos 5
Rufus 103
– "Grey Gardens" 103

Saari, Ron 172
Said, Edward 147f., 151–153, 159, 161f., 170
– *Out of Place* 152, 161, 170
Sanin, Camilo 120, 136–139
– "Louis Armstrong" 120
scat 136f.
Schiller, Lawrence 83, 95f.
Schmitz-Emans, Monika 123, 125, 127
Schultermandl, Silvia 2, 4f., 191, 206
Scorsese, Martin 75
– *Raging Bull* 75, 81
sculpture 3, 11, 38, 41
Sedgwick, Eve Kosofsky 169
– *Dialogue on Love* 169
Seijas, Esteisy 228
self-definition 4
self-expression 2, 4, 147, 151, 191, 194
semiotics 2, 10, 52f.
Serfaty, Viviane 205
Sex and the City 104
sheet music 76
Shelley, Percy Bysshe 219
Sherley, Glen 126
32 Short Films About Glenn Gould 95
simulation 129
Singer, Ben 77, 103, 105
Smith, Sidonie 2, 37, 42, 99f., 120, 129, 148, 185f., 191–196, 205, 212, 240
Snively, Susan 5, 233
– *Composing Yourself* 233
– *From This Distance* 233f.
– *Skeptic Traveler* 233

– *The Heart Has Many Doors* 233, 236 f., 241
– *The Undertow* 233
– *Voices in the House* 233 f.
social criticism 220
social media studies 3
social networking sites 5, 191, 195
socioeconomic implications 3
Social Network, The 95
song 1, 77, 103, 107, 110, 123–126, 136, 211, 216 f., 222, 227, 229, 238 f.
Spamilton: An American Parody 213
stand-up comedy 4, 78
Stein, Daniel 4, 119
Stein, Thomas Michael 153
Steiner, George 170
– *Errata: An Examined Life* 170
Stevenson, Adlai 182 f.
Stewart, Maria 46
still image 4
Stone, Augustus 62, 102, 195, 222
Storify 191
subjectivity 83, 167 f., 195
Sucsy, Michael 111
– *Grey Gardens* 111-114
Summers, Tim 119, 127
Surtees, Bruce 76, 79, 86
suspension of disbelief 54
Sweet Smell of Success 89

Taylor, Diana 67, 211–214, 216, 227 f.
Taymor, Julie 77
television 1, 76 f., 79–81, 85, 89, 96, 104, 106, 113 f., 121, 130, 141, 178, 183, 187
temperance 46
testimony 41, 99, 168
theater 51–56, 62 f., 65, 67, 76 f., 79, 82, 94 f., 211–214, 219, 222, 224
Threepenny Opera, The 110
Todd, Mabel Loomis 237 f.
transculture 4, 147–149, 151 f., 154, 159 f., 162
transmedia 140, 211–213, 221, 229
transnationality 3–5, 151 f., 191 f., 195–197, 205 f.
Tappan, Arthur 44
travelogue 150, 156 f.

Turkle, Sherry 206
Turner, Frances 66
Twitter 191, 196 f., 204–206

Uricchio, William 65 f.
Urvater, Ernest 236 f., 240
– *Berthe Morisot* 240

verbal representation 150, 219
verbal–visual relations 3, 9–12, 16, 19, 22, 24, 26, 147, 149
– visual–textual games 4, 168
Verne, Jules 175
– *From Earth to the Moon* 175
Vertov, Dziga 77 f.
– *Chelovek s Kinoapparatom* 77
video 1, 3, 104, 121, 213, 229
– video games 2
– video installation 52
Villard, Fanny 41, 46
visual culture 9–11, 26, 155, 197, 202, 247 f.
visual culture studies 3
visuality 2 f., 10, 14, 20, 59, 90, 112–114, 119–122, 125–127, 129–131, 133, 135–137, 139, 141, 149–153, 156 f., 162, 168 f., 172–174, 182–185, 191, 193 f., 198–201, 203 f., 208, 212, 215–217, 227, 234, 240, 247 f., 250
Vitagraph girl 66
vlog 2

Ware, Wilbur 140
War of the Worlds, The 176
warts-and-all 80, 111
Washington, George 59–62, 66 f., 103, 178, 223, 225 f., 228, 238, 245
Washington, Martha 59-61
Watson, Julia 2, 99 f., 120, 148, 185 f., 191–196, 198, 201, 205, 207, 212
Weems, Mason Locke 13, 59 f.
– *The Life of Doctor Franklin* 13
Weiner, Sonia 161 f.
Weld, Horatio Hastings 26
– *Benjamin Franklin: His Autobiography* 26
Wells, H.G. 175
– *The First Men in the Moon* 175

Welsch, Wolfgang   148
Wenders, Wim   89
– *Der Himmel über Berlin*   89
Wesley, Cynthia   142
Whitlock, Gillian   2, 192–195
Whitman, Walt   77
– "Song of Myself"   77
Wilmer, S.E.   52, 62
Wilson   76, 104
Window Washers, The   176 f.
Wineapple, Brenda   5, 245, 249
– *Ecstatic Nation*   245, 249
– *Genêt*   245
– *Hawthorne: A Life*   245

– *Sister Brother*   245
– *White Heat*   245 f., 249 f.
Winehouse, Amy   248
Wolf, Stacy   106
Wolf, Werner   53
Wolff, Francis   140
Words of Garrison, The   41
word–photography configurations   4, 147, 149

Yankee Doodle Dandy   76

Zefirelli, Franco   220 f., 226
Zimbardo, Philip G.   220 f., 226

www.ingramcontent.com/pod-product-compliance
Lightning Source LLC
Chambersburg PA
CBHW031804220426
43662CB00007B/527